AF473587

Karen, The Girl That Would Be A Plumber

Also by Petra Ceason

West Novochester Chronicles Group
Delia, Chef In A Wheelchair.
Rita--Who?
Janie, Mechanic On A Motorbike.

Work Related to Creative Writing Course
Collected Short Stories And Pomes,
{And No. It's Not A Typo.}
Rough-cut
Rosalind And Timothy, An Essay On Deflated Self Worth.
Richard, Jim And Friends, Finance And Fine Art.
Frank, An Essay On Health.

Work in Progress
Anna, CEO In Short Socks.
Ash And Cindy.
Fred And Louise, Reluctant Athletes.
Jennifer And Sylvie, Flouting Convention, But Politely.
Maxine, Ma(i)d(e) In A Hard Hat.
Jill.
Jo.
Pealle, Sporty Sparks.
Samantha, Under Age Working Girl.
Shelley And William, Autistic Artist.
Shirley And John, Monta's Secret Weapon.
Stewart And Jean.

Autobiography {Whimsy (in progress)}
Writes En Passion.

Petra Ceason

Karen, The Girl That Would Be A Plumber

Karen, The Girl That Would Be A Plumber

First paperback edition printed 2014 in the United Kingdom

A catalogue record for this book is available from the British Library.

ISBN 978-0-9930419-0-7

Published by Double-Sausage.

For more copies of this book, please contact the distributor, on line book facilitator, Lulu: www.lulu.com

Designed and Set by Petra Ceason: www.petraceason.co.uk

This website carries a link direct to books by Petra Ceason.

Printed in Great Britain.

Acknowledgements:

My thanks to Renée Cuthbertson for editing this work.

My thanks, also, to Jean Bullivant Flowers for permission to use their name in Part Two, Chapter 3; and Irwin Tools, and to The Zoological Society of London, for permission to use their web-photographs of a Stillson wrench and the feisty little Rockhopper penguin, Eudyptes chrysocome, respectively, on the book cover.

Dedication

For my severest critic,
the severest one that I listen to, anyway,
my wife Joan,
and Angela Lloyd and Alison Geggie,
I hope you like it.

Any dodgy commas,
incorrect its, your or who's
are not bad grammar, just typos
and are down to me.
As for the rest,
blame Petra.
She did it,
all I did was hit the keys,

Mervyn Waine.

Declaration

The use of the word 'canoe' in this novel is generic; the one person boats involved are actually kayaks throughout the book.

The characters and events in this story are fictitious, any similarity to persons living or dead is purely accidental.

Except for Karen.

Karen is my way of remembering with fondness two girls.

One who was dragged unwillingly to canoeing by her friend. She came with her friend, to accompany, but returned, alone, to excel. If you ever read this, you will recognise the dangerous seconds of the scene involving surfing on Tynemouth Beach and know who you are. The other served in a plumbing wholesaler as a warehouseman and dispensed wisdom and quality advice to a DIY pond-builder and did it FOC. Once again, there are not that many girls with dirty hands in warehouses, so the available short list here is similar to Pealle's in her diary.

And Bill Carpenter, half the inspiration for whom is dead and sadly missed.

And Shirley. You will know who you are, Big Mamma.

And Anna; a blonde, right-handed little firebrand, who canoed left-handed. There is only one candidate here too.

Karen's, and everyone else's, other wild-child character traits, free thinking and non-mainstream exploits are, however, entirely their own.

Consequently views expressed by characters in this book are always theirs, but occasionally mine too.

Petra Ceason 2014

Sex

Parasites outnumber non-parasites in the World by many to one. It's the nature of things.

Any animal or plant behaviour that occurs regularly is likely to be targeted by parasites for their own devices. As an ecologist I cannot think of any behaviour where also I cannot quote an example of parasitic exploitation.

Sex is no different.

From the misguided souls who consider it sinful, all the way down to those troublesome life forms called viruses, which are scarcely any more advanced than complex chemical compound groups, sex is under attack for a multitude of hidden agendas.

Petra can fight the ignorance and allow me to be sybaritic and ignore the venereal diseases in her books, but Dear Reader, please do not ignore them in life.

Sex is not sinful, it is neither wrong, nor likely to kill you, but the parasitic hangers-on are!

Sex is lovely; please keep it that way by practising safe sex always.

Jennifer Jackson 2014

Contents

Part One:

Part Two:

Part Three:

Karen,
The Girl That Would Be A Plumber

Epilogue as a Prologue

She sat at her computer, finishing her report,

'-- I was just about to test it. My warning was ignored.

From that height, a cage in free fall hits the ground at crushing speed.'

She paused, phrasing her next sentence, it would be the final sentence of the account proper, then she just needed to write the Conclusion.

The report was just a few short pages, but, bearing in mind the quality of the hovering Silks waiting to present it at the inquest, in effect a

'Get away with Murder' card --

Well--Manslaughter anyway, she thought.

To ensure a verdict of Accidental Death, however, she had had to write it carefully.

Such a lot missed out--the door behind her opened, breaking her thoughts.

Two gentle hands massaged her shoulders, two more teased elsewhere,

"Can you take a break, help me fulfil my dream?"

"Yes. Virtually done. I can finish tomorrow."

The others went up to bed, while she saved the file and shut down.

Such a lot missed out, all the way back to--to--years back-

Part One:
School
Chapter 1
Seth: Western Scotland: August 1998
Karen

Just one week Girl! That's all you've got.

Karen Robinson, loath-to-be-maiden of a distant parish, interrupted her thoughts to concentrate on alighting from the short-wheelbase hopper bus, automatically ducking her head as she stepped through the door. She eased the big rucksack into a more comfortable position on her shoulder. The little one bumped uncomfortably against her leg. The holiday would still leave her nearly a month to gird up for the Sixth Form; Seth and Duncan would have a shorter time before starting their Highers' Year. As the bus drew away, the sight of one of her three favourite boys approaching re-focussed her thoughts,

You do not go home still virgin. Make sure.

Seth grinned broadly, stepping out quickly towards her.

"Give me those," he called across the narrowing gap.

"This one's nothing. But --"

Her cousin had already taken the big ruck. She leaned in to

kiss and, as always, he offered his cheek.

You're pretty enough to be a mate Karen, but far too ugly to bed. No, don't! That way lies failure. She shook the self-contemptuous thoughts out of her head and chatted brightly during the half mile walk through peaceful, fence-lined lanes. Occasionally a bridleway winding down from the Ben above joined the farm road. Sprinkled sporadically among the encroaching heather that lined these narrow ways were wild bilberries that were fruiting, and ripe; Karen made a mental note to be sure to collect some. Together they turned into the track that led eventually to the farm and its sprawling outbuildings.

"That'll be the new free range pig field then." She waved to her right, where the distinct family groups of pigs were scattered randomly about.

"Just for a month, just Piggy Heaven for now, once these turnips are harvested." Seth waved at the sea of dense foliage on his left, already half processed by the tractor and squaddies busy in it. "We'll move them over here."

"They'll be the happiest pigs--This side of --" she shook her head defeated.

"Happy pigs give tasty pork, that's the theory anyway. If it's right, you're looking at the tastiest pies in Scotland."

"Seth!" But she was laughing too.

During the holiday Karen did everything she could think of to hurry things along, although to be fair, most of it came naturally anyway. She smiled and cleaned, smiled and tidied and kept out from meddling unasked among the family squabbles that to outsiders seem so futile, but have the principals seriously hurting.

The first morning, she woke early and was showered and downstairs dressed, before anyone else was stirring, quite an achievement for a city girl in a farmhouse deep in wild country. Uncle and Aunt appeared briefly, before leaving to do the before-breakfast half-shift.

Creaking floorboards heralded the next set of bodies moving, then the explosion of noise.

The eldest siblings were rending their World upstairs.

Joanne's inability to leave things alone was the bane of Seth's life. Feet drummed down the stairs and Jo went into the garden close to tears. Moments later she was furiously beheading the roses, faded blooms flying off like spray, an angry little Jack Russell killing rats. More sober, heavier feet followed, he stopped in front of Karen,

"Well say it."

"Good Morning Cousin."

"Oh, sorry. Morning." They looked at each other. "Well aren't you going to say it?"

"And interrupt you? When you're saying it far better than I ever could."

"She makes me mad, I'll go for something and she's moved it."

"Is it always in the same place?"

"-- After she's moved it, yes."

"So who are you really mad at? Jo for tidying it away. Or Seth for leaving it lying around."

Seth hung his head and sighed deeply,

"Where do I go from here?"

"Easy. It's not the tidying you're bothered about. It's doing it without permission. Taking away your rights. What you see as your right. To be Master in your own room. To live in a midden. Give her the permission. Insist she lists where everything is."

"She won't listen; we're always rowing."

"When did you last cuddle her? Told her she was lovely? That you were glad she was your sister? You're her big brother. She idolises you. Believe me, I know."

"I couldn't let her loose in my room."

"In case she finds your Girlie Mags? My guess is she knows exactly where they are. And borrows them regularly. Len used to tell me. When he'd found a really nice story." She'd shocked him, deeply. "You're the adult. Go out there and do what you really want to do. Say sorry. Give her a hug. Give her permission. Mention the magazines." He was wavering, wanting to obey her, all he needed was justification. "Go on Seth. You love her; she's your kid sister. Just sometimes you don't like her very much. Try harder, try to like her. She's okay. Thoughtless sometimes, headstrong. But they're fleabites. She's okay really." She stopped, pointedly waiting.

Seth turned away and went out into the garden. He spoke, waited, spoke again. The rose-heads fountain slowed and stopped, he stepped into his sister and enfolded her, the girl's shoulders shook and she clung to him tightly. Presently he kissed her on the forehead and said something that made her laugh. Together they returned to the house and mounted the stairs. When Seth returned a few minutes later,

"She's tidying my room up, making a list. And she did know where the magazines are."

"Can I borrow if I need to? If I get lonely and frustrated?"

He swam right past her fly,

"Yes, of course. How did you know I had some?"

"I didn't. Not until now."

"Bollocks!" The expletive became a coughing fit, but he grinned as he got it back under control. "I walked right into that one, didn't I."

After dinner, with a long day's farming behind them, the family was lying about crashed out. Karen considered that the evening programmes had boring writ in gross script across them, but later on there was a documentary about building and enjoying a sailing dinghy.

Faint heart never launched a boat!

"Does anyone want to watch a programme? At nine o'clock."

The leisurely responses gave rise to hope,

"No."

"Don't know, what's on?"

"There's not a lot on but that sailing programme looks a reasonable bet."

Thank you Seth, you're a mind reader,

"Can we watch it then? The sailing programme. I'd like to."

"Can we watch it?" The twins, testing the boundaries.

"No, you'll be in bed."

"And I'll fall asleep," said Aunt Morag and promptly did.

Karen glanced at the clock. If she washed up now, at ten-thirty she could go straight from the end of the programme to bed and dream herself to sleep, deep in her virtual sailing hobby. She nodded her head firmly and began rounding up the dishes. The water, heated directly from the Aga was always scalding hot; she slid the dishes into the huge washing-up bowl, added the water and a generous squeeze of detergent. By the time she'd found the rubber gloves the stains on the crocks and irons had surrendered and lifted off with the merest wipe. She had dried and stowed most of them when Jo had chivvied the twins off to bed and dragged Seth in to help her.

"You were quick."

"No. It was your water temperature."

"You've done enough. I'll do the pans."

"I've got the gloves on. You dry."

The programme on sailing dinghies was the first in a series and showed the presenter researching her requirements, choosing from several options and the first stages in how to build one. Karen was smitten; the only problem was the cost. Buying a kit boat might give her a couple of fingers change from an arm and leg, which she didn't have in the first place. The ancient trust fund was fat and healthy, but specifically designed to stay that way, for her and Len's offspring and onwards. Although she could have had a hack, or even a gig, with no questions asked, a bike had nearly needed an Act of Parliament,

A boat, amnesia reigns or something, I forget.

And that was ignoring the fact that when she turned sixteen her clothes were no longer paid for either, ergo even less fritter money available. Aunt Morag woke up and wandered through to the kitchen,

"Who did the dishes?"

"We did," Karen hadn't even looked away from her programme. Aunt Morag returned and looked at her kids who both pointed to Karen and mouthed,

"She did."

"Thank you, who ever it was."

The following day the sibling truce had extended to include

the house. When Aunt Morag returned for her morning break,

"Who cleaned up?"

"Jo tidied, Rockhopper vacuumed and I got in the way."

"You helped," and "He did his share," said Jo and Karen together.

Daily, Karen fed the rabbits and hens and patrolled the newly harvested field where the tasty pie fillings, paused only momentarily in their snuffle-snorting piggy activities, to blink short sightedly at her, before happily thrusting their snouts back into the earth. Two short expeditions provided enough bilberries for tarts whilst at Bencaillie and a tub for home.

Aunt Morag had taken advantage of a few days hot dry weather recently to cut the hay fields. The forecast for later in the week wasn't good and getting the crop in was a priority. Karen, Seth and Duncan drove the tractors leading loads of hay bales back to the barn, for Jo and Duncan's sisters, with a motley crew of other youngsters, to sort and stack. Then, a couple of bale ties mysteriously popped on Karen's last load and she eagerly joined in the maelstrom and squealed with the rest, as the boys grass-pied the girls.

When order was restored, she held still for Seth to extract the prickly stalks from her undies.

"I look like the Pillsbury Dough Man. That's a miniskirt, not a hooped crinoline. You've filled my knickers. I'm all prickles. And my bra."

"That's the idea, now I can offer to get it all out again, caress the prickles away."

"Okay." She turned away from his stunned expression and slid into the walkway, between the stacks of bales, temporarily out of sight. Seth followed her in and she stood side on to him with her arms above her head. It took a few minutes, a lovely few minutes of him rummaging in her bra and knickers, tentatively at first, then when she didn't pull away, caressing her sensuously with the backs of his hands and, then bravely, the front, as he searched for the last few stalks.

"You're empty," he said.

Her thoughts,

Hadn't you better take them off to make sure, died unsaid as Aunt Morag's voice from close by called,

"Seth."

"Yes."

"Take this chutney over to Benguthrie, to Grandma. You can use the quad, if you promise to stick to the high track. I've got to take the twins into the village."

Seth shrugged and left her standing, panting-ready for sex and no partner to share it with. She walked slowly to the door of the barn, when Seth got back from his delivery everyone would be home. Nothing for it but to take him up on the permission to borrow.

Seth's door was ajar, Jo was lying back on his bed, Karen could see a narrow strip of her cousin through it; the view though restricted, was enough to see what the youngster was doing. She stopped, stepped back down a couple of stairs and coughed, then walked up and into the room. Jo had pulled her skirt back down and secreted the magazine under a pillow.

"Seth said I could borrow a Fiesta. Where have you put them?"

Jo glanced at the pillow and then at the bottom drawer. The magazines were under a neatly folded Tee shirt. Karen took the top one and went to her room. She had barely lain on her bed when her cousin followed her in,

"Do you read those?"

"Sometimes. When I'm feeling randy and neglected."

"You don't think it's --"

"Naughty? Wrong?"

"Yes."

"No I don't. I work hard during the day. I would like to play hard in the evening. But I can't. Not yet. So I pretend play hard."

"The Minister says it's wrong."

"Rubbish! Sorry Jo, I feel very strongly about this. Wrong is hurting others. I try not to hurt others. So I don't do things that are wrong. But, when you see the boy you fancy and think of him in bed. If you don't let him touch you what happens? You can't sleep. You lie awake getting fractious. Then, you give in. And, then you feel guilty."

"Yes," her young cousin replied nodding, with cast down eyes. "Is it always a boy? I mean-- Sorry--"

"It has been known to be a girl. I don't restrict myself. And, I don't feel guilty about **that** either."

"Oh, oh, okay."

"I come to bed. Take my pretend lover with me. Reward myself for a day's hard work. Sleep sound. Get up refreshed and ready to do another hard day tomorrow."

"What could I do that would deserve rewarding?"

"Did you do your chores today? Properly?"

"My chores, yes, but I should do them properly without reward."

"Why?"

"The Minister says so."

"Not good enough Jo! More please."

The pretty little face showed puzzlement. Eventually,

"What then?"

"Lots of reasons. Because you want to. It's your Duty. You feel a Commitment. To satisfy your own Honour Code. Because you owe it to yourself. Only a few of the possibles. Are they any reason not to say 'Well done, here's a reward'?"

"You make it sound so simple."

"It's a lot simpler. Than merely being punished if you get it wrong. If punishment is okay, so is reward. And nicer."

On her last full day, Karen set up a walk to look for deer. She tailored it to appeal precisely only to Seth and herself. It succeeded in getting him alone for a few hours, but they walked and looked for deer, ironically successfully, as deer and hart were both spelled the other way to what Karen had in mind.

She'd got dressed, had a long think, discarded the bra and knickers and exchanged the shorts for a short, tight and tarty skirt. She had reached the stairs before returning and regretfully, reluctantly, replacing her knickers.

Late in the afternoon, they'd been caught out in the rain. Initially, she'd run for shelter, but then thought it through, stopped, dropped her little day sack down and strutted on a catwalk, up and down the path, spreading herself to the falling spray.

"Come in out of that, you daft bint, anyone would think you're enjoying it."

"I am. It's warm; it's got no taste. So it's clean and fresh. The rain at home always tastes of industry. This is good enough to put in a single malt."

"Only if you want to ruin it, with single malts the emphasis is on the word single." He slowly joined her to get soaked too. "But I know what you mean."

She knew that he would be able to see everything through her soaked Tee shirt. She had pretended she didn't know and walked and strutted and posed in front of him, and all for nowt. She hoped that her body had been admired; it certainly hadn't been lusted after. He must have guessed she was flaunting herself for him alone, surely. When they cut back through the village, she had unslung her day sack and bundled it across her front, and she'd done it again later when they arrived home. Seth was one thing, but the village youths who leered, and did casual work on the farm, were a different breed altogether.

Seth's friend, Duncan, excepted, of course, he wasn't lumped with the casual workers from the village, she wouldn't necessarily hide the goodies from Duncan, just not give him first refusal.

But, her cousin could have a Gold Access Card anytime he wanted

The trouble was he didn't seem to want it.

She needed to know.

Even if merely to know that she could pull.

Or not.

As the case may be.

Then right at the end of the walk, back in the farmyard, with folks crawling all over them every few seconds so that the conversation was punctuated with long gaps, he steered it round to sex.

"Didn't you find it strange, sleeping with your brother, I'd hate to be in bed with Jo, well, I'd have hated it before this week anyway."

"Can't remember not doing it. The strange bit was not sleeping with someone. Waking up and finding the rest of the bed empty. No one to snuggle into when the Black-Bats came."

"You used to snuggle?"

"Yes. Len was very patient and understanding."

"I meant--Sorry."

Karen waited, but he wasn't going to elaborate; she guessed that he couldn't.

"Yes, we snuggled. But, if you're asking about sex. I'm still virgin. We didn't snuggle quite that far."

"Sorry, I was being rude."

"You were being interested. And, that's okay." She raised her eyebrows.

"Yes me too," he paused plucking up the courage. "Have you ever had any--you know--with anyone else?"

"Have I come? With someone else touching me?"

"Yes."

"A few times." *Why didn't you ask that question hours ago dammit?* She was almost annoyed. She pressed her hands flat together, fingers to her chin then straightened her arms until her palms were flat against the wall. Her fingers were still flat together. People seeing this for the first time usually made some fatuous comment that alerted Karen to what she was doing, Seth had seen it so often that he didn't even register it.

"Any one I know?"

"Could be. Would it matter?"

"No, of course not, it's your body and your life--You wouldn't cuddle up to the local Mr. Big just for the danger kicks."

"Would age matter? Or gender?"

"No."

"I've had fun with Jet. On sleepovers. She'd cuddle me and play with me. And make me come. But, she wasn't bothered about me touching her. I think she just liked feeling me."

"I don't understand that, I like being felt more than feeling."

"I wanted to give back. I even pleaded once. She said I didn't need to; she'd already come. She came when I did."

"How long did it go on?"

"Years. Every month or so for the last few years. After I moved back into my own bed."

"Oh! Yes! Len would have loved that, I doubt that his snuggles against Jet would have left her virgin."

Karen rolled her eyes, in a moon face,
"Halliards! No!"

The following morning, her last morning, Karen woke up, the weather forecast had been accurate, her bedroom ceiling was distinctly grey, instead of white. The irregular swish and occasional rat-tat of the heavier drops of rain beating on her bedroom window were interrupted by the 4x4 as it started up and squelched off down the track taking the rest of the family to their various destinations; the week was finished, her bus would leave past the end of the farm lane at noon, in less than four hours. It was now, or wait until it's dry, at Christmas.

"At Easter you said, 'Now. Or wait until after G.C.S.E. in the Summer,'" she murmured to herself. "So how about making it now?" Karen knew she wouldn't have him alone for long; Aunt Morag would be back. How long did it take to drive twelve miles? She glanced in the mirror and stood up, straight and tall; the nightie wasn't her sheerest sexy one, but definitely the nicest sexy one she possessed. Karen read it as transmitting a blatant come on, but still falling well short of trollop, and walked purposely through to Seth's room. It smelled of sweaty boy, but not unpleasantly so. Playfully she took a penalty kick with one of his socks, netting it low into the corner of his bedside cabinet. On the lee side of the house she would be able to watch the rain bleaching past the gable, whilst remaining dry, she parted the curtains, opened a window and leaned out.

"It's a lovely day to end a holiday. We'll need an ark to get to the main road."

There was a long pause; she looked at her cousin over her shoulder. He was awake, half-sitting up in bed, looking up at her, hands behind his head supporting it.

"Would you let me see you?"

Now he had her undivided attention, she turned and stepped back into the room near to the bed.

"You've seen me. You saw me yesterday."

"But not bare, not for years, not since you grew them. They must be lovely, because they stand right up with no support; I'd love to see them."

Karen was excited, apprehensive, thrilled to her core, his soft Scots accent adding even more romance to the words. She wanted to be brave and naughty and let him see her breasts, feel her breasts, suckle her breasts. She silently coaxed him on,

Persuade me, urge me, con me into obeying you.

"Show me yours and I'll show you mine, I'm hard looking at you in your nightie, I'm just as embarrassed as you are."

She took hold of the hem of the loose shift garment,

Don't stop, persuade me, encourage me.

"Just lift your hands, that's all it takes, just lift, higher--higher I can see your lovely hips, higher, your pretty belly button--just another few centimetres--your beauties are nearly there, yes, they're lovely. I knew they would be. Look what they've done to me." He rolled the bedclothes back, his manhood stood up hard, proud, erect, thrilling, frightening, so big, huge. Even bigger than Len, how could a girl ever take that, when her little cunny squashed two fingers so tightly? Her eyes, were fixed on him, all thoughts as to her own lewd display forgotten.

"Would you like to touch, you can if you want."

Karen closed up to the bed,

"Yes."

He slid over to give her space and she climbed on and knelt beside him. Now, that her stilts were folded away under her, they were nearly the same height. Her left hand was still holding her nightie up around her neck.

"Take it off."

The thin shift looped upwards and side slipped to the floor.

"Touch me."

She reached out, she didn't know what to expect. Did all boys feel the same?

"Oh, he's hot. He's rigid hard. Is he all right?" Her voice was full of concern.

"He's fine now that you're holding him, that's what he wanted." Seth had already begun to caress her voluptuous breasts. Her nipples slammed out to greet him. She was always amazed at how smooth a penis was, skin so silky it rivalled that of her own baby soft hands. She felt him all over. In his mind, would he be pretending he was having her? If so, she could help there. She wrapped her hand gently around him and caressed sensuously.

"Oh Rockhopper. Don't stop. Don't stop! Don't stop!" His hands gripped her breasts firmly, she pushed them into his grasp. He swelled up, hardened even more, pulled back and climaxed in great jets of pale, whitish, gloopy fluid up his tummy. Karen, working on the principle of what one boy liked, another probably did too, kept pumping him in a smooth rhythm. It was several seconds later when he released her, covered her hands with his and asked her to stop. She sat back on her heels and grinned at him,

"Was that nice?"

Seth mirrored her grin and tried to acknowledge that it was, the cough caught him again and he had to wait for a few seconds to get it under control.

"Yes, it was lovely, thank you."

"You've had that cough since I came up. It hurts you. I can see it does. Are you going to get it seen to?"

"I'm allergic to this new mousse. I've stopped using it. It'll be okay." He reached over for tissues and Karen gave him space until he began to mop.

"No, let me do that. I thought they were for the cough." She cleaned and tidied and threw the ball of tissues into the bin. "Can I cuddle in?"

He shuffled down offering the crook of his arm. She slid into place and guided his hands in to caress her, then turned her attention to his body, caressing him with languorous, feather-light touches on his breasts, tummy and thighs. Presently his caresses became more charged with purpose and his flaccid penis, rolled around and lifted off him.

"That's better," she murmured, as she eased up, swung a leg over him and sat on his thighs, just not quite touching the now rampant pole. She leaned forward circling his nipples with her fingers and smiled straight into his eyes. "Is he ready to be loved again?"

"Just about."

She tickled downwards, her hands and pubis closing on his manhood to provide a three-way caress.

The 4x4 noisily changed gear up the track.

Karen jumped off the bed, grabbed her nightie, and scurried through to her own room to get decent again. The call came up the stairs a few seconds later.

"Are you two still in bed?"

"Just going for a shower," from Karen and,

"Yes," from Seth.

Karen said her Goodbyes, and Thanks, and picked up the smaller of her bags. Seth shouldered the large rucksack and took the letters off the dresser,

"Is this all the post?" he called to the house generally, no reply meant yes. The pair walked down the track, heads bowed against the weather and along the minor country road to the lonely, stone-built bus stop. Karen loved the aura of civilised society that permeated the deserted shelter, no graffiti, there was untended post in an unsecured rack and, although dust dry inside the building, it still smelled only of freshly rain washed air. All so different from those in her deprived inner city home. The bus wasn't due for twenty minutes. It wasn't quite an 'Oh you've just missed it, it went yesterday,' service, but it was kept afloat by carrying the mail too.

"Thank you for this morning, it was lovely." He looked embarrassed, fearful, his eyes, not meeting hers. "I wanted to do it to you."

"Oh. I thought you didn't. Why didn't you? I wanted you to. I wanted you to do it. All week. For years, I've dreamed of you doing it. I thought I wasn't pretty enough."

"You're lovely, of course you're pretty enough, you're pretty enough for anyone, never mind me. I didn't know, come here." He put his arm around her and felt her through the front of her dripping skirt, below the hem of her cagoule. Her eyes, closed, she hunted around his face for his mouth and kissed him. Seth pulled up her skirt at the front and petted her through her knickers; she spread her thighs in welcome. Then, he was up her knicker leg, fumbling his fingers into her, rubbing, rough, hard, a boy's fingers, quite unlike Jet's gentle probing, her first boy was into her, except for Len of course, but he didn't count.

Karen went down like a marionette with its strings cut; the orgasm ripped her senses apart in a dead faint. Seth was struggling to hold her, the sudden effort made him cough. It was long seconds before she had her head back together again sufficiently to hold a compos mentis conversation.

"That was lovely, holding you, feeling you, making you come, sorry I didn't do it this morning. I didn't know you wanted me to feel you."

"I didn't. I mean I did. But, not just to feel--I wanted you to do it. You know, do it."

"I tried, yesterday, on our walk, but you didn't want to; you wouldn't stay in one place."

"I did. I wanted you to ask. To persuade me. To make me. Gently make me. I had to do something. Nice girls don't. So I moved about."

"That is one of the nastiest, most sexist insults ever thought up by chauvinist bullies, don't ever say 'Nice girls don't' again. It's a mental chain, padlocked to you, to deprive you, have you ever heard 'Nice boys don't'? Dearest Cousin, I confer freedom upon you. You can do what you want. I want to share losing my virginity with you, when you come back at Hogmanay, but you're free, you can do what you want."

"Why wait until Hogmanay?"

"I haven't got anything."

"I'll risk it."

"I want to take my time and love you. I want to make it special. I'll get everything ready; we'll give each other the best Christmas present ever." Outmanoeuvred and with another passenger heading towards the only place in the district not smarting under the slashing rain, Karen surrendered,

"Okay. I'll wait until Hogmanay."

The other passenger joined them, guillotining further details. The bus breasted the rise across the valley; its headlights dimmed by the downpour. Seth carefully loaded her up, with ruck and day sack, ensuring her hands were free,

"I've got something for you," he said and eased a large hand-sized, gift-wrapped box out of his poachers pocket and gave it to her. "It's heavy and fragile, so don't drop it. I was going to give it to you after, but I changed my mind. Now that we know about Hogmanay, you can have it in anticipation." Only seconds later the bus swished to a stop, Karen kissed her cousin goodbye and climbed aboard, with the box in one hand and the clutch of mail in the other.

She waited and waited.

Heavy and fragile, so don't open it until you get home, one deep pothole and you'll lose it.

However, waiting until she got home to Novochester, across the border, into a different country, was beyond her. Once aboard the train, where she had a little table to rest on, she gave in and peeled her present.

Lead Crystal
40% PbO

The sticker on the side of the box proudly announced, so it was made from seriously good-quality materials.

It was a decorative object, a truly beautiful work of art.

A piece of green and brown cliff, framing a small ledge of rocky shore had green and blue sea, with white highlights, raging against it. Standing on the ledge, just not quite centre stage and looking into the water, was a crested penguin. The bird was clear white glass with a frosted finish, the essence and spirit of coloured plumage achieved by the thinnest layer of dark enamel. From above the eyes, scarlet and yellow crests stood out, long slender and delicate. Karen chuckled and chuckled at it as she twisted and turned it. She got out her reading glasses and looked at it more closely. It had grey-blue barnacles and brown and green seaweed, a single violet anemone provided the solid artistic anchorage from which to enjoy the scene. She chuckled again at the look of intense concentration on the bird's face. The beady eyes, stared straight down the beak into the water, like a child at the kerb reciting the Green Cross Code, with sudden death a major player for both if they make a mistake.

But, you won't die little Rockhopper; you can stay up on your ledge forever. No lurking leopard seals for you to worry about. No speeding trucks for us. I'll make sure of it. When we're old and grey, we'll still be chuckling at you.

As soon as she got home, she telephoned to thank him.

* * *

When Jet's timing was off, occasionally it was spectacularly off. This time on the telephone,

"Can I come over tonight? Discuss the Sixth Form Courses with you."

Karen's eyes rolled, as her knuckles on the hand holding the telephone whitened.

"No, not tonight please Jet." She was desperately groping for excuses. "Anyway there's nothing to discuss. You're doing Tourism. I'm doing Plumbing."

"There's General Studies, we're both doing that."

"General Studies is just to balance up the curriculum. It doesn't need discussing. I'll talk about it with you on Saturday."

"Saturday's shopping, I want a dress; we won't have time to talk about school."

Karen dropped the receiver onto the top of her desk with a clatter, picked it up and dropped it again.

"Oh. Sorry." She gave it another knock for good measure. "Look Jet, I've got problems. I've got to go. I'll see you on Saturday." And hung up. Her Dad looked up from the model car that he was building,

"It's Thursday! It's nine o'clock! And it's Sailing!" He called, paraphrasing the famous introduction to Crackerjack.

"It's my one time of the week. I know I'll never own a boat. But, I can dream for one hour a week. Surely!"

"An hour and a half! Never curtail your dreams girl!"

That night the presenter completed varnishing the boat, that she was building as a centrepiece to the sequence of programmes, and moved on to choice of sails and sail care.

In bed, Karen fell asleep dreaming of becoming such a successful plumber, that one day she might even consider owning a boat of her own.

On Saturday, she smoothed Jet's ruffled feathers by talking General Studies throughout the shopping morning.

The following week in her local library, she found the address she needed to facilitate the main event of Hogmanay and a few days after that, went to get herself fixed up.

What if someone sees me? They'll know. She stopped. *That's a typical 'Some people might say' bullying Media tack; I look 'em straight in the eye and stare them down. Nobody, but Nobody is going to take Freedom from me.*

With her head up and back straight, she aimed straight for the last door of the row of buildings, that decades ago had been a terrace of huge, luxury town-houses and now were homes to Legal firms, Dentist Surgeries, Training Centres and, her destination, a Family Planning Clinic.

A girl, in jeans and top, with her long blonde hair in a single plait down her back was walking ahead of her, obviously heading for the same destination. She was doing so furtively, her little knapsack with its tennis gear protruding from it responding in an agitated manner to her unease. Karen's heart went out to her; this was the true legacy of Victorian hypocrisy. The girl hesitated, lost it, turned and walked straight into her. She didn't even look up.

"Oh sorry."

The tall brunette had to grab hold of the other girl to stop her from sliding away, she had obviously not been recognised. Despite the incongruously-bulky arms and shoulders on the otherwise slender frame, the huge owl-glasses, single blonde plait and tennis gear, Karen hadn't put the clues together and realised herself who it was, until they collided,

"Hello Pealle."

"Oh, sorry Karen, didn't see, I was--"

"Come on. I'm going too," Karen linked the other girl, spun her around and assertively guided her up the stairs and in through the door talking all the time to prevent the blonde from saying or doing things she later regretted. "It's difficult. Coming in to places like this. Best to do it your way. Just barge straight in. As if you owned the place. I've never been before. Do we ask at reception? Well, I'll have to anyway. Stay with me."

She managed to keep a neutral conversation going through reception, waiting and in to see the doctor.

"Are you coming back into the Sixth Form?"

"I think I'll have to, I've had five job interviews and lost every one. A couple of them I lost before they spoke with me, as soon as they saw I was a girl."

"What do you want to be? Brickie?"

"Electrician."

"I want to be a plumber. Girls aren't plumbers apparently. Wrong species. I'm going to change all that. I'm going to do Mr. Carpenter's A level course. Vocational Engineering. It's modular. Five modules to qualify. At least three of them are electrical. Well, they've got electrics in 'em. I know 'cos I'm doing them."

"What? I mean which?"

"Domestic, Heating and Electronics."

"You need all those for plumbing?"

"I'll be a better plumber with them."

"It's exactly what I want."

"You'd have to do the Heating anyway. It's core, it's an essential part."

"Do you think he'd have me, I wasn't great at technology; I'll just scrape through."

"With what?"

"A 'B' with luck, but Mrs. Pentland--"

"That's why you weren't that great. Forget anything about the potato. It's Mr. Carpenter. A real teacher. Why don't you ask him? Tell you what. After we leave here, we'll go to school and see him. The worst that can happen is he says no. You'll be no worse off than you are now. Oh, we're on."

She grabbed the other girl's hand and hauled her into the consulting room to get herself fixed up. Then, she carefully excused herself; telling Pealle she would wait outside.

When the elegant blonde rejoined her, the two girls headed back out West, to school.

Karen checked at the school office that Mr. Carpenter was on site before they signed in, it was a long trek through to Technology merely to find the cupboard bare, but he was. Several minutes later she knocked politely on his door, opened it, went in and stopped abruptly.

Face to face with Mrs. Pentland.

“Oh hello Miss. I’ve just come to see Mr. Carpenter.”

“He’s busy. We’re all busy.” Her eyes, shifted focus to behind Karen. “You shouldn’t be here. Make an appointment.”

“It’s okay Mrs. Pentland, Karen did make an appointment and she’s right on time. Come in girls. Thank you Mrs. Pentland, I’ll see to these.” Mr. Carpenter waved some papers. “Straight away.” He drew the girls inside and ushered his second in department outside. “Straight away, I promise.” Then he shut the door. “Back room,” he said pointing. “Sit down.”

“I didn’t make an appoin--”

“Yes, you did, we agreed you could come to see me any time to discuss your future. It happens to suit me to talk to you now. You did make an appointment, it might have been a bit imprecise, but you did make it.”

Karen had never before been on the receiving end of the baleful glare now turned upon her, but she’d seen it used on others.

“Okay. I made an appointment.” Like butting walls, she thought, So nice when you stop, as the glare was replaced by a smile.

“Good, I’m glad we got that straight. What can I do for you?”

“Not me, her.”

“The face is familiar pet, who are you?”

“I’m Pealle Tumpkins; I was in Mrs. Pentland’s set.”

“Ah, yes, the girl with the lovely name.”

“But difficult to live with Sir. I was hoping to get a job as an apprentice electrician, but they don’t want to know, from the second they see the skirt. I’ve discussed it with Karen.”

“And you think it might be better if you were to get some better qualifications?”

“It couldn’t be any worse. Your A level course seems to be exactly what I need, would you consider me for it?”

"Right. First, you pick your subjects, you need one or two more besides mine and then you make an appointment to see the Head of Sixth Form, find out if he'll accept you. He's much more likely to do so if he thinks you will be staying to complete the course, not leave and jump into the first dodgy apprenticeship that offers you a place. You can tell him I'll take you if he does and make sure you say it that way around."

"I'm not that good at Technology."

"You're good enough if you work hard and I think you will." He turned away and began rummaging in a cupboard. "I'll give you the documents you need, syllabus, equipment lists 'n that." He gathered a fat wad of papers into a neat pile and slid them into an envelope file. "It's just to save you trekking all the way back, but don't thrust them under Mr. Pling's nose, let Big Kay carry them or something."

With the primary objective of their visit achieved, the girls headed back towards the school office and their next target, an appointment with the Head of Sixth Form.

"It is a lovely name you know," said Karen gently.

"Well at least it's better than the other one they were considering, 'Triplebobmajor'."

"Oh dear. Just think. You could have been called 'Freakouttraverse'. Had your parents been pot-holers."

"'Chasmdrop' or 'Boulderfalls', thank goodness they're campanologists."

"What other subjects could you study?"

The blonde grimaced as she replied, she had obviously foreseen problems,

"History, Geography, not a whole lot of use to an electrician. My Physics is good in Magnetism and Electricity but useless otherwise. Anyway you can't do it without doing Maths and I've heard that's very hard at A level."

"I'm doing Business and Economics-Two subjects, for when the time comes to set up on my own."

"That sounds like a nicely balanced selection, would you mind?"

"No; of course not. Jet's doing Tourism. It would be nice to be with someone I know."

When they reached the school office again, they discovered that for the second time they were in luck, Mr. Pling was in and available.

An hour later Karen bounced off home, feeling completely on a roll. A girl whose sporting prowess she'd admired for years and whom today she had discovered was nice, with human foibles, was joining her on her Sixth Form courses.

She hadn't minded being the only girl, assuming she was, she didn't know for sure, but now there wasn't even that to not mind. Pealle had arranged to come over for a final discussion before the end of the holidays and thanked her, as they parted,

"Thank you."

Karen had shaken her head and turned away, only to be restrained, turned and have her face cupped in both of Pealle's hands.

"No--Thank you--For everything."

The blonde was staring meaningfully into her eyes. Karen nodded,

"Any time. See you next week." She nodded at the pile of paper Pealle had had to lay down to hold her. "You have a lot of work to do."

"Next week." The elder girl had released her, scooped up all the administration that Karen had had for months and gone off herself, to catch up.

With her head full of her news and her priorities a short list of one, telephone Seth, and tell him not to bother getting everything ready, she'd already done it, Karen hurried joyfully up the front path at home, her emotions matched by the massed ranks of bedding dahlias either side of her feet that were now approaching their brief dazzling best. Prematurely they would be cut down by autumn's frosts,

Blaze now, she thought. *It's your time--and mine.*

Her Dad opened the door to his grinning daughter and closed it behind her. Her rucksack and his case, bulging with clothes stood side by side in the hall. She turned to him puzzled, he was grey, haggard.

The Severed Head
Part One

The Birmingham Trade Fair was as bad as the Novochester delegate had feared. It consisted of hours of waiting around fawning to minions, with no guarantee of a sale. That this was his chief gripe was not a secret, he'd said it in so many words in the Sales Bar.

"You price are too high, for poor Country," replied a portly man, breaking into the delegate's tirade.

"I know that. But quality costs."

"Little sacrifice on quality, big save on cost, big sale, big profit."

"I sell what we produce, have made to order, branded products. Quality stuff."

"You good seller. Sell cheaper goods no problem. You become Buyer, buy from me, you sell, you make profit."

The big man turned away,

"Just another sale trying to turn a trick, I'm selling, not buying, or hadn't you noticed."

"Not you company, you Mr. Man. You are Buyer, you sell, you profit. Think to it. I see you at Europe Fair. Next month. You buy from me, big profit." The portly man waved Goodbye and sauntered off through the throng, occasionally stopping to speak with contacts, arrange meetings. At his own stand, later that night, in his own language, he spoke with the unacknowledged colleague, he'd left watching the delegate.

"Well?"

"It was easy. He is a bully; he likes to beat weak ones. He tries to beat everyone, but the weak ones, he beats without mercy. We will buy a girl, for him to beat."

"Girls are cheap enough."

"That's not what we will tell him though, is it?"

Chapter 2

Loss: August 1998

Karen

"What's up?"

"It's a big shock. Be brave. Seth's dying."

"No!"

He's not expected to last the night."

"It can't be!"

"I'm sorry darling, so sorry. We have to hurry. We're probably too late as it is though."

While her Dad loaded the car, Karen, coping in denial, threw together some food to sustain them. It was a solemn pair that dashed north-westwards through the evening and on into the darkness. She fed him little snacks from time to time and, at his insistence, forced some down her own throat.

They didn't make it.

Capability Karen kicked in and bolstered up the distraught family, all through the post-mortem findings and funeral arrangements.

An early task was to separate Jo from the crowd.

"Have you taken the magazines?"

"I tried, there was never a good time, always somebody bustling in and out and then it didn't seem right somehow, with

Seth lying there, but not there, under that sheet."

"I know what you mean. But Seth wouldn't mind. Cheering you on more like. When the undertaker has been, we'll do it. Get a box ready." She cut her Dad out of the throng. "Dad, Jo and me. We need some privacy upstairs. When the undertaker is busy down here. After seeing to Seth. Make sure everyone else is busy."

He nodded.

"Right Jo. We've got a few minutes to plan. Then, we might only have two minutes to do. You know where the magazines are. What about videos?"

"I've got it."

"Only one?"

"That's all we had."

"CDs? Computer Stuff?"

The younger girl shook her head,

"Just the Mags and a video."

"Sure?"

Jo sniffed, fighting the tears, nodding into to her tissue.

"Yes, I'm sure, we've been good mates since you--since the summer holidays. We pooled our money, bought the video together. To learn what to do, it's sex education, not just sexy fun like the magazines. Oh Karen, you gave me my big brother back and now I've lost him again." The threatening tears won and the taller girl hugged her sobbing cousin. It was several minutes later when the talking and general activity outside the door helped her get the grief under control. Dennis Robinson put his head around,

"All clear for now." The girls hurried to their task. A few minutes later when Aunt Morag appeared, Seth's room was tidy, his bed stripped of the soiled linens and protective sheeting and remade for the living. She sat on it. Karen waited until the racking sobs ceased before going in and asking, with a gentle smile,

"Can I get you anything? Tea? Bun?"

"No I'll be okay."

Nevertheless, a few minutes later she pressed a sweet mince pie and cup of tea into her Aunt's hand.

"Carbohydrates. Nature's comfort food," she murmured and

stayed to watch as her Aunt pushed it down.

* * *

"Show me the video."

Jo rummaged the box out and handed it over,

"Sex Tips for girls, Volume One, Making babies, it's by Stevie Bollard."

"I know of a Stevie Bollard who designs work clothes."

"That's her, she does all sorts."

"Where did you get it?"

"Mail-order, there's a whole series, at least I know what to do now, most of what my mates say is wrong."

"What's the most wrong thing you've ever been told?"

"If you do it and get pregnant, do it again, gets rid of it."

"Yes, that's just about as wrong as I've ever heard. And a boy thing?"

"It was a boy."

Karen made a moon face.

"Have you straightened your mates out?"

"No--Should I?"

"Up to you. If it's any help, I would. If they were mine."

Karen was magnificent, but it was a front. Her Dad waited for the cracks to show and the edifice crumble. It happened at the graveside, as the coffin was lowered. He turned her to him and hugged her. The service finished; he waved the rest away.

"We're alone darling; you can say Goodbye now."

Father and daughter moved over to the edge and kneeled down side-by-side, oblivious to the hovering sextants.

"Why? Why did you make me wait?" Karen blindly groped for soil and dropped it into the grave along with her tears.

"You should have had me. In your bed. Now, you never will. I wanted you to fuck me. In the bus shelter Seth. I wanted you to do it. Not to wait. We shouldn't have waited."

Dennis Robinson massaged his daughter's taut back. Slowly she stood up and turned; he folded her in.

"I'd have lived with any consequences. Now, I have to live with these consequences. And I don't know that I ca--" Her protest petered out to silence.

The younger gravedigger was struggling not to leer, but the elder man's face was full of compassion. The sobbing racked her slim body.

"You weren't to know pet; it's not your fault."

"We were going to do it at Hogmanay. We agreed to wait until Hogmanay. Make it a super special Hogmanay. Be each other's first. When I came back up. And now he won't be here."

"It's not your fault."

"I'll bring his present up. And he won't be here to have me." The tears were pouring down, but the gut wrenching sobs had eased, catharsis was near.

"I know pet, I know."

"Why do people do what I don't want? Why do I agree to it?"

"I know. But we'll talk about it later, get it all out now, don't hold any back, then we can talk and remember him with joy later."

As he turned to walk them away, Dennis waved his thanks at their audience. The younger man was now tuned in; he got two lots of compassionate gentle gestures in return.

Pealle

One hundred and sixty miles roughly to the southeast by crow flight, but many more by car, Pealleovbelles Tumpkins was patrolling her club's premises, furtively checking the courts and changing rooms for mad people prepared to play despite the driving rain. The gifted young tennis player failed to find any, both her intentions and the countryside were uncomplicated by competitors.

Eager now, she slid into the admin-block. Once inside she straightened up and walked confidently towards the office. Harold was here. His car stood tucked away in an obscure corner of the otherwise empty car park, she'd had to look hard to find it, nobody would know they were here, together, alone. Noises were coming from the gym; he wasn't in his office after all. Grinning, she turned and bounded down the short corridor to the open door and stopped dead. The noises had become words, foully abusive words, of which slag was the least offensive. A man was foully abusing a protesting woman. The youngster crept up to the door ready to jump in, or run for help, which ever was required.

Her help wasn't needed. The woman was protesting encouragement, not objection. Pealle realised that she had been completely wrong; her intentions had a major competitor.

She didn't watch for long, when Harold stopped beating his mistress, and mounted her, the blond retreated and moments later left the building.

Back home, in her room, with the door firmly closed she hauled out her Diary, found the relevant page and reviewed the situation. Slowly, sadly, she drew a line through a name on her short list of acceptable candidates to deflower her; the only problem was that the list had only been one name long, there were none left, not even unwritten ones.

"Okay, life goes on," she murmured. "Start again."

Karen

On the drive back home, the following day, Karen apologised to her Dad.

"I'm sorry. I didn't mean to tell you all that. Hurt you."

"I'm not hurt, you're sixteen in a few days time, you can fuck whom you like. It's entirely your business." He paused assessing an overtaking opportunity. "Seth was a good choice, waiting turned out to be the wrong one, but it was a reasonable thing to do at the time; you weren't to know. It won't be the last wrong choice you ever make." Mirror, signal, down two gears, he slammed the throttle to the floor, flicked out onto the right hand side of the road, five seconds later he was back safely in left and top. "With luck, you'll make fewer as you get older, but it's not an inviolate rule. And I'd much rather have a relationship with my daughter where she feels that she can tell me with whom she's fucking, rather than her feeling that she can't tell me."

They were silent for a while, then Dennis broached the subject that had intrigued him since the leaving graveside

"Did I understand correctly, that you're still virgin?"

"Yes. Is that a problem?"

"No, a pleasant surprise. When Mum died, I had to carry you back to bed, every night, but every morning you were back in with Len, I guess it was your way of coping, making sure that another loved one didn't slip away while you weren't looking. You were only six, there didn't seem any harm and so after a while I just let you. Short of locking you in your bedroom, there wasn't much else I could do. Then several years later one night there were strange noises, I looked in, you were passively lying there, while Len was having you from behind, his hands pummelling your breasts. I didn't know what to do, it didn't look like the first time you'd done it, you looked so serene, completely acquiescing to what was going on, so most probably it was too late to do anything, so I just left you to it and lay awake all night worrying."

"He was having my bum cheeks. Not me. Not properly."

"That's what he told me. So I belled the cat, told him that if he got you pregnant I'd skin him alive."

"It wasn't just him you know."

"I didn't blame him; I didn't blame either of you. You were clinging to each other for comfort and support, in all respects but one, it was natural, and bearing in mind the love you have for each other, understandable. I just reacted, I had to do something, I didn't know what to do for the best, so I went for the possible consequence."

"Did you tell him to send me back to my own bed?"

"No, but the following night that's where you were."

"He told me to go. That he couldn't guarantee not to do it to me. By accident. We haven't stopped completely. The occasional shower. Sometimes a friendly cuddle when we're alone."

"But you managed to preserve your virginity."

"Yes. Amazingly. I mean if he'd asked, I'd have given. But yes,--Is it always going to be like this? Loved ones sneaking off when my back is turned? There's only you and Len left."

"Sometimes they say goodbye to your face, I don't know which is the harder to bear, but yes, it doesn't stop--He didn't mean to sneak off behind your back you know, he'd much rather still be here, waiting for his Hogmanay present, panting with anticipation."

Karen tipped her head in agreement, but knowing and accepting are sometimes different fish in disjoint seas.

A few miles further on,

"Do you really want to know why you end up doing what other people want?"

"Yes."

"You like to please, it's not fundamentally a problem. The problem arises when you let go. Relinquish control, in order to please. You don't like doing that much. Or you agree to something, which you don't really want, and later decide it was wrong, and have to live with the consequences. We all have to live with consequences, from decision to decision. Think things through thoroughly and make decisions where you can live with the consequences."

"Thanks Dad."

"If you must please, and it carries as many problems as refusing to, do it in such a way as you can stay in control. That way at least the consequences will be down to you."

Later that night, Karen joined her Dad in the shower.

"Can I sleep with you tonight? Give you my cherry. Please."

"No darling."

She wasn't surprised, but the pain was intense, he hugged her to him to comfort her and his penis responded at once.

"No, I want to, as you can feel--"

"Just this once. I know you need to relieve your frustrations occasionally. You must be able to hear me sometimes too. And tonight it's particularly bad."

"It wouldn't be just this once. I told you the truth, the last time you offered. I don't know how I've kept my hands off you sometimes, but I have, and it's important that I do, you'll find your man soon and I might trip over a lonely widow somewhere and we'll be fine."

"You haven't been fine for ten years. Not taken a girl to your bed. Unless you know something I don't."

"That management course I went on? When you were eight?"

"At the college. You went several times. South Berkshire?"

"I paired up with this lady from London, we had a lot of laughs. We met again the following year and the year after that she'd obviously got sick of waiting for me to take her to my bed so she took me to hers. We were about to begin when the telephone rang; it was her husband wishing her Goodnight. I had no idea; I had been sizing up the long-term possibilities, how to close a three hundred mile gap. I just left--"

"Oh Dad." She hugged him again.

"Without a word, carrying my clothes. Stark naked and feeling utterly betrayed. It put me right back to square one. The only good thing about it was we hadn't done it, so I hadn't helped betray her husband."

"Unknowingly."

"When I got over the shock and anger and self recriminations, not having done it, even unknowingly, was the thing that buoyed me up enough to get back."

"I'm sorry. I didn't know."

"A young maid asked me if I were all right and helped me back to my room. She offered to stay and look after me. She made it plain that she meant in bed. I turned her down and she was a bonny little thing, but I was smashed."

"You went only on day courses after that. Now, I know why. And why no girls. You haven't been looking."

"I'm about ready to start looking again, until then--I'll try to keep my squeals to myself."

"Don't you dare. Okay I'll sleep in my bed. On one condition. Tonight, you squeal your head off. Shout rude words. I'll do the same. But, if I don't hear you, I'll be in to sleep beside you. With you. In every sense."

"Okay I'll squeal my head off."

"Leave your bedroom door open. I want to be sure."

Her own bedroom door, open wide, left a darker shape against the pale wall, with a red edge all the way down it, Dad hadn't switched his light off yet. He'd promised, if he failed her, she would carry out her threat.

She waited.

She'd waited long enough, the short nightie slid sideways just as it had in Seth's bedroom, a month ago and a moment later she stepped across the landing and stopped. His bedroom door opened the wrong way, into the bedroom, instead of against the wall, and was standing at a right angle to the opening forming a short corridor into the room. Through the gap she could see her Dad from the chest down, lying on his back, star fished, naked on his bed, and he was relieving his frustrations after all. He was holding his local depot's annual report in his other hand, with a picture of the bosses boarding a plane facing away from him. The page he was looking at, Karen knew, showed a group of youngsters from the accounts office, dressed for a party, in clothes that virtually had 'Bonk me quick' written on them.

"Are you going to fuck me?"

For a moment Karen thought he was speaking to her.

"You can if you want, all of you."

No, he was fulfilling his part of the bargain.

"Yes,--Oh!--all of you--I don't mind--all fuck me--Oh fuck me." He came hard up his tummy, jerking. Karen nodded and returned to her own room, to see to her own needs.

The Severed Head
Part Two

In a dingy back room, less than a mile from the glittering facade of the European Trade Fair, a girl was cowering away from her punishment. Unable to see, scream or dodge she waited meekly for the next punishing blow to descend on her unprotected back. It never came, instead there was much shouting in a foreign language, which she didn't understand, but which was almost as frightening.

The portly man had plucked the stick from the big man's grasp as it was raised for the next blow. The other was beside himself with fury, screaming for it to be given back.

"No, no, my friend, you not kill her yet, she is not paid for. Girl are expensive; you must pay before you break." He assertively drew the other through into a different room and began to negotiate their contract. "Here is portfolio; I can supply anything. At a price." He waved into the room behind him. "Even girl, at a price. Speak to you client, if you cannot make sale at company price, try my price. You Buyer! You buy from me, you sell, you make big profit, you able to buy girl."

Karen

The series on building and using a boat continued to captivate Karen and each week the presenter had guests on her show whose faces were familiar from the box, but whom previously Karen had not realised were boat people.

Lesser celebrities, when required to be themselves, occasionally show as featureless ciphers, but she was intrigued to note that the boat owning guests obviously had substantial depth to their characters. This was spectacularly so in the case of two of those featured, themselves Natural Earth programme presenters.

The pair had always impressed Karen with their style and she strove not to miss their programs. To her surprise they turned out to be fisher-girls, whose mastery of boats, kayaks in their case, allowed them to pursue their hobby into otherwise inaccessible places.

On screen, they made a formidable pair, the familiar Geordie accent of the redhead, contrasting sweetly with the blonde's cultured Yorkshire.

A boat became the trainee plumber's most desired material asset.

Pealle

Pealle was hurrying.

Having decided to return to the Sixth Form, despite none of her friends doing so, it had been a relief to the nubile blonde to be befriended, mentored even, by a pleasant acquaintance, who might yet become a close, supportive ally. She had every reason not to be late for their next meeting.

Five years in the more and more, dog eat dog world of competitive tennis, had taught the blonde to choose her soul-mates with care. Even more so when the string of consecutive victories began to stretch out behind her for weeks, which became months and now stood at two years.

Now, increasingly, she felt the need to watch her back. There were those on the circuit that, behind a friendly smile, possibly wouldn't stop at ground glass in her yoghurt, to topple the champ.

Karen had already shown herself to be supportive and tactfully understanding. Pealle was sure she'd found a friend who would be the perfect foil to her highly competitive sporting career.

Karen

The blonde dropped her tennis gear down in the hallway.

"I've come straight from training, I showered off, but I'm a bit sweaty again now, I'm afraid."

Karen retrieved a hand towel from the nearby cloakroom and began to wipe the other girl down with it,

"Nothing wrong with the fruits of honest toil. No worse than me after a morning digging the potatoes. And that's dirty too. I've got everything ready. We'll do it in here. In the shade. Then go and laze in the garden. Once you're cool again."

With the school business safely completed, the girls took their coffees out into the back garden.

"Foot Faults! What's that?" Pealle headed across the lawn towards the dominant feature.

"The pond." The tall brunette watched her new friend surveying the garden and tried to imagine seeing it for the first time. Half an acre was in clear view, beyond that, the mature trees, heavy with nuts and fruit, extended at least as far. On the left, a bedding scheme of dahlias, antirrhinums and African marigolds presented a carnival of colour; large ethnic pots overflowed with lobelia and fuchsia. To their right the kitchen garden, already heavily plundered, could still keep a hungry scout troop happy until Christmas. The huge greenhouse, sheltering in a sunny corner, displayed, as well as standard varieties in red and yellow, trusses of cherry and beefsteak tomatoes. Flashes of other, even more vibrant colours peeping through between them, showed that the far side was devoted to exotic flowers.

And of course, straight ahead across the lawn, framed by the mature rock garden, lay the pond.

"The lake, the main reservoir for Novochester and District, not to mention the miles of river flowing into it. Is this where you caught your love of boats?"

"Deranged child. But, it is quite large, I never notice. It's just our pond."

A dozen golden torpedoes turned down the river from just

below the bridge and cruised around the edge of the pond to Pealle's feet. They circled and weaved in a mesmerising maze, darker shapes joined in, followed by a slower moving under storey, poised, waiting.

"Complete with--No they're not, they're Golden-Orfe, aren't they. I knew they grew big, never seen them that big."

"They were fingerlings. When we got them." Karen held a little finger up. "Eight years ago. Pinkies. The dark red ones are Golden Rudd. They're older than we are. Some of them. They'll take their flakes from your fingers. First thing in the morning. And the ones on the bottom are Tench. Golden Tench."

"It's fantastic. Red lilies, yellow ones, that's water hawthorn isn't it?"

Karen nodded. The blonde walked along to the river that curled around in a loop and back towards the pool, but climbing through the rocks, as you walked upstream, to about a metre higher,

"What's this pair of stretched wires all around?"

"Heron proof fencing. Herons like to land and walk into the water. Seems to work. We haven't been hit. Lots of people have. In the neighbourhood."

Pealle stopped a few metres up the river, her attention grabbed by a rocky pool.

"That's the minnow pool. They can't get out."

"And vacuum up every living thing smaller than they are."

"Yes. There's fine mesh netting under the bridge too. To keep the big fish in the bottom pool. Most of the river is a wildlife paradise. No fish predators. Reach into the water and turn a stone over."

Pealle did so,

"Heaving! Invertebrate soup, that's why the Orfe were up the river, gorging on the succulent morsels being washed down."

"Yes. They're always up there."

"I take it that it's not a real river."

"No, closed system. Pumped. Well accelerated really. Mains power. Battery power. Wind power. Whatever's handy at the time. Right now, it will be mostly sunlight. With a fair bit more topping up the batteries." Karen turned to a little cairn and withdrew a jar of pellets. "Okay you lot. You win. Want to feed them?"

Pealle walked back holding her hand out.

"Two good handfuls. Sprinkle them on their noses."

The mesmerising maze accelerated to feeding-frenzy, a fast-rolling-boil of fish soup. How they avoided crashing into each other was a mystery.

"What are these?"

"Trout pellets."

"Flake in the morning, trout pellets in the afternoon and the natural menu all day, little wonder they're that size."

Presently the pair wandered back to the patio and sat together in the swing bench.

"What a lovely seat."

"And it doesn't tip you out. When you swing it back. I'm told it used to, not now."

"No it doesn't. Oh I see, it's hanging from four pivot points, where did you get it? I've only ever seen them with two."

"It was a Wedding Present. Dad altered it."

Pealle tipped her head back and examined the frame; the additional supports for the extra anchorage points were indistinguishable from the original wood.

"Your Dad is a craftsman."

"Yes. Not bad. Like Ernie Wise's rug. Even up close you can't see the join. I've looked. He built the wardrobes in the bedrooms too."

The blonde nodded thoughtfully and sipped her drink. There was an undemanding silence, new friends growing together, easy in each other's company.

"Is it his job?"

"No. He's a postman."

Pealle looked around at the large mature garden, behind the impressive house. Karen guessed she was too polite to ask,

"By choice. He inherited the imposing pile. And there's funds to run it, just about. Keep it safe from termites. Virulent Venusian Fungi and such. The odd Band Aid. Most Posties do it to feed their kids. Dad does it because he likes it." The easy silence resumed, presently a pair of butterflies weaved their courting dance through the tranquil scene, triggering Karen's comment. "I wish he'd find someone. He's lonely." Which in turn seeded Pealle's next question,

"Who's your boyfriend? The one Maggie would claim that you're poisoning your body, solely for his selfish pleasure."

"Haven't got one. He died last week. Mebees week before. It's blurred. It was the day we went to the clinic. Don't sympathise Pealle, I don't need it. I'm coping, just. We had--I had long term plans. We were to become lovers at New Year. All sorted, agreed. Now, it won't happen." She smiled, painting on the brave face. "I'll tell you sometime, just not now. The pain's not dry yet. If you don't mind."

"Of course not."

"So there isn't anyone. Not yet. Just trying to be a good Girl Scout. Prepared and all that. I wouldn't want to pass up the opportunity. Is your boy suitably appreciative?"

"I haven't got one either, I thought I had, well not exactly a boy but someone who would do the necessary for me, get rid of this virgin millstone but--" Karen caught the vibes clearly, her friend was agitated,

"You can tell me if you want. If it'll help. If it's too private that's okay too."

"I want to tell somebody, I need to tell it, but it's shocking, I don't want to shock you."

"You won't shock me. Not now I'm warned. Now, that I know. Just tell me."

"It was Harold Wreagues, he coaches tennis, at the club. You know the vibes you get when a man's shoved his hands in his pockets, to avoid grabbing you."

Karen smiled,

No Pealle, I don't, but it was nice of you to suppose that I do.

"Well Harold's wanted to get in my knickers for ages. I went there last week specifically to seduce him."

Karen nodded encouraging,

"Good for you."

"It's not that I particularly like him; he's loud and pushy. But, the idea was to go for a pushover target for my first try; you know, where I stood a chance of succeeding. That was the plan, but he wasn't alone; he was busily engaged in riding somebody else's wife around the gym."

"And you didn't fancy it? Becoming a member of his harem."

"The harem bit didn't bother me that much, I'd just wanted a friendly fuck and then move on. But, I did want it to be friendly. When I said he was riding her around the gym, there was a riding crop involved. I thought at first she was being assaulted, he was beating her and shouting abuse and she was squealing. Then, I realised she was screaming for him to hit her again and be rough with her."

"I'm told some girls like it that way."

"Fucked up the bum?"

"That certainly. I find the idea exciting. I'm definitely going to try it some time. But, not so sure about the beating bit. Not my scene. I don't think."

"It wasn't even the beating bit." Pealle heaved a big sigh. "To be honest, it wasn't actually the beating bit. I've thought about it since, they were both enjoying it. They had lowered the vaulting box to just the right height, the other sections were all together to one side, so she most likely helped lower it. She was lying along it face down; she could have dodged or got up and run away, but she didn't, she was very obviously agreeing to what was going on. Like you said, exciting, I'll try it someday." She stopped then after a moment, sighed again. "The whole truth is; I've been going to try it ever since I saw them. I wanted to run over, push her off the box and spread myself in her place, are you shocked?"

"Of course not. So you're Miss Pleespankmee. So what? That's okay."

The blonde chuckled as the tension flowed out of the situation.

"I've never been beaten, afterwards at least I'll know what it's like, and if I don't like it, I'll be able to refuse from authentic knowledge."

"Don't knock it until you've tried it? There's always that I suppose."

"That and--and up my bum, you could be right; I'm feeling all gooshy at the thought. It wasn't the beating and it wasn't the buggery, it was something else, I didn't even mind his enjoying it, what I didn't like, what stopped me from running over, was the way he was enjoying it, I didn't like the look on his face, I don't ever want anyone to look like that and say those things in quite that way, while doing it to me."

Karen nodded and lay back closing her eyes,

"Yes, I understand. Be careful who you tell about all that." Then, after a short pause. "I'm quite surprised. That you're still virgin. What with going on tour. Playing matches away from home. Staying over. Loads of opportunities. I would have thought."

"Two main problems. The team manager's wife was a portal guarder that made Cerberus look like a pampered lap dog. Would be seducers stood a better chance of building Venice on Venus." Pealle paused. "And boys don't make passes at girls who wear glasses."

Karen looked sharply at the pain behind the blonde's eyes and attacked it aggressively,

"Yes, they do."

"I believed they didn't, so the successful Venusian Architect's advances were not recognised, eventually, they asked someone else."

"Ah, beliefs." She reached out and touched the other girl gently. "Yes, I understand. There can be few lies so damaging as those we make up to tell ourselves. So we have a couple of bruised virgins sitting in this swing."

"Yes. Slightly handled fruit--I hope?"

Karen grinned back at the enquiring expression,

"Oh yes. Definitely handled."

"But as yet unplucked, well it's a start, infinitely better than nothing at all."

"Was he really sodomising her?"

The blonde nodded.

"Not just doing it doggy style?"

"No, the look I got was short, but very good, clear. They were right inside the door, only a couple of metres away, he specifically pushed it straight up her bottom. That surprised me as well, that he slid straight up."

"KY jelly."

"Yes, I didn't get a clipboard and researcher's pencil poised and go in to ask, but you'll be close."

"Names? 'Ravishing Roger' and 'Lusty Lady.' Question one. Which brand? Ah yes. Question two. Do you press it into the hole? Or wipe it on the phallus? Hmm. Question--" The conversation dissolved into giggles.

A little while later,

"It was nice of you to assume I get lusted after. But, I have to own up. I don't."

Pealle began to laugh, then stopped, her mouth open in shock,

"You're serious aren't you?"

"Nobody sends me 'I want your knickers off' vibes."

"Yes, they do Karen, I was with you for one morning recently, in the presence of three attractive men. The Doctor and Mr. Pling both fancied both of us, but you had Bill Carpenter all to yourself."

The enormity of such a preposterous statement had Karen groping for dust,

"He's married."

"That's why he stuck his hands in his pockets, because he's a good man, not a love rat, but he still fancies you something rotten. It's not the vibes that are missing, it's you that's missing them, as I used to, tune yourself in better kid, I promise you they're there."

The subject of the conversation was temporarily changed by a call of,

"Fruit juice?" It had come from the house.

"Fruit juice for three," replied Karen. Moments later, her Dad appeared carrying a tray with jug and glasses to join the girls for a laze before lunch.

"Dad this is Pealle Tumpkins. She's on my course. Pealle this is my father, Dennis."

Man and maid greeted each other and Dennis sat down.

"We have been bemoaning our virginal state. Pealle's had a near miss too."

Pealle's eye's widened, but she obviously quickly regrouped when Dennis replied,

"Sixth Form will rectify that rapidly, or least provide the

opportunities for it."

By the time they took her home Pealle had begun to call Dennis by his name, apparently without thought and later that evening she had another serious conference with her diary.

* * *

The car drew away, paused for the junction and accelerated down towards the bypass,

"Now, that we are alone, who is that? I've never seen her before."

"That is the reigning County Tennis Champion. She's also the Under Sixteens' Champion naturally. I've always liked her. But, just knew who she was. Not as a mate. We're on the same course. So we might be seeing her often. Is that a problem?"

"Far from it, I liked Jet for your sake, I just like Pealle, she's nice."

Yes, Dad! Even I got the messages. So Pealle would have been swamped. Did you know you were transmitting? But, carefully avoiding potholes she said,

"Not on a tennis court she's not. But she's really taken with you. Hanging on your every word. Probably because she likes the swing. Wants one."

"Harrumph!"

* * *

"I'm going up to bed; I've locked up."

"I'm coming Dad. I've got a whole ten pages. Saved them up. For bedtime."

"Whose idea was it to ration your reading?"

"Mine. Makes the books last longer. Ten days of pleasure instead of two."

Dennis shook his head, grinning and climbed the stairs. His daughter carried the wine glasses through, washed them and checked around as she put them away then followed him up.

"Night Dad."

"Night." Came the reply through the open door.

Karen regretfully placed her bookmark and closed her book.

She'd sneaked another two pages onto her self-imposed daily allotment.

As Elizabeth toured Pemberly, she was falling in love with the house, as well as its Master and Karen was sure some sort of crisis was about to befall the little firebrand, but she had to stop and savour the anticipation. It would read all the sweeter tomorrow. She tiptoed to the toilet, but the lack of light on the landing wasn't because her Dad had gone to sleep. His light was on but the door was shut. As she passed the soft murmur of voices reached her through the door. She set about her ablutions briskly and returned to bed, she knew exactly what was happening in the Master bedroom.

Dennis

Dennis tried to read, but shortly after Karen bid him Goodnight he gave up, he'd not read a whole sentence anyway. He slid the bedroom door shut as quietly as he could, fluffed up the pillows and sat up on the bed. His wife grinned at him from the dresser; Jane, taken on honeymoon, reaching out to pluck the Eiffel Tower out of its landscape. The linkup didn't take long, suddenly the girl in the dazzling white dress released the famous landmark, slid over to the bed and lay across it, propped up on her elbows, looking up at him.

"She's very nice, sensible, down to Earth; a very nice girl."

"She's the same age as Karen."

"Dad's twenty years older than Mum, you know that and in those days it mattered, it doesn't now."

"Are you saying you approve of this one?"

Jane half leaned up towards him, gesticulating expressively like she always did,

"Of course, she's lovely."

"But you approved of the whoring expedition too, at least you said you did."

"I approved, because I knew it wouldn't be necessary; I wasn't wildly against it anyway, preferable to Karen providing for you."

"I wouldn't allow that."

"That's why it was preferable; it would have bothered neither her, nor me, but you were tearing yourself to pieces."

"I like Pealle, obviously I'd like to take her to bed, who wouldn't, but I really like her too."

"I know, that's why the age difference doesn't matter, because you don't just want to use her and discard; you want to honour her and cherish her, as well as take her to bed for the rest of your life. When did you realise it?"

"Sitting in our swing."

"You can impregnate her there, if you want to, I don't mind, conceive all your offspring in that swing if you like; I think it would be nice. Tell her first though, she might want to be different."

"Aren't we taking a lot for granted here? I can't see a bridge yet, never mind planning how to cross the fifth one down the line. Especially when I don't know what Pealle wants."

"So ask her, or give her the chance to tell you; my generation wanted equal rights, modern girls expect them."

"I'll ask her; I wanted to anyway."

"You still haven't wrapped Karen's present from me."

"Yes, I know, I promise I'll do it tomorrow."

"She's going to bed, and you should too; give her my love and don't neglect her; she's hiding it well, but she's hurting bad over --"

The conversation covered the usual leave taking between lovers, eventually,

"Dennis, go to bed darling, it's late."

"I am, how do I--I mean I can't just--"

"She plays tennis doesn't she?"

* * *

"You were talking to Mum again? Last night?"

"She sends her love and told me off for neglecting you. Sorry. Is there anything I can do?"

"Yes. But you won't. Just be here for me please Dad. That'll do. I need you."

Dennis Robinson spent several minutes on the telephone to the local branch of the L. T. A. later that day. The upshot of that being that he was able to catch a challenge match on the Saturday.

Karen

“Happy birthday darling.” Karen opened her eyes and squinted at her Dad’s dark silhouette outlined against the bright, late-summer-morning window.

“Thank you.” She struggled up to meet the kiss, and he pressed a card and present into her hand, as he sat on the edge of the bed. The humorous card, about the misadventures of a penguin in a nightclub, made her giggle,

“Thank you.” The shape of the present’s box suggested bracelet or necklace. She opened the packaging apprehensively, her Dad knew she wasn’t into jewellery surely. Of course he did, it was neither bracelet, nor necklace, not with Waterman in gold letters on the top of the box. Inside was a leather pouch, with a high tech, magnetic closing mechanism. It was so strong that for a moment she struggled to open it. The matt-black fountain pen with gold fittings, that it contained, looked every bit a class act.

“It’s got a broad nib. I wouldn’t let them fill it with ink; you can do it yourself.”

She hugged him tightly, “Thank you so much.”

“There’s more downstairs and breakfast.”

“Okay.” She had a quick shower and, downstairs, opened the rest of her cards between munching toast. At the end, when she went to gather up the cards into one pile, cheques and notes in another and envelopes to discard, Dennis gave her another small, oddly shaped parcel, with corners situated where middles usually were.

“And that’s from Mum.”

“Oh. Right.” Karen broke open the wrapping paper and several packs of three fanned out and fell to the floor. “Oh, thanks Mum. I’ve already got some. But thanks.” She grinned broadly and hugged him tightly again.

“Belt and braces. If you ever discover you’ve missed a pill, or you’re taking antibiotics for instance. Use a condom too.”

“Yes. I know.”

“I’d rather you didn’t need to use one as disease protection.

I'd rather potential partners were not disease risks. Anyone you suspect you might need a condom with, shouldn't be inside you in the first place."

She gave him the eyes,

"Abso-jibing-lutely!"

Pealle

Halfway through her match, Pealle noticed a middle-aged man in tee shirt and slacks watching the game from an unobtrusive position.

When she next passed her partner, Beth, she whispered,

"Up a gear."

Beth looked at her startled for a moment, then replied,

"Okay."

They finished off their opponent with all dispatch and all through the hand shakes and congratulations that followed, Pealle tracked her target with her peripheral vision, ready at any moment to cut free and pursue if necessary. He drifted slowly towards the clubhouse apparently waiting for something. Despite her attempts at keeping them severely in check, Pealle's hopes rose and rose. When he finally stationed himself at the clubhouse door and for the first time standing in full view, he was very obviously waiting and his attention was solely on her.

Hoping changed to planning,

Right Pealle Tumpkins, the chances are he'll make an offer, if he doesn't you do! Right? Right!

"Hello," she said as soon as she was within comfortable speaking range, "This is my doubles partner, Beth. Beth this is Karen Robinson's Dad." She paused to allow the greeting to be concluded with a handshake then added, "We won."

"I saw. Well done." Dennis paused and Beth slid quietly away from them murmuring thanks. Dennis waited until she had detached from the group, then continued, "I was wondering if you could do with a coke after all that running about, I could, would you like to join me?"

"Yes please. Mum, Dad, this is Karen's Dad. Dennis, Felicity and Fergus my Mum and Dad. Wait right there, I'll be coming straight back."

Dennis had barely begun some small talk before Pealle was back.

"I met Pealle on Tuesday, my daughter, Karen and your

daughter are doing the same 'A' level course at school."

Fergus and Felicity nodded.

"But the elegant young lady I met was not that, focussed solely on kill, tigress that plays tennis."

Felicity laughed,

"No, it's not. I'm quite glad that she exists, to cope with life's pitfalls, but relieved that mostly she leaves her behind on court."

"Dennis and I are off for a coke, Dad," Pealle had returned and was thrusting the little knapsack into her father's hand. "I'll make my own way back home. Bye."

She had already linked arms with her friend's Dad and drawn him away, as she bade her parents farewell.

Several hours later Dennis returned Pealle to her home. The blonde had been planning the event,

How am I going to handle the goodbye?

By the time they got to her home, she had decided.

If he doesn't bet, I will. If he does, I'll raise.

The car stopped. She turned to him, the silent pause became too long. Dennis leaned minutely towards her, telegraphing his aim for the cheek, but when Pealle mirrored his actions, it was to close up lips to lips, guiding him in softly with the fingertips of her cupped left hand. Her eyes closed on contact. Although brief, the kiss was anything but dismissal, she smiled at him with her eyes,

"Monday afternoon, are you doing anything?"

"I'm free from about two-thirty, say three o'clock to be safe."

"Would you come shopping with me, for my school clothes, tell me what you think? I'd like an alternative viewpoint, I have to buy a boiler suit."

"Ah, right. Yes I'll pick you up at three."

"Three o'clock." She closed with him for a second kiss and, confident now, tenderly caressed the short hair at the nape of his neck.

Karen

"I was wondering where you'd got to."

"I've been watching a tennis match. When I saw who it was, I stayed to watch the end. I agree with you, off the court she's Snow White, on the court--"

"She's Lady Macbeth, with attitude."

"We had a couple of Cokes in the café afterwards. After she's qualified I know exactly who's going to rewire the house."

Karen looked up to tease, but her Dad had gone and, on second thoughts, that was an area in which she didn't want to meddle.

In her bedroom later, the question was raised by the girl in her mirror,

Given that you have to have a Step-mum, how would you feel if it were Pealle?

"Well, it's not very likely, but given the choice, she's the one I'd choose."

Let's hope then.

"And pray."

Yes, that too.

Dennis

The following Monday Dennis returned from the Shopping trip, he ran Karen to ground finishing jobs in her room; he was heavily laden.

"I have been shopping, I hope you like them," he said as he dropped the pile of bags on her bed and left. It was several minutes later that his silent daughter presented herself for inspection, wearing a boiler suit over blouse and skirt. He nodded and she turned the full twirl,

"Yes, very nice."

"Thank you so much. I've been trying to work out how to get them. With money so tight."

"They're in the budget, that's exactly what the trust fund is for, it buys school clothes no questions asked."

"I thought it stopped at sixteen. It did for Len."

"It stops at the end of your full time education. For Len that was sixteen, when he got his first job. You're still at school, and they're needed for your course, so they're funded, no problem."

Karen shucked the boiler suit down and lifted her skirt, revealing the shear and sexy underwear,

"And these?"

"Do you like them?"

"They're gorgeous. But, school regulation they're not!"

"The trust doesn't specify what style your knickers have to be, just that you must have them. I see no reason why Sixth Formers have to wear unflattering garments, just because they won't be on general show. Pealle was buying her course clothes and helped me choose yours, so I got some undies for her too, from me, not the trust, as thanks, slipped them in her bag without telling her, she'll find them soon, I'm expecting an irate call any minute."

The telephone rang.

Karen

In the Sixth Form all the students were registered in the Sixth form common room, Karen found herself with a dozen or so from her Year Eleven form class still with Mrs Carter as her Form Tutor, so her class designation was 12MC. The first morning of term, on their way to their first lesson, out of earshot of the masses for the first time,

"I've seen your Dad a couple of times."

"Yes. I know."

"Do you know what he did? Dennis the Menace."

"Bought you some sexy underwear as a thank you. It's okay, he got some for me too."

"It's not okay, he was helping me buy my Sixth Form Gear, all I did was say thank you. Sometimes people are so nice you--you--"

"Want to scream. I know. But you'll find a way to get your own back. Be so-nice-to-him-back. You'll make him squirm."

* * *

Day Two; and 12MC trooped down into the English department to their first General Studies lesson. For English, Maths and General Studies they were taught as a Form Class and consequently one of the few the new friends were taught apart. Of these only General Studies carried an examination. The other two were there merely to maintain an acceptable standard of literacy and numeracy.

Karen had followed her sequence of sailing programmes religiously, never even thinking of an alternative, but Llew Smith who took them for General Studies, used anecdotes from canoeing in his lesson.

"Life's a constant compromise, like canoe design. The ideal canoe is long, short, wide, narrow, flat bottomed, with a sharp keel." He shrugged at the grinning youths in front of him. "My experience of life is something similar and I bet yours is too."

Jet gushed at length about how they would join West Wild Water and learn a new sport,

"Let's go canoeing, it seems like fun, nobody else does it in our form, they're all football and hockey, we won't have to put up with Trevor and Maggie fighting. We'll go on Thursday. Start canoeing, start a whole new phase in our lives." There was quite a bit more. When Karen managed to get some words in,

"Have you considered sailing? Instead of canoeing--"

"Don't be silly, we've never considered anything like this before and now we've got a Heaven sent opportunity to do something new and different and straight away you want to try something completely off the wall. We'll go and join Llew Smith's absolute beginners' class, they're Year Sevens, so nobody will know us, we'll be the only people we know who do canoeing and--" Jet was thrusting the error of her ways so forcibly down her throat that the possibility of a hidden agenda occurred.

"Pealle, Jet wants me to go canoeing. Mr. Smith's group, on Thursdays. D'y'want to come?"

"No thanks, I tried it on holiday once, not my scene, I'll stick with the tennis. Does that mean we need to change the homework night?"

"No. You go and make Dad squirm. I'll join you later."

Consequently, as the Globetrotter dragged the reluctantly acquiescing Plumber down to the swimming baths, on that first Thursday evening, the Electrician made the journey out to tea, alone, her heart rate jumping wildly.

Chapter 3

Canoeing: September 1998

Pealle

The door was opened for her as the athletic blonde walked up between the dahlias; the short conversation was solely for any neighbours who may have been listening with boom mikes.

"Karen's gone to her first Canoeing Session."

"Yes, it's Thursday."

"She said to come on over anyway."

"Yes, that's fine."

Greeter and greeted were careful merely to smile at each other until she was inside, only then did they kiss, their first ever, full blown gather into arms, smooch. Even then, it still wasn't comfortable. They disengaged, he with a wry smile, she a nervous giggle. Their first meeting alone, in seclusion, the kiss was only their fourth and the others had all been goodbye. Despite the telephone conversations which had covered the preliminaries nicely, Pealle was desperate not to grab and spoil things. At the same time, she needed to signal to him that she was willing and eager to meet him halfway.

Karen

In the swimming bath, the beginner canoeists drew their equipment from the stores and, after warming up; they performed exercises, Press-ups, Squat thrusts and Vee-ups.

"You start with only five of each. I know you could probably do ten, or even fifteen, but you wouldn't be able to get out of bed tomorrow," said Mr. Smith to the assembled kids. "We'll work up to a big score over the year."

They learned how to get into the tiny one-girl boat that sat so serenely whilst empty, but wobbled like a ball on a stick with someone in it.

Then how to eject correctly after a capsize and soon after that, how to paddle, feathering between strokes.

Karen dipped her paddle into the water on her right and pulled, flick of the right wrist and dip into the other side, pull, un-flick and repeat.

Dip, pull, flick, dip, pull, un-flick, repeat in a controlled sequence.

The end of the bath was approaching fast.

Almost without conscious thought,

she exaggerated the slight snaking of her canoe's course through the water.

The bow came around in an accelerating curve.

With a controlled power stroke, she straightened up and sped back up the bath.

All around her youngsters were travelling in circles;

or bumping into each other;

{a neat extra dip on one side avoided a collision of her own}

or swimming towards the side of the bath, towing an upturned canoe behind them.

Jet surfaced scowling and with her hair rats'-tailing down her face. She was struggling with her boat. As Karen watched, it completely submerged beneath the surface and began to sink away. Llew Smith was going to her aid, chuckling.

Karen weaved her course among the wreckage, swapping chitchat with bobbing heads and testing ideas that occurred to her, for steering and turning.

Mr. Smith called time.

Time!

Astonished, she checked the clock,
an hour had gone,
gone from her life,
leaving the warmest glow she had ever known.

In the changing room, Jet dried herself furiously, her skin was covered in a purple network. Karen knew better than to say anything when her friend's chin took on its annoyed tilt, but all calls of sails plucking at her heart's strings were forgotten.

The Globetrotter could hump and grump as she pleased; the Plumber had discovered Canoeing.

* * *

Karen arrived home to find her friend seated at the table in the conservatory, working at the Economics homework. Together the group ate their evening meal, while the new convert to canoeing regaled them with a splash by splash account of her introduction to the sport and shared her laughter at the amusing incidents that often happen when beginners tackle something new.

"There's a Canoeing shop down Gallows Chare. Can we visit on Saturday? Check some prices."

"Of course."

"I might be able to afford a cheap wet-suit. Now that I don't have to buy school clothes. It won't be a dry wet-suit; of course. But--"

"Dry wet-suit is an oxymoron, but you meant it!" murmured the blonde gently.

"A wet-suit holds the water in the suit stationary. In a spongy layer next to your skin. A dry wet-suit the spongy spaces don't link up, they are sealed. So they stay dry, full of gas. Oxymoron, true, but warm too."

Pealle laughed; by the end of the evening all three ended up generally feeling very good.

A hard mental day at her desk had been followed by a hard physical hour on the water and further mental gymnastics on the homework, Karen was ready for her bed and declined the invitation to accompany her Dad when he took Pealle home.

It was the right decision on several fronts, not least that she fell asleep before she'd pulled the covers up around her. Dennis had to tuck her in like a child when he got back an hour later.

Pealle

The lay-by, a few hundred metres from her house, was empty, Dennis signalled and pulled in. Pealle made no comment, waiting, ready to respond to his lead,

"Thank you for an incredibly wonderful evening."

"Thank you too, I loved it, every second of it."

"I want to do it again."

"So do I." She caressed his face, leaned over and kissed him. "What do we tell Karen?"

"The truth."

"I didn't mean that."

"I suggest we wait until she asks, then tell her the truth."

The blonde was silent for a while.

"Okay."

Dennis

The wet-suit waistcoat was the only one left on the rail for a girl. It was reasonably priced and scarlet and yellow and black. It was her shape, but too small. Karen had rarely gone for something as unconditionally as she had for canoeing and Dennis was really disappointed. He'd come shopping with her, full of intentions to spend serious money from the savings but,

"It's too small."

The assistant stretched the neoprene over Karen's bust and zipped it up tight, she shook her head,

"No Sir, it's exactly right, it's supposed to be a very snug fit. If you splashed out on a made to measure, it would be no different from that, I promise you. I'm so confident it's right you can try it out for a week and return it if I'm wrong."

"Oh that's very fair."

"No. You won't be back, not to exchange it anyway. You'll be back to buy other things I hope, but not to change that, it's perfect." She nodded at Karen. "You're very lucky, we hardly ever get them in your size--"

"You mean. In my shape!"

The girl shrugged,

"That was an end of line bargain lot."

Even now Dennis wasn't wholly convinced,

"Okay we'll take it on a week's trial, what other things will we be buying later?"

"Crash hat, paddle, spray deck, buoyancy aid and when you leave West, a canoe. Who's your instructor, Mr. Baques?" She waved generally at the shop. "He's responsible for all this, taught me a hobby which became my career."

"Mr. Baques takes the Year Nines. But our instructor's English Mr. Smith."

"After my time, but I've heard he's good too."

"Go and take that off," said Dennis and when Karen was safely out of earshot. "Is there anything in that list of yours she needs now?"

"For the swimming bath, crash hat, paddle and spray deck.

How good is she?"

"No idea, she's mustard keen, always been interested in boats, but I've never seen her so keen, ever. Why? Does it matter?"

"If she's good, she'll need spoon blades on her paddle. We do a self-assembly, asymmetric-spoon-blade kit. It's lightweight, high quality stuff, but reasonably priced."

"How much for all three and the suit?"

The girl offered an attractive discount and the deal was struck. When Karen returned folding the wet-suit, she surveyed the pile of desirable acquisitions,

"What's all this?"

"Happy Saturday Darling, you pay for the wet-suit; you can have these on me."

She flung herself at him,

"Steady girl, I've got fragile stamped on my bum." They paid the bills, while talking more generally about Karen's new sport, finally they took their leave,

"Call back regularly," the girl nodded at the bulky bag containing the wet-suit. "We often get other end of line bargains in, but they go quickly, and don't forget to put the drip rings on the shaft of your paddle before you fit the blades."

"With a drop of washing up liquid?"

The girl nodded,

"I won't."

By bedtime, each blade had an exaggerated cartoon-style, humorous drawing of a crested penguin under the first of several coats of yacht varnish and she had remembered the drip rings.

Karen

The following Thursday Mr. Carpenter turned from his white board and surveyed his small group of sixth form would be engineers with attitude. "Okay tartan paint, long stands, left handed cups. I want ten Bully-Boy send-ups of your own for tomorrow, at least half of them from your own imagination. You can go when you're ready."

Karen gathered her work and mathematical instruments together, popped her reading glasses into their case and loaded them all into her briefcase, then she hefted the bulky, but obviously not that heavy, shoulder bag up off the floor; the strap pulled her top tight, revealing the shape she usually tried to conceal. She paused for a moment while Pealle too finished loading up and then with a smile and a wave at their craft teacher, the girls followed the boys out of the room, body swerving elegantly around the benches. On her way, Karen plucked her paddle from its out-of-harm's-way position in the corner. Sid had held the door for them, as if he intended to escort them away, but then veered off in the other direction,

"Sorry, just remembered it's Thursday, you're not going my way. See you tomorrow."

Karen smiled her acknowledgement of the courtesy,

"Thanks. I'm not. Pealle?"

"I'll see you up there."

"Okay bye."

"Bye Sid."

"Bye. I'll come around again, do the homework with you."

"You're expected. For tea. Come any time. No need to ask."

"Thanks--Vibes?"

"From Sid? Friendship vibes."

"And the other, but he's got them severely bolted down, a very proper young man, our Sid. Anyone else, somebody in your registration class, not Vocational, Academic subjects for instance?"

"Trevor makes the hairs on the back of my neck stand up."

"And so they should, thank goodness, he's besotted with and

terrified of you."

"Pealle!"

"That's why he's such a prat when you're around, he's just mildly annoying when you're not there. At last you're starting to receive transmissions, even if only warning ones. I suppose if you're not getting them all, at least you're getting the personal safety ones, it's something anyway, see you later then."

The end of school bell rang just as Karen joined Jet coming down from Tourism and they walked slowly with the current in the main stream of kids flowing homewards. The shorter, plumper girl was carrying only the normal complement of school equipment, books and briefcase, "Where's your gear?" Karen asked.

Jet prevaricated for a minute, waiting until the wall panels became scenes from classic literature, heralding the English department, and Mr. Smith's room, before dropping her grenade. It produced the justified explosion,

"What d'y'mean? You're not going?"

"I don't like it."

"Jet! I started because you wanted to go. I've got all my stuff. I've bought stuff."

"See ya, I'll miss my bus."

Karen disconsolately watched her exasperating friend disappear out of the bottom door, there were times when--

"Karen, could you open up? You can get them out, but nobody goes on the water until I say so." Mr. Smith had come out of his classroom and was handing her his keys.

"Jet's not coming,"

He was disappointed, but philosophical,

"Okay." He dived back into his room and began teaching from his board again, to a small group clustered around it. Jet's departure was small beer compared with a child who couldn't do her homework; Karen had no argument with those priorities.

Jet had sat in the tiny, wobbly, bouncing cockleshell and her interest in the sport had gone head-first into the ground, from gush to buried in spectacular, record breaking time. Karen's had done the reverse journey and the discovery that their young teacher, although when dry was merely a passably attractive man, when wet he became a star, hadn't exactly been a disappointment either.

And now she had no friend to go with.

Except that she was about to discover, that she had.

She organised the eager young brood of Year Sevens, getting the canoes out, paddles sized to match the assorted bodies wielding them, crash hats issued.

"Right, time for exercises. Paddles and hats in boats. Boats stacked against the wall."

"Miss, is it okay to put my boat here?"

"Yes, you boys at the end. You can all leave yours there. But, on their sides. And it's Karen. Not Miss, I'm in the Sixth Form. Right everybody down this end."

They performed their exercises on the wide walkway where the diving boards used to be, before removing any chance of being sued became more important to the LEA than adventure. The extra space meant that every child could fling about or lose their balance with less risk to those around. Before leading off Karen checked individually with each one how many they were at, and when they intended to increase it, she herself was at twelve, fifteen on Sunday. The main exercises were press-ups, squat thrusts and canoeist's sit ups, up like a V, touching your toes at the high point. This last was the one she hated, but it really did firm up the tummy, even at twelve, four times a week, she was aware of the difference.

When Llew Smith arrived into the baths hall, squeezing into his wet-suit waistcoat, he found the group neatly lined up along the water side, each standing with one foot at the edge with their toes curled over the gunwale of the canoe, holding it still against the side. Karen was at the far end of the line, standing tall and slender, with her long brown hair done in bunches Pocahontas style, to match canoeing. The boats were kayaks as she well knew, but what the floppies. Her brand-new wet-suit waistcoat that had cost the carefully conserved Birthday, Baby Sitting and other monies, which had, up to a fortnight ago, been earmarked for Boiler Suits, briefcases and other student bills, was heavily tailored and she filled it.

"Exercises?" Produced a chorus of positive responses. The

pretty little dot right next to Llew said,

"I'm up to twelve, same as Karen," her eyes, were shining.

Karen watched as the young teacher blossomed from fern to orchid as he stepped into a canoe. She recognised the alteration intimately; she did it herself.

"Right everybody in."

She sat on the rear deck of her canoe and slid in two footed, not the way she had been taught nor a recommended way, a proud piece of GRP would open your legs to the bone, from ankle to knee, but Mr. Smith had relented and allowed his long legged student to use it, as the only guaranteed way of getting them in. The legs stayed unopened, there were no proud snags, but she'd checked anyway.

"Boys to the deep end, girls to the shallow end. Go!" The canoeists turned and made their way, five to each end of the bath, Llew waited until they had adjusted and aligned themselves in shallow W formations, all eyes, were on him, alight with eagerness, waiting for the command.

"Two lengths forward. Go! Go! Go! Come on! Let's see some water fly!"

The formations accelerated towards each other, meeting in the centre in a Motorway pileup; there wasn't room for six canoes to pass each other never mind ten. Then amazingly, they were all through, back into open water. They turned and plunged back into Charybdis but in ragged formation now, the second length was always easier, with the canoes spread out along the bath. Karen turned into her corner and watched the others completing their lengths and getting back on station; several had already taken up the paddle position in anticipation of the next instruction. She smiled, as she realised that she had herself.

"Two lengths reverse. Go! Don't forget to look!"

"Well done Cyd!" Called Karen as the normally timid, pretty little dot dived bravely backwards through a gap. "Nice one!" The space had opened only long enough to allow her passage, before closing tightly again.

The session progressed with known skills being practised and new ones learned; the committed, enthusiastic urging and praise of the young teacher and his gifted pupil instructor, sowing seeds of enthusiasm for the sport which would grow and in years to come, blossom and scatter their consequences world wide. They finished off with a game of Canoe Polo, where the girls proved themselves as adept as the boys, at playing dirty.

"Okay. Paddles and hats in the rack, canoes emptied and carried through into the store, then everyone gets a shower."

"I'll give you a hand. In the store. It's not so cold in there with a suit on."

"It's desperate without one."

Karen chuckled,

"Yes."

Pealle

The second Thursday's meeting was much more controlled. Neither spoke until she was safely inside away from prying eyes and then they kissed first, a passionate, deep, lovers' kiss. When they surfaced she whispered,

"I'm all of a dither, so take me straight to bed and make love to me. Take me completely; I'm so ready you wouldn't believe, but I'll make mistakes, do it wrong--"

He gently silenced her with more kisses; but as soon as he stopped.

"Just keep me right, I want you to do this, I want us to do this--"

This time his finger across her lips worked.

"It's all right darling, just take it steady and you'll be fine. Shh, we'll both be fine."

She nodded through the insistent silencing pressure of the finger,

"As I had time to plan it, I tried to make the location special, as well as the event. I hope you don't mind?" Now, he lifted the finger only just enough to signal an answer was required.

"I'm sure I won't."

"Close eyes." He led his girl up the stairs and into her defloration chamber. "Open."

The Severed Head
Part Three

Buyer met his business partner in a small, unfashionable, out of the limelight bar.

"We've been offered some goods for sale that'll earn us a fat profit. I can sort out the administrative side, I haven't found a way to make the switch yet, but I'm working on it."

"I've been thinking about expanding our business. No doubt, your seller will want his cash up front?"

"No doubt."

"Will we have to raise the price of protection?"

"We'll need a loan, raising the protection won't be enough."

"We'll do it anyway, they're getting it cheap enough."

"I'll see about a loan; you sort the rest."

Karen

The Canoe Store was a large walled in area next to the bath hall, with a corrugated translucent plastic roof. The ventilation at the eaves was more than matched by that under the outside door, as such it was light and airy during the day, but at night with wet skin and no clothes, very cold. The canoes had been posted through the interior door and lay spilled out like a broken fan on the floor. Karen and Llew worked steadily feeding the short, light boats into the rack and then straightened off the racks of paddles and hats that eleven-year olds, with the best intentions in the world, left askew. They took a last look around, it was clean and tidy; the irregular wet splodge would dry within hours, leaving no sign of their presence, as per instructions.

Llew followed Karen back into the bath hall,

"On a cold January night I've seen the fog in here so dense after the clean-up, you couldn't see across the bath."

She pulled a comic face.

"Only for a minute or so, after shutting the door it quickly cleared. Erm--If I split the group into a couple of sets, do you think you could teach the better one some advanced techniques? Techniques you've mastered yourself."

"Well--Yes, if you want me to."

She waited patiently while he locked the store, then walked down to the girl's showers with him. Together they discarded their waistcoats and rinsed the chlorine out of them.

"Can I wash your hair for you?" Karen smiled at him to cover her embarrassment at the effrontery of her request, *What on Earth had made her say that?*

Chapter 4

Games: September 1998

Karen

"Yes, I'd like that."

She leaned against the tiled wall directly under the shower head giving the most even spray and guided him backwards towards her. They hardly spoke as she shampooed, washed and rinsed his hair twice and he gradually snuggled against her until he was leaning against her and she was sandwiched tight between him and the wall. She gently, sensuously wriggled against his bottom as much as she dared, using having to reach around his head as cover. His erection stood proudly up in his bather, she could see it over his shoulder. Had their positions been reversed, she could have snuggled into him and held still while he cuddled her tighter and tighter, like she had done for Len all those times.

Or even pushed his trunks down, pulled her bather aside and let him back shuttle her, up her bather leg, without either of them moving from the spot.

"Can I wash yours now?"

They were children throwing lighted matches into boxes of fireworks, who couldn't stop.

"Yes." They changed places. She leaned back against him, snuggling the rigid bar nicely between. Half way through washing, while she was still making up her mind, he slid his hands down onto her hips and gently pressed her to him. Obediently she pouted her bum, snuggling gently against the urgent, insistent thrusting and a moment later he was spurting into his bather gasping and grunting. It wasn't as nice for her as pleasuring Len had been, two layers of bather were probably responsible for that, but he had obviously enjoyed it. He stopped, straightened up and finished her hair,

"If you bend forward."

She leaned against the wall and let him wash and rinse her bather-clad bum, fondling, washing, feeling, rinsing.

"Thank you."

She smiled, in reply and walked through to the changing room, which by now was quite deserted. She peeled off the bather and knelt down stuffing it under herself. She draped her towel around her, hiding herself, even though there were no watchers and caressed her clitty. Seconds later she had collapsed jerking and squealing through clenched teeth as the orgasm rampaged through her.

Pealle was working in the conservatory when Karen arrived home. She took the tea her Dad had prepared for her through with her. She ate it slowly whilst working and trying not to look at the tell tale wisps of drying hair clinging to Pealle's neck, nor the unbroken vista of flawless skin showing through the back of her blouse. She could clearly remember a brassier strap being there earlier, at school. She smiled inwardly at the new developments; things were progressing quite nicely apparently.

The previous week, when they had invited Karen to accompany Pealle as her Dad drove her home, besides being exhausted, she had sensed the vibes, apprehension, reluctance even. Her Dad and her friend had both relaxed when she declined, she waited.

"I'll just take Pealle home, Karen. Don't wait up, I might call into The Club for a game of dominoes or such."

"Okay. Goodnight." Dennis Robinson settled his young passenger into the car and Karen waved them off.

And remember not to ask how the game of dominoes went, vulgar thoughts about double one and one blank, had her giggling rudely as she locked up and went to bed to face her own sexual progress.

The night's academic work had allowed her to clear her mind of the emotional turmoil. The light-hearted end to the Vocational Homework had, in addition, been uplifting, she was particularly pleased with a 'Water knot' for tying hose pipes together, to restore water flow and a dozen 'Missing Links' to do the same to short pieces of chain. That both of these actually existed, in a different context, added to her satisfaction. At bedtime however, the situation had to be faced. Karen was addressed by the slim, brown, naked girl with the big tits and fat lips that lived in her dressing table mirror.

If he'd tried to do it. What would you have done? She knew the answer, just didn't want to admit it.

Okay. What if he tries next week? If you feel this good next week? Still no answer.

Okay. Do you want him to do it? Feel his hands on you. You can only give it away once. Do you want to give it to him? This time the girls' heads nodded firmly.

Right, it's next week and he's pulled his bather down. What do you do? The reflection sat quite still.

He's moving your bather out of the way. What do you do? Karen had made her decision, the girl in the mirror sat back in her chair,

"I'll do nothing. I won't help. I won't stop him. If he wants a fuck, he can have one. I'll just wait and let him. If he can get up me without my help, he can have me." She rose and retrieved one of the small oblong boxes of contraceptive pills from her bedside cabinet. She read the instructions again, noting when she needed to start taking the medication. Her period almost filled the days between now and the next canoeing session, she would need to start late the following week. While nodding the decision home, she replaced the box.

What about the bather?

No answer.

Dare you?

The girl in the mirror stirred uncomfortably then Karen replied,

"We'll see."

The following day, would Llew be embarrassed or ashamed? Karen knew that she was a bit of both, but more excited than either. There was only one thing to do. There was a simple canoeing question that she was sure she knew the answer to, but it would do as a topic of conversation. She walked Pealle down to his room, when she turned the last corner, he was only feet away walking towards her. She stopped, turned and matched his progress,

"When you do a bow rudder on the left. You must have to feather first?"

"Yes, but only for a left turn."

"I thought so, it had to be." Another pupil wanted his attention. "Thanks." She turned and rejoined Pealle, leaving Llew Smith, hopefully, as unworried as she was, but equally hopefully, as pleasantly bothered.

"Don't claim you didn't pick those up," said the blonde.

"No. Even I receive transmissions. When they're that strength."

"And no wife to get in the way, take care kid."

The week passed with a couple more gentle, utterly neutral exchanges between Karen and Llew and a jolly General Studies lesson, in the middle of which the most ardent member of the Politically Correct Sisterhood was spitting spleen, over nothing, and to the obvious intense annoyance of most of the rest of 12MC. Mr. Smith politely asked,

"Maggie, when you're arguing, are you ever accused of being a female chauvinist pig?"

When order had been restored, Karen questioned the questioner,

"Are you? A male one I mean?"

"Not and it being meant and I hope I'm not. I've based all my life on trying not to be. I'm not claiming that I always succeed. I do get a bit ruffled when somebody accuses all men, or talks about New Man, or lets the side down by ungracious treatment of the opposite sex."

"Why New Man?" asked Jet, herself a fully paid up member of the PCS, even if not as ardently blinkered as Maggie.

"There's no such thing. My Dad changed nappies. Pushed the pram. Did housework. New Man was invented by the Media one afternoon when they had nothing better to do. And, like all Media inventions, it's all froth, no substance."

"You don't pull your punches. Do you?"

"Challenge it! Apart from Michael Buerk's Famine in Africa Awareness programme and the various spin-offs it triggered, the Relief Charitable Efforts, which were mostly down to performers and athletes and the like, not Media people, name one that's worthy, life enhancing."

Karen turned sideways in her seat, next to the window and surveyed the room. He certainly knew how to stir the soup; at least six separate arguments were raging. Jet and Maggie were close to coming to blows with Trevor. General Studies might qualify for a lot of dubious descriptions, but in Llew Smith's room, pointless, dull or boring weren't among 'em.

* * *

The Sixth Form Common Room was full of bustle as the students geared up for the day ahead. Jet surveyed Karen's baggage suspiciously,

"What's all that?"

"It's Thursday, canoeing gear."

"I wanted you to go to town."

"Well you should have said. It's your fault. I went canoeing to keep you company. Found my sport. It's the one thing I do well. Look around you." Karen waved around the room. "Beauty over there. Stylish fashion to your right. Brains everywhere."

Pealle, having discovered tennis only when she idly picked up a racquet during her first Summer Term at Novochester, interrupted,

"But the best canoeist in the room is right here, it's your fault Jet, Thursdays she goes canoeing."

The session had gone well, Karen had taught her little group the bow rudder and then been taught the hanging draw herself.

"It's a very useful stroke to have if you are shooting a rapid and suddenly realise that the standing wave you're heading for is a Quality Street!"

"Shooting a rapid! That'll be the day."

"Next summer and you'll be surfing next spring."

Karen thoughtfully concentrated on mastering the hanging draw. The wild claim Pealle had made in the Common Room that morning was absolutely true, but solely because West Wild Water had its main canoeing talent bulked in Tuesday evening's Year Nine class, Mr. Baques' group, several of whom were good, but surfing and shooting? The prospect had definite attractions.

Presently, when she could do it without attracting too much attention, the pretty little dot closed up to Karen and murmured,

"What did he mean, a Quality Street? They're chocolates."

"Canoe slang. Some chocolates have hard middles. Not necessarily Quality Street. But hard middles."

Cyd looked puzzled.

"Some standing waves hide standing rocks."

"Oh! Oh, yes!" The little one giggled nervously.

Karen helped Llew Smith put the canoes away, but then checked to make sure the changing room was empty, before joining him in the shower. He had already discarded his waistcoat and was holding the shampoo ready, waiting for her.

"Would you mind if I took my waistcoat off?"

"Mind?"

She pouted her hip, pulled up the skirt as far as the under crutch flap would allow and pointed to the piece of ornamental string revealed, the entire side panel of the virtually non existent briefs she hadn't dared wear in Scotland.

"It's a monokini, no top. There's hardly any back either."

The eyes, she was gazing into opened wide, but the double take was quickly under control, his answer was calm enough,

"Ah. In that case I think we'll use my shower. Come on." He led the way down to the staff changing room and locked the door behind them.

The male staff shower room was dingy and depressing. The

paintwork was chipped and sad, the lone skylight yellow and stained. Long lost linens hanging morosely from an incomplete row of decaying pegs, like rejected chickens too scrawny for sale, contrasted sharply with Llew's clothes grouped neatly at the other end of the rail. A tall stool with a cracked seat recycled from the science labs competed with a chair with a bent leg for hiding space in the corner. Had she wanted to sit, the choice of risk would have been between a pinched bottom, or being unceremoniously dumped on the floor. The whole place reeked of neglect and studied ignorance of its plight. Not quite the powdered, scented, defloration bed, Seth would have prepared for her. Like the staff who used it, Karen resolutely closed her mind to the surroundings and stepped down from the changing area into the shower well. The floor was rough, non-slip, she shrugged the top off her impressive bust as nonchalantly as she could and leaned against the tiles. Llew closed up to her, but facing her this time, his bather already bulging.

"Is this okay?" he asked.

"Sure." They reached up and began to wash each other's hair, as he pushed against her and frotted her bare breasts with his chest.

The hair was finished, his penis like an iron bar against her thighs and pubes, he dropped his hands and caressed her hips sensually.

"Do you want to push against my bum?"

"Yes, please." He eased away from her. She guessed to give her space to turn, but she pushed the monokini panties down first. It was a voluptuous naked bottom that she presented to him for his pleasure. Llew only hesitated for a moment, before pushing his own bather down around his knees.

Karen reached behind her and wiped a smear of shower gel between her cheeks, like Len had done to her, the last time they were on holiday together, just before he left home to take up his first live in position. Together they'd smuggled her into the male campers shower block and he then waited patiently while she frigged herself to a peak, before having her bum cheeks, while she squealed and flopped about in his arms.

Okay girl, that's far enough, now it's up to him. But she

couldn't help just one more. She glanced around her shoulder straight into his eyes,

"You can hold me steady. If you want."

She waited unco-operatively until his roaming hands stopped fluttering 'accidentally' over her breasts and took hold of her, then she slid her hand down between her legs and gently pouted her bum. He panted and grunted and squeezed her tits quite firmly. His raging erection was squishily having her bottom. She frigged her clitty sensuously, she was going, she imagined pouting just that bit further, forcing him to poke her up her bottom.

Go on, do it, she thought, began to lean forward and she'd gone. Squealing her joy as he spurted up her naked back.

When at last she could stand unaided, she waited half bent forward until he had washed her clean.

"Can I wash him?"

"Yes, please."

She delicately coated him with shower gel and rubbed him to an even foam, peeling back his foreskin and washing between, as Len had taught her. By the time she had rinsed him off he was firm although not erect.

"Thank you, that was lovely, you are lovely."

Reading that as dismissal, she wriggled back into her waistcoat and replaced the monokini,

"Thank you. It was nice."

He unlocked the door for her as she gazed around the grim little room once again and then with total aplomb she walked back to the girl's changing room to dry and dress.

Still virgin then, she thought. *Oh well.*

Thursday nights are becoming a set pattern, she mused later, but the work was different. She laughed. It was the only thing that was. When she got home, Pealle had been wearing a very similar skirt; an identical blouse, with no ghosts of bra straps that it had had at school and the same damp curls, as a week previously.

* * *

A week later Karen sat at her dresser putting on the minimal school day face. Thursday had long since become the week's marker, days to Thursday, days past Thursday, but now it was even more special.

"Will he fuck me tonight?" she softly asked the girl in the mirror, "I wouldn't mind--All right. I would mind if he didn't!"

Even in there?

"Even in there. I agree. It's the vomit corner of a Victorian Workhouse."

Are you prepared to ask him, out loud, up front?

"I think so--Yes."

Exactly what will you say?

That night's canoeing session had gone well, the two friends stowed the canoes in an easy companionable silence. Karen was in no doubt. She'd made up her mind. Tonight, if he didn't, she was all tooled up to ask. She'd rehearsed the request again and again, she knew exactly what she was going to say. They came back into the bath hall and she waited beside him as he locked the canoe store door.

Deep breath, go for it.

An explosion of noise greeted them from the changing room. Karen looked at Llew in astonishment and walked through the girl's shower and on into the changing area to investigate. The canoe club should have been long gone by now and Year Seven voyeurs were decidedly not in her plans.

The canoeists **had** long gone; the changing room was full of junior school boys, stripping off.

"Miss! Miss!"

Karen suddenly realised that it was she who was being addressed,

"Yes?"

"John's got my peg."

"No I haven't."

"It's mine, I had it on Monday."

"I had it yesterday, it's mine!"

It was several minutes before Miss Robinson, newly promoted to the teaching staff, had restored order. She returned to the bath hall, where she found the man she had intended to be fucking by now, engrossed in conversation with other teachers. He introduced her.

"Miss Lee, Mr. Cuthbert, this is Karen, my senior pupil instructor."

"Hi, I'm Siew Mui, get your stuff, bring it into the female staff room away from that lot." Thankfully Miss Robinson collected her gear and joined the slender Chinese girl in the female staff changing room.

Unlike the male staff room, the female staff changing room was sweet smelling and friendly, with welcoming clean mushroom coloured walls; the row of shiny brass hooks for clothes had none missing and they all lacked dead anorexic poultry. The furniture was purpose built and in good repair, a couple of star grades higher even than the girls' changing room. All the same,

"I'm not a teacher you know."

"It's okay the kids don't know that, just behave as if you were. Call me Siew Mui, not 'Miss'." Siew Mui was already naked and wriggling into a bather.

Karen had shucked off her waistcoat before she remembered what wasn't underneath it.

"I hope that zip's secure, wouldn't do for it to come down, half way through a roll up."

"Could be an exciting next few seconds though."

"There's always that." The slightly built but luscious Oriental stood and watched Karen strip the remaining tiny triangle of material off, before she put a track suit top on over her Speedo. "Very nice," she said, nodding at the younger girl and departed.

When the Sixth Former emerged, showered, dried and dressed, Llew was waiting for her,

"It's for the duration apparently, several junior schools are coming, every night is filled up. They would have been here at three-thirty but for our prior booking."

"Oh well."

"I'll see you in school."

"Yes, bye."

"Bye."

* * *

Llew held Karen and Jet back from the last General Studies lesson of the term,

"Would you like to go out to look at the Tyne during the holidays. Scout out some of the rapids?"

"Yes, please, are you coming Jet?"

"No, I'll be busy at work, they're having a big sale."

"We go to Scotland for New Year. On the Thirtieth, to the Second."

"Okay. I'll miss those days."

"I'll see you later. About the details Sir."

The following day, Llew was waiting for Karen outside the Sixth form block, he drew her out of earshot,

"Can you go on the twenty-ninth?"

"Yes. I'll bring a lunch if you want. Give us more time."

"Would you mind where we had lunch? I've got a nice place in mind, all facilities for eating, relaxation and freshening up, but it's secluded, we would be on our own and we wouldn't be disturbed."

"Sounds lovely."

The pause stretched out while vibes were swapped,

"What are you going to do when Jet changes her mind and decides to come?"

"She doesn't know which day. I have been invited to lunch with you. Just you. In a nice secluded place. With all facilities. Where we won't be disturbed. No way will anyone else be there."

The Severed Head
Part Four

"Did you get the loan?"

"Yes, have you sorted out the switch?"

"Yes."

"Who do we have to pay? How much?"

"That's the beauty of the plan. Nothing. The lorry tracking system is simple, that's its strength, hardly any moving parts to wear out. But, it is also its weakness, all I did was add a moving part, well strictly speaking, two moving parts."

The more athletically built man leaned forward,

"I like it already, explain."

"You're HGV qualified, aren't you?"

Karen

"Are you sure you'll still be going?"

The weather-girl's comment about the rain, the night before, had been 'Novochester, 30mm and counting,' they were still counting.

"Yes, it'll just make the river even more impressive. I might be late back. Very late back. After the river, we're going on somewhere. Somewhere nice and quiet."

"Where?"

"He's got a place in the country. The old station at Coquetdale Halt. There I guess."

"Karen, he's one of your teachers."

"And consequently unlikely to boast about his conquest all over the locality. He's a bit immature. But quite nice. And single. To me that's far more important. You said you'd prefer I could tell you. I'm telling you. I'd rather not have a hard time over it."

"How long has it been?"

"Starts today I hope." Dennis hugged his 'all-growed-up' daughter to him,

"First time?"

She nodded against his shoulder.

"Put an old towel under your bum, saves a lot of embarrassment over stains and goo."

"Thanks Dad."

"I think I'll give Pealle a ring, see if she's housebound with all this weather. Ask her over to look at the wiring in the garage."

Yes, you do that Dad. That's if she's not already secreted around the corner, waiting anxiously for me to leave, getting soaked.

"I'll probably not see her. Tell her I'll give her a call after New Year or whenever."

The car she was waiting for turned into her street, swishing through the puddles beneath the avenue of desolate, leafless trees. "He's here, Bye Dad." Karen pulled the door shut behind her, picked up the cool box and rucksack and dead heated at her gate with the stopping vehicle. She dropped her load into the back seat and got in the front, the car had only been stationary for seconds.

“Hello,” she said brightly. “It’s a wonderful day for sightseeing,”

He laughed, she felt the tension lifting, the canoeing friends were going out for the day.

“No I’m serious. There’ll be nobody else there. We’ll have the countryside to ourselves.”

Wylam rapid was enormous. The belching-swollen Tyne, milk chocolate brown in colour, writhed its sinister dance below the bridge. A huge reverse-current, standing-wave, aptly named a stopper, rolled backwards at the tail of the chute. Downstream a line of canoeist-friendly standing waves, known as haystacks, exploding at impressively random intervals, marked the main flow of the current. Undeterred two intrepid canoeists were frolicking in the waves. As the couple watched from the bank next to the bridge, one powered straight down the chute into the stopper, intending to punch through.

The approaching canoe gave the scene a sense of scale.

The wave was truly enormous.

The canoeist seemed to hit a wall.

The prow of the now stationary canoe
lifted sedately straight up into the air,
until the tiny craft was vertical,
and then an unseen grab
plucked it down from below,
like a trout taking a fly.

Karen clutched her companion’s hand,

“He should be okay, he’s probably gone deep enough like that. Yes, there he is.” The upturned canoe had been spat out a couple o’dozen metres downstream. “He’ll have gone along, right on the bottom, under all that aggro.” A moment later the canoeist rolled up, broke out of the current and started calling excitedly to his colleague.

“It just stopped him dead. And he powered into it really hard.”

“Yes, stoppers do that.”

“It’s a bit big for me,” said Karen, relaxing her grip. Llew kept a hold, so she held him again.

"It's too big for me! Come on, let's have a look at Ovingham."

At Ovingham, they approached from the South bank this time and parked in the otherwise deserted country walk car park. Karen closed up to her teacher and slid her hand into the small of his back, he accepted the invitation, slid his arm in under hers and cuddled into her. Obediently Karen raised her arm around his shoulders, almost tucking him under it. Ovingham rapid was a big disappointment. The Tyne was too big; the rapid was just a huge shallowly sloping chute.

"No good, Chollerford, then lunch."

At least at Chollerford there was a stopper at the base of the weir and haystacks further down but it still wasn't a patch on Wylam.

"I'd like to walk Warden Gorge, but we probably can't with the river this high. Can I invite you to dish up our lunch in my country estate."

Karen disengaged, stood facing him and dropped him a full curtsy.

"As my Lordship pleases," she said and they both laughed as they cuddled back together again.

They drove off North Westwards.

"It's a railway station, well a railway carriage, a hundred metres of track and a station cocooned until I have the money to renovate it. But the carriage has all mod cons, I live there most of the holidays. Granddad bought it, as one of the chips flying off, when the Beeching axe fell. I was the only grandchild the least bit interested, so he left it to me in his will."

The station building had seen better days, but the vibrant colours of the dogwoods and snow white trunks of the birch trees, promised that the bare soil beds beneath them were hiding a multitude of joys when spring deigned to stroll on stage. Through the entrance, the freshly rain washed platform was furnished with plant tubs in two groups containing interesting rocks and attractive foliage. The gleaming engine, in its original L.N.E.R. livery and the stunning carriage, freshly restored to Pullman specification, were glowing with pride. They were artistically framed by the broad lustrous white stripe along the edge of the platform.

Inside, the carriage had been converted to kitchen, living room, bathroom and bedroom, all tidy, snug, warm and welcoming.

Karen stripped off her hooded waterproof and fleece, revealing a matching, white, collared-tee shirt, sports miniskirt and knee-socks combination, with discretely artistic, but nevertheless, vibrant red and blue piping that could have graced Wimbledon on Finals Day.

He gave her the conducted tour, ending up in the bedroom. She caressed the duvet cover whilst looking at the curtains.

This is more like it.

This was a boudoir worthy of a truly momentous moment in anyone's life.

"You have an eye for fabrics. Unusually so for a boy. And colour."

"Mother, not me, outside is me."

"Which is also stunning,"

He smiled, pleased, perhaps also a little embarrassed, nervous.

"Right what would you like?"

"I'd like to rest in here with you for an hour or so. Afterwards, we can try the lunch I brought. This afternoon, we could rest together a bit more. That shower's enormous. Built for two, playing games. We must road test it before I leave."

"I turned the heating up earlier, so that we could dress more comfortably if we felt like it--"

"I feel like it. I'd really like it if you helped me get more comfortable."

"Can I do it all myself?" She'd succeeded, he was obviously more confident about the situation now. Karen discarded her trainers and lay back on the bed languorously, trying to relax and encourage him even more. That her stunning breasts had been liberated from their bra for the day, became even more twin peaked apparent, as her excitement built.

"Yes, please."

"There's something I've never done to you. But I would like to do it."

"Yes, please."

"You don't know what it is."

"Just do it Llew. Have me for Christmas. Anything you want. Anything! Just--Before you mount me. And we strive for Nirvana. I've got a little towel in my ruck. Stick it under my bum please. Towels wash easier than duvets."

Llew was puzzled.

"First time--Don't look like that. I'm panting eager. Do it. On a towel."

Afterwards,

"These were a revelation." He stroked the silky globes and kissed the erect nipples. "I hadn't noticed in class just how busty you are, a loose top can hide the Alps if a girl really wants to, but the canoeing waistcoat was heavily tailored and snugly full, nowhere to hide."

"It was the only one they had."

"In class I was aware that you were attractive and neatly groomed, deliberately holding yourself out of the limelight; in a bather, neoprene top and crash hat, you can't hide, you look stunning'.

"I look like a caricature. Spitting Image would need more foam for my lips than for two other puppets. My parents had to take my bricks away. When I was little. I could get them into my mouth."

The lips and mouth were tenderly kissed, licked, loved.

"You look lovely and with this amazing all over tan, you must have spent all your holiday on a naturist beach."

"No. On the Scottish farm. Where we celebrate New Year. The all over tan is permanent. Grandma was a Zulu."

"What?"

"Is a Zulu. There's nothing was about her."

"Karen, be serious."

"I am. Grandma is a Zulu Princess. So am I as it happens."

"Really?"

"Well twenty-five percent of me is. That's how I see it. I might have trouble persuading hard line conservatives. We're a wild offshoot from the main line."

"How come?"

"Diplomat's daughter with a posting to Kenya. They sort of smuggled, not quite illegal, their daughters over here as kids. Granddad was a German Scientist that ran away from Hitler. They had to get married because Mum was on the way. Dreadful crime in those days supposedly."

"The worst crime a girl could commit, believe me, the worst."

In a pig's bum, thought Karen, but said. "But, then, they fell in love. They're still together. Granddad's a bit frail now. But he can still shout when necessary. The tan really is permanent. This level. I can deepen it by sunbathing."

"How tall is Grandma?"

"A hundred and eighty-eight. Six foot two, in old money. Well she was. So was Mum."

"That explains the legs. You are amazing and as far as being a caricature is concerned, to slightly misquote you, 'there's nothing caricature about you.'"

The girl regarded him in mild scorn.

"It's true--You have nice eyes, in an attractive face, your mouth is licentious, your bottom voluptuous, your waist and hips wanton, there is more than a suggestion of a six pack appearing here." He traced the lines on her tummy. " And these are big--"

"34D's not that big."

"Don't be embarrassed about them, be proud of them."

"I am," said with no conviction whatever.

"No you're not, but you should be. 34D is big enough, but you're tall and slender and so they look big, but you interrupted me, the real point is that they are pert and pretty and they stand right up with no support. Perfectly round, with perfectly circular, large, dark brown nipples, which come right out to kiss back, when they are kissed. Karen, I used to measure myself against others and get depressed, short, fat, ugly--"

"You're not."

"Quiet baggage, then I realised I should measure myself against me. How well was I doing compared with how well I could do. I can't be taller, but I can be fair and just, I can't do much about my build, but I can be tolerant. Look in a mirror and settle for that, it's a pretty good package. Then look inside your head and ask if that's the best you can do, if it isn't, that's when to be dissatisfied, when to change something."

And,

"I know you're on a Vocational course, which one?"

"Plumbing. Industrial Plumbing. Pipes and pumps and hydrodynamics fascinate me. Dunno why. I saw a picture of ICI when I was a kid. Just a maze of pipes. I wrote to them, got posters for my wall. I read manufacturer's product releases like other kids read novels. I read novels as well."

"So what career are you looking at?"

"Plumber."

"With your brain?" he asked gently. "Your aspirations are your business, it's not an argument, just a question."

"Choose between happy or rich! Have you? You can only get decent money in teaching outside the classroom--You're getting hard."

"Can I fuck you again, but from behind?"

"Of course you can. Again and again. As often as you want, I want you to."

Get your clitty going Karen Robinson and you might come this time.

She eased herself up onto hands and knees and grasped the headboard with one hand and sensuously frigged her clitoris with the other. Her man, like in the shower in his changing room, again made no comment about her self stimulation, as he cuddled up behind her and gently pushed in. Her breasts were gently pummelled as she felt herself fucked. Yes, this time, smoothly up onto the top of the roller coaster and suddenly down the other side. Down onto the bed too, helpless on knees and shoulders,

"Yes, it's there--coming--I'm coming--come." The words squealed out among his,

"Oh yes,--what a shag--what a lovely shag."

"Where do you see our relationship going?"

"I don't think of you as my boyfriend. Is that what you mean?"

"Yes. Don't you mind being used for fucking?"

"Is that what you're doing?"

"Some people might think so, but I don't mean it that way."

"Many girls in Africa are forcibly butchered, circumcised. From then on they have no feeling. Down there. They get used for fucking." She sat up, turning away. "Holes for men to stick their dick into. Unless a baby happens to be coming the other way at the time."

Suddenly, he must have realised she was desperately trying not to cry and cradled her, comforting her.

"The worst bit. The very worst. It's often other women who do the dirty deed,"

He turned her around to face him and cuddled her and stroked her.

"Many of their husbands wish the girls were entire. So that they could get pleasure from pleasing the girl they love."

"No I certainly don't mean using you that way."

"I don't mind. I'm astonished to say it, but I don't. You could--can use me for fucking whenever you want. It's my choice. My mutilated sisters. Their option to choose was taken from them."

"Let's just say I'm fucking you then, rather than using you, I'd prefer it and you are choosing, so using isn't accurate." He paused for a moment, plucking up the courage. "Is that what happened to Grandma?"

"No. They got her out while she was a child. Her and her sisters. But she was going to visit later. Kenya, not Natal. In her early teens. She was advised against it, for exactly that reason. They thought it was only a small chance, but --"

"Somebody put his foot down?"

"Granddad and very hard. They weren't lovers then. But he'd heard things from relatives in Kenya. Turned out they had it all planned. Just waiting for the girls to return." She sniffed and determinedly put out of her mind problems over which she had no control. There were enough within reach, crowding her. "Are you going to fuck me at school? You can if you want. I don't mind. I won't stop you. It's just. If we're caught, we'll get fired."

"I could already get fired for what I've done to you at school. I could get fired for this."

Karen looked at him nodding, waiting for an answer. He sighed,

“Yes, I won’t be able to keep my hands off you, if there’s nobody else around.”

“Getting fired. Just a minor inconvenience for me. If I said sorry. They’d probably let me back in. It’s your life.”

“The bottom end empties very quickly on a Friday. Could you wander down later on Fridays, help me pack up for the weekend?”

“Be your ‘something for the weekend Sir?’ Yes. I’ll come down for a Friday fuck.”

“Karen!”

“You’re getting hard again.”

“On your tummy wench, stick that voluptuous bottom up, I want to give us another good time.” Karen giggled, but didn’t immediately obey. She knelt up, pulled some pillows down and laid the towel over them. Then she lay face down snuggling herself spread wide over the hump in the middle of the bed. Her fingers were already at work on her eager clit.

* * *

Karen came out of assembly and walked straight into Siew Mui Lee. The young teacher had been visiting West Novochester on junior school business. When she finished she had asked at the Office for the Sixth Former.

“The Sixth Form are in Assembly, they will be coming out in a tick.”

“Where do I wait please?”

“Just there, she’ll walk right past you.”

Karen had appeared only a couple of minutes later.

“You wouldn’t like to be Miss Robinson for the Swimming Club this Thursday as well would you? Give me a hand with the little ones; Mr. Cuthbert can’t come any more. Just the organisation, no life saving or teaching stuff.”

“Okay, why not?”

So after helping Llew put the canoes away, while he showered and dressed in lonely isolation, in his bleak little room, she helped Siew Mui in her swimming club for tinies, with the supervision nuts and bolts, those not primarily devoted to swimming. To her surprise, Karen found she was enjoying herself.

The parents arrived towards the end of the session and presently the girls had no charges left to pack off home.

"Lovely. I like doing it, but it's so nice when it's all finished and you can relax. Now we can have our shower, can I bathe you, wash your hair and that?"

Chapter 5

Lisa: January 1999

Karen

Karen had missed Llew's fondling and loved her hair being played with,

"Yes, please. I'd like that."

Siew Mui pulled the little wooden stool in from the outer room and stuck it under the falling spray.

"Take that hanky off. Sit."

Karen got her hair delicately, sensuously washed and hardly noticed it, because as soon as Siew Mui got her naked under the shower, she cuddled up to her and rubbed her naked soapy body against Karen's. The taller girl interpreted the first rub as a firm request, 'Can I do this?' She answered by putting one hand in her lap and the other arm around the Chinese girl's waist, her hand gently resting on her hip, and guided her in to sit straddling her; two fingers gently mashed the Oriental cunny, breasts together erect nipple to erect nipple, transmitting 'Do anything you want.' Siew Mui responded to the message and washed Karen's hair with her hands and the rest of her with her body. Karen concentrated on holding her new friend to her and pressing her fingers into her in response to the rubbing.

"Come home with me." Panting and breathy, Siew Mui was

still in control, but only just. “Come for tea.”

“I can’t, I’ve got arrangements tonight. I could come next Thursday.”

“Yes. Come for tea, stay over.” The control was slipping fast, already having lost the tongue. “Sleep over. Sleep with me.”

“All right. You’ve nearly gone Siew Mui. Relax. Let it go. I’ll hold you.”

The smaller girl’s hands snaked down to Karen’s breasts squeezing, feeling. She squealed and folded, her arms fell limply away. Karen held her up and took over the lovemaking, probing deep into the other girl. When she closed with her to kiss softly, Siew Mui returned the kiss, eagerly, with tongue, moaning in her passion.

Later, after their homework,

“I’ll just take Pealle home-’

“Don’t be too late back. There’s something I need to tell you.”

“Okay.”

* * *

“Do we have a problem?”

“No Dad. No problem. You said you’d prefer I could tell you. I’ve got something to tell you. Siew Mui asked me to sleepover next Thursday. So I’ll be out. Thursday morning to Friday night. But I’d like Pealle to come over. Look after you for me. If that’s okay?”

“Erm--Yes, okay by me--When you say sleepover--I mean--”

“Yes, Dad, in her bed.” She kissed the man she loved. “Goodnight.”

At the first opportunity the following day, Karen drew Pealle aside,

“Next Thursday night, I’m helping Siew Mui again. After canoeing.”

“You’ll be late again, okay.”

“No. I won’t be there at all. I’m going to her house for a sleepover.”

Pealle looked desolated,

“Oh--Okay--I’ll --”

"Still come around though. Dad wants you to."

Giving presents is more rewarding than receiving them, thought Karen, as the scene of desolation was swept away with a sunburst of a smile.

"Oh, okay."

* * *

The following Thursday, with all their charges collected, Karen took Siew Mui into the shower and cleansed and snogged her.

"Don't make love to me, not here, later darling at home, yes, kisses, lots of kisses, but I've got to be able to drive. I don't think I was very safe on the roads last week, don't get me so hot I can't drive safely."

The evening meal was in the family restaurant in China Town,

"This is Karen, she helps me in the swimming club."

Several extended family members came, ate and departed and the Sixth Former earned brownie points with her caring attitude towards some little ones. Presently they said their goodbyes and walked the few metres to Siew Mui's little flat above a hardware shop.

* * *

When Karen walked into the Sixth Form Common Room on Friday morning, Pealle was re-packing her bag,

"Hello."

The blonde completed the pirouette airborne. A large, awkwardly-shaped, multi-secondary, step-down-transformer slipped from her fingers and thudded to the floor. She bent to retrieve it and stuff it into the bag.

"Oh--Hello." The transformer swerved clumsily against the lip of the wide-open bag, folded it shut and slid down the outside before crashing to the floor for the second time. The hands that delivered serves that grown men respected, shook, uncoordinated and feeble.

"How was Dad?"

"Fine, on good form--I--I stayed over, is that okay?"

"Course it is. Siew Mui's asked me to sleepover every Thursday. So you can too. Look after the aged parent. If you want to that is."

"Oh--Yes,--That would be nice, thank you." Pealle slid the fitting neatly into her bag rather than swerving past it and onto the floor for the third time. She didn't have Parkinson's Disease yet after all. "I had to leave later and lock up, set the alarm. Dennis said to give you the keys." She rummaged the spare set from her pocket and held them out, stepping towards her friend.

"Keep 'em. You'll need them every time I'm away. No point in keep giving them back. I'm sure to forget them one day. Then we'll be stuck. You need a fob. With a bell tower on it." The taller girl turned away to her own locker, struggling to keep the belly laugh under control and hidden inside. Pealle looked as if Karen had just served an ace past her.

Why do some people do hurtful things just for kicks, when doing nice ones is so much more good clean fun and causes so much more serious aggro?

Later, when she went down to his classroom, Llew's door was open, but he was nowhere to be seen. Although most of the room was neat, with the chairs tucked under their desks and basically tidy, Karen knew that was solely due to the kids automatic reaction to whose room it was. The signs of a supply teacher were obvious in the higgledy piggledy piles of exercise books and disarrayed papers on the front desk and the floor around the waste bin. Llew arrived as she was finishing the clean-up.

"I was beginning to wonder if you were here. You don't look good. Sit down. I'll get you a drink."

"Exam moderation. I've been forced to spend four hours doing a job we could have done in ten minutes. I've got a splitting headache and all for nowt." Karen rolled the cool can across his neck and forehead.

"You poor thing. Tell me."

"I mark my candidates' work and submit it to the board with a list of marks and recommended grades. Then the moderator comes and relates my grades to those of everyone else, to ensure consistency."

"Yes. We get moderated in Vocation as well. You could be a hard marker. Or generous to your kids. Wanting them to succeed."

"Exactly. He insisted we look at every paper to study the quality, after five minutes it was obvious that I was being consistently half a grade generous. I said so, offered to move my grade boundaries half a grade and look at the new borders, but we still spent four hours to get to exactly the place I offered to go at once."

"You look trashed."

"I am. Never again. Next time I'll demand to see his list first, he had one, right from the start, the list we agreed on at the end. I'll demand to see it next time and, if it's okay, we'll agree it straight away."

Karen caressed his brow and massaged the tight muscles in his neck.

"Why do idiots insist on negotiating, when the deal they want is there for the taking?"

"I don't know. Perhaps he's paid by time. Does this mean you want to go straight home?"

"Quite the reverse, the prospect of my Friday fuck is all that kept me going."

"Well in that case, I'd better lock your door."

* * *

The General Studies lesson was on Morality. It was the third in the series and they had already discussed Murder and Theft, it was the turn of Sex to be put through the wringer. The class was smaller, four girls, one Jewish, two Christian and one Muslim, had all been withdrawn by their parents from the discussion. The class still represented the United Nations though and Llew's intention was that precise thinking would come out of it. He clearly stated his objective at the start,

"At the end of this discussion I want you to know why you make the choices you make. I don't care what the choice is, Celibate; Chaste; Promiscuous; I don't care and I don't care what the reason is, Religious Morality; Pragmatic Reality; because You Want To; I don't care. I care passionately that you know why!"

"Would you really not care if your wife was promiscuous?" Maggie, in Female Chauvinist Pig mode, having a go.

"Firstly: it's a cruel and offensive question and it was meant to be. Naughty!" He wagged his index finger at her. "Secondly: What I said was that I really would not care if **you** were promiscuous." He had to quell the resulting riot. "Finally: I'm not married, but if I was and if she was, I would hope that I loved her enough to work out an agreed settlement with her about it." He skilfully channelled the responses into a discussion, occasionally looking hard at Craig and Trevor, when their more immature side rolled to the surface and they tried to make it personal and score points. Somebody mentioned the word slut.

"Define slut! A proper, emotion free definition."

"A girl that will have sex with anybody."

"That is a girl, not a slut."

Karen jumped into the resulting explosion,

"No! Quiet everybody. I think I know what he means. Any-girl will have sex with any-body. Provided you press the right button."

"That's not true, there are people in this room that I'd rather die than have sex with them," Maggie spat back at her.

"Maybe," said Llew, "but what if it wasn't you that was going to die? What if it was your Mum, or your Sister, or your **Daughter**? What if it wasn't die, but be tortured? There's a right button somewhere Maggie, even for you."

The silence was broken eventually by one or two half hearted attempts at a definition of slut, but Llew criticised them all as being emotive.

"What is the male equivalent of slut?"

"There isn't one."

"Whilst reserving my position on that statement, can you think of any male, any male at all, who, if he was female, her behaviour would be regarded as that of a slut?"

"We can probably all think of several," said Karen.

"So I'm shepherding you towards thinking of slut as a sexist, emotional word, can we have an emotion free definition please?"

The resulting failure of the class to come up with an emotion free definition, allowed him to introduce the concept of forcing others to conform to your view by irrational bullying insult, rather than rational argument.

"Leading directly on from irrational insult to irrational behaviour, I know it's unusual to have General Studies homework, but you have this week. Here's a handout, with a drawing of a common woodland, fungus fruiting-body." Mr. Smith was walking around the room, placing papers onto desks. "It happens to be poisonous but that's not the question of the day. I want you to look at the shape of the toadstool, read the absolutely true rubric underneath the picture and comment upon it. Try to limit your comment to 500 words or less, because if you break through the superficial skin, and really come to grips with all the innuendo involved, you could easily get carried away and write a book."

He paused while the class took stock of the drawing, a diagrammatic, inkjet-print of a drawing of a stinkhorn toadstool, with underneath,

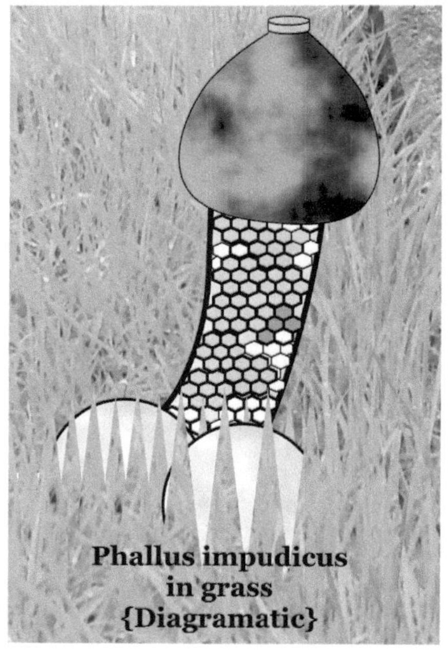
Phallus impudicus in grass {Diagramatic}

The Stinkhorn's suggestive shape caused Victorian Gentlemen to issue orders to their gardeners to go out every morning and destroy the fungi, lest their wives, daughters or other Victorian maidens should be offended by the sight.

Karen put her glasses on. Yes, no doubt about it, the stinkhorn was very redolent of--

"What shape?" whispered a girl sitting behind her, to her friend, genuinely ignorant.

Trevor sniggered.

"It's a very close approximation to the human male penis. Ready for copulation. Hence its Latin name," said Karen generally to the whole class. "Trevor's sniggering because he thinks they don't come that big. They do Trevor. And bigger."

The guffaw of belly laughs around the room, suggested to Karen that she had scored, probably highly.

"Enough!" Barked Llew before the irate boy could reply. "The fact that in these permissive times there are still sixteen-seventeen year old girls who are unaware of the shape, is the crux of your homework. Can we move on to sin? When is sex sinful?"

Karen listened with amusement as 'Conceived in Sin', was paraded and 'Sex inside Christian Marriage' was hoisted up as the only 'non sinful' kind and kept in prime place by the debating skills of the two very bright devout Catholics present and the aggression of the female chauvinist. Llew was going to butt in, but she held her hand up, palm out and mouthed 'No! Wait!' at him. The three girls carried the day, to the obvious discomfort of several boys who nevertheless were unwilling to argue their corner any further, only then, as the silence lengthened, did she hold her hand up.

"Karen."

"I have a bunch to say. I've listened to you. You listen to me. Your point of view of chastity being desirable, is one I applaud. But." She held up fingers and ticked the points off. "One: An engaged couple have loving sex. Twelve hours later they get married. Fall out, have a big row and he rapes her. The first was sinful, the second not? No! Silence! You've had your go. I'm not going to dignify that example with any further comment."

Trevor was desperate to reassert himself,

"It's fornication, the cities of Sodom and Gomorrah were destroyed for it."

"The one good man to get out was Lot," Karen replied. "Yet, he was prepared to give up his virgin daughters for debauching. To save his own skin. Other skins too, I do admit. The girls got their own back later. Got him drunk. Got him to knock them up. The pair of them. A pair of incestuous relationships that went totally unpunished. Strange that. Must have been because he was a good man."

Several grins appeared on tuned in faces.

"I thought both girls died, raped to death," said Llew, confused.

"So did I. But I checked last night. Revised Version 1884. I was surprised too. Could be different in different versions. Any more?"

Trevor tried again,

"Onan. He was killed."

"Onan has given his name to onanism. Coitus interruptus. People use it, wrongly, as a polite term for masturbation. Which the poor soul wasn't even guilty of. Not as on record anyway. He just didn't fancy fathering children. On his dad's orders, on Tamar, his brother's widow. So he withdrew and spilt it on the ground," Karen paused and looked around significantly. "The recommended Roman Catholic contraceptive. The Lord slew him, I wonder who wielded the blade? But his dad wasn't slain. When Tamar pretended to be a whore. Tricked Judah into impregnating her. I've still got two. And plenty random shells."

Prudence, the more aggressive of the devout Catholics said,

"Nice girls don't."

"A boy I love and respect beyond measure fried that one for me. A while back. How about, 'Nice boys don't!' Have you ever heard that? There are nineteen people in this room. None of us is married. Who is claiming they're not nice?" Nobody moved or spoke, so Karen continued, "I know for a fact that there are not nineteen virgins in this room. I would guess there's not as many as nine."

This time there was silence, with several students glancing uncomfortably at others.

"Go on Karen."

"Okay, Secondly: Just a few hundred years ago. Few people in this room would expect to get married formally. Marriage was for the nobility. Not the peasants. Did that make their sex sinful? Utter tosh. Two thousand years ago. All sex, everywhere in the world was sinful? Greasy dishes!" She ticked the next finger. "Thirdly: The Native Central and South Americans had sinful sex before the Spanish arrived. And, bullied them into Christianity? Even more greasy dishes! Sex is not sinful. It's how it's done. You want to see **real** sin. Take a look at what the Christian invaders did to the Native, Human Sacrificing, Americans. Not the glossy, sanitised version. Mere rape and pillage. What they **really** did!

That's Sin! Loving sex is not sinful. Sadly it may involve a third party in betrayal. Rejection. Loss of self-esteem. Those are the sins, not the loving sex. Calling sex a sin is just a handy gun to hold at your head. It's all about control. Sin has nowt to do with sex. And vice versa."

"It's against a commandment!" Maggie wouldn't hesitate to break commandments if necessary, today it served her purpose not to.

"The commandment is, 'Thou shalt not commit adultery'. That requires at least one to be married to someone else! The authorities carefully forget that awkward fact. If the authorities can interpret to suit themselves. Then so can the squaddies."

Maggie persisted,

"Twenty years ago, a book came out, 'The Joy Of sex', it was castigated, as an exploitation of women, and rightly so, you'd think Victoria was still alive and we were still men's possessions."

Karen gazed steadily at her as she set up the reply,

"One incensed respondent even hoped the author would rot in hell. Just for writing a sex textbook."

The response was spat back, white-hot spleen being vented,

"For writing a Sex is Pleasure for Men book, a Degradation of Women book."

"But that wasn't the problem. Was it? And it **still** wouldn't have been the problem, even if it were true. The problem was that it was a **sex is fun** book. Not degrading of women. But written by a man. Of course he wrote it from a man's own viewpoint. How else could he write it. The problem was he said sex is adult play. The Establishment couldn't stomach it. The Feminists couldn't stomach it. Misogynists, Misandrists, Clergy and especially the Media couldn't stomach it. So they joined forces to slander the book to criticise it. Personally I would not have liked to be the author's wife. But his mistress had a ball. The Joy of Sex, is her sex manual written over several years. For the two of them, by him. Later published. Sex is merely adult play. Not sin. I've said my piece."

"You would have sex with a boy if you liked him enough? And not consider it sinful?"

The room was quiet, waiting, Karen decided to stand up and

be counted,

"Not would. Did. And, not one boy either."

Utter silence, then Lisa, the nicer of the two devout girls murmured,

"A gang bang?"

"As it happens, it wasn't. Different occasions."

The questioner was completely tuned in, nodding her head gently, throughout her question and Karen's answer,

"But you would?" Lisa had barely breathed it into the hush.

"I don't know. It's not a no go area. I'd think about it."

The lesson change bell caught them all by surprise. Llew wound up with,

"Many of you have expressed your views bravely. Well done. They shouldn't be repeated, to bully outside the room. Trevor has already been soundly spanked for trying to bully **inside** the room. There will be no bullying. Have I made myself clear?"

There were a few moments of embarrassed shuffling, then murmurs of,

"Sir."

Back in the Common Room, Trevor just had to disobey Llew's instruction. As soon as it became apparent what was afoot,

"Ye! Shut up!" The normally polite and quiet Sid, voicing the view of the majority. Pealle edged over to Karen,

"What's up?"

"Llew Smith's General Studies lesson. We had another riot. I slapped Trevor for being rude to Melanie. He was getting back."

"I wish we had him, Mrs. Pentland dictated notes to us the whole lesson, there were only three of us there. There might only be two next week. Well, there **will** only be two next week."

"Notes about what?"

Without a word Pealle opened her notebook and stuck it under Karen's nose,

It is important to preserve modesty at all times. A husband should be able to assert that he has never seen his wife's body above the knee or--

The tall girl looked up,

"This is a joke?"

"No. It's deadly serious, Marie Stopes lived in vain, or so she is trying to ensure."

"Don't you discuss it. Challenge it?"

"With the Potato?!"

"We're free to--No. We're encouraged to challenge anything Llew says. He's hardly ever wrong mind. But all the same. Look we've got homework."

Pealle stared at the sheet.

"He warned us not to get carried away. Write too much."

"Can I discuss this with the Potato?"

"I'd do it formally. Through your Form Tutor. If you obey the rules. She can't put it down to spite. And she will if you don't. And anyway Miss J'Enson'll listen."

"I'll go now."

Pealle returned grinning.

"How did it go?"

In reply Pealle waved her own homework sheet,

"I'm to turn up to E9 in future, not E1, just not tell anyone, what the eye doesn't see --"

"Welcome aboard."

"Erm, there's some things building up in the Heating Unit plumbing work that I'm unsure about. Dennis suggested I come on Tuesdays to work with you, if that's okay."

"As well, not instead though. If that's all right with you."

"It's fine, I hit it off with your Dad nearly as well as with you."

No you don't, for a moment Karen feared she'd said it, she shook her head and turned away.

"I do."

"No you don't. You fit better than a coat of paint. I'm just a good friend. Come for tea. Telemarks, look at the time, we'll be late."

* * *

"Are you going to tell me?"

Karen had gone down to Llew's room for their Friday session, but he hadn't immediately locked the door behind her, as he usually did, he'd fired the question instead. She didn't need clarification,

"Whom you're sharing me with? No. My business. I've never asked you that question. Your business. Are you going to chuck me out?"

"No, sorry Karen, your business is your business. I've never walked around the table and looked at it from the other side. I bang on, in lessons, to others about doing it, but then don't do it myself, sorry, you're not sharing me with anyone else."

"Well you are. Do I get fucked or dumped? I'd much prefer the fuck."

"Okay, do you want me to back shuttle you as usual?"

* * *

Karen, Jet and Pealle left the Sixth Form block and Karen bore away towards the main building,

"Where are you going?"

"Just calling in to see Llew Smith. About the homework. You need to see him too. About women being possessions."

"No. I'll not bother, I saw him at break."

Karen didn't get a chance to answer, Jet was making separation distance as if from a plague victim.

"Oh dear," murmured Pealle, heading for the door. Llew was on duty just inside,

"Sir. Sorry to bother you. But I'm the wrong side of a thousand words already. And I've still got loads to do."

"Try précising it."

"The thousand is a précis. Down from three thousand."

"Summarise the rest under self explanatory headings. I'll have a look, if necessary you can say it to me, if it needs expanding, multimedia and all that."

* * *

The following week several members of the Upper VI had a communal Eighteenth in downtown Novochester; in a trendy bar, noted for forgetting to check ages. The members of the Lower VI were invited as a matter of course. Trevor was boasting about his down in one prowess,

"I'll take anyone on, never been beaten yet."

"Ever taken a girl on?" Maggie asked innocently. Trevor looked around, Karen was watching the exchange.

"Nobody can beat me," He said straight into the tall girl's eyes. She shook her head sadly at him mouthing,

"Don't--Don't."

Trevor grinned,

"Nobody."

Maggie grabbed Jet.

"I don't want to."

Maggie ignored her and thrust her forward.

"Let's make it interesting, a fiver each in a kitty, winner takes all?"

"I told you I don't--"

"Let's make it ten," interrupted Trevor imperiously, whilst flicking away in Jet's general direction with his fingers. Her eyes, narrowed; her chin took on an annoyed tilt.

"Okay." She rummaged in her purse and plonked the note down. "Ten it is."

"Tenner to play. Down in one, winner take all." Called Maggie. "Anyone else want in?"

A couple of Upper VI boys looked into the circle then withdrew.

"Not with Tissue's eyes, aflame," murmured one to the other.

"No-way, if I'm going to drop a tenner, St Oswald's can have it." Came the soft reply. Despite her urging Maggie couldn't get anyone else to join the competition and so it was Trevor and Jet who squared up across a small table, a brimming pint in front of each.

"You start on my say so, no spills, no stops, nothing left or you lose. Right?"

The contestants neither moved nor spoke.

"Take your pints."

Trevor took hold of his glass.

"Go."

Trevor upped his pint and noisily gulped it down. Jet leisurely reached out for hers, lifted it up, disposed of it down her throat in one, swallow-less pour and set the drained glass back down. Trevor, saucer eyed, missed a swallow in his shock and sputtered to a stop, a gill or so short, with beer fanning down his front like an unkempt beard. Jet picked up the stakes,

"Don't like it that way, you can't savour it properly. Come on 12MC Girls." She waved the notes aloft. "The drinks are on Trevor."

A few minutes later, clutching their free drinks, Lisa managed to corner Karen alone and asked to speak to her in private. Karen had wondered at it taking her so long, it had been obvious in the General Studies lesson that a private meet was required. Lisa assessed her friend's reaction correctly,

"You're not surprised."

"I'm only surprised that it took you until now." There was a long pause. "Do you want me to ask?"

"I don't know where to start."

"Is it about being gang banged?"

"Yes."

"Have you had one?" It didn't match her stance in the lesson.

"No." But the look in her eyes, added the clarification.

"But you've been invited to have one?"

"Yes."

"Tell me about the invite."

"A friend of my cousin Jack, they live in High Loblom, behind the lake. I go there almost every holiday, have done forever, in the summer we go swimming in the lake, skinny-dipping. We did it as kids, then when I grew these." She waved a hand across her chest. "I got embarrassed and I didn't want to swim without a costume any more. The boys were nice and understanding and we talked it through. As kids they had shown me everything they had, stuck out in front, I had shown them a mound with a crease down it."

"Not quite as interesting."

"Now I'd hidden even that behind a crop of hair but grown some beautiful extras to compensate. They would understand if I insisted on hiding them, but they would be disappointed at being deprived of so much beauty. And anyway, the embarrassment would be all theirs when they got hard."

"Understandable. Devious but understandable."

"Yes, I knew that I was being conned, my own debating skills being turned on me."

"But deep down you wanted to. All they had to do was clear the way. Make it easy. And not rock the boat. Not too obviously force you. You wanted to tread down that road anyway."

"I just took my bather off and dived in. When we finished swimming I walked about naked for a while, drying myself, as if I was alone."

"While the boys jacked off? Watching you."

"Yes."

"And it made you feel good. In control."

"Yes--You really do understand, don't you?"

Karen shrugged.

"That was Year Ten Summer Holiday, they hid behind bushes or stayed in the water, but I knew what they were doing. I told Jack that I knew and I didn't mind. Last summer they did it in front of me, I shimmied the shoulders, wobbled the tits about a bit and watched the boys spurting their appreciation. That was so exciting, the feeling of power, control; when I picked my bather up one of them asked, 'Can we put them into you, give you a good time too?' I said, 'No way,' and put my bather on."

"And, if he'd said, 'Go on. You're lovely. Please Lisa. You're so beautiful. Make everybody's day. We'd love to give you a good time too. Please. Go on.' It would just have been a question of time. Your bather would have been off, discarded, forgotten. On your back. Knees up in the air. Legs wide open. Arms out in welcome?"

"Barely half of what you said would have been needed, I don't know how I put the bather on, my mind was screaming 'Yes, please,' while my body was protecting my virtue."

Karen cuddled the distressed girl,

"Oh Lisa and now I've started you thinking again. Just when you had it all sorted. Sorry."

"It's not your fault, it's mine, my faith isn't strong enough to cope with my brain. I want to know Why? And in Robert A. Heinlein's words, 'To how many decimal places?' and my faith isn't strong enough."

"What are you going to do?"

"I'm going back up for a week at Easter, I don't know. That's a lie, I do know, I don't know how I'll live with myself when I come back."

"I'll take you down to Streetwise after school one night. Get you fixed up. Have you thought that through? You're not allowed contraception either."

"Something about hanging and sheep and lamb?"

The tears welled up and cascaded down her cheeks, Karen cuddled the other girl even more tightly into her, soothing her sobs, caressing her back and feeling very randy. The sobbing slowed and stopped.

"Are you okay? Because this is making me horny. Some of our friends are trying not to look. Unsuccessfully. Shagging you in public would be naughty nice. I'd love it. But it would complicate things still further."

Lisa eased her top away, gently; the girls were still pressed tightly together from the waist down, which wasn't giving Karen any respite at all.

"Oh sorry Karen, I thought you did boys?"

"I do. The odd girly feel, on sleepovers. Like most people. But until a few weeks ago, I thought I did; **only** boys. Now I know different. Now either have me or let me go Lisa. Please."

The shorter girl pulled her in and gave her a full wet smacker all over her mouth,

"Thanks!" She said, as she released her.

The following Tuesday the two girls emerged from the specifically for teenagers, family planning clinic, walked briskly across the road and almost at once onto the bus for home.

"Have you told your parents?"

"No."

"Could you?"

"Not my Mum, I might be able to tell my Dad, I don't know."

"My Dad got me my first supplies. Just about. Part of my sixteenth birthday present."

"Can I tell mine that, test the water?"

"Yes. That's why I told you."

Lisa nodded, smiling; the smile thinned,

"What's--Sorry."

"Ask. I can always refuse to answer."

"What's--What's it like--with a girl I mean?"

"Lovely. Soft. Gentle. Lovely. And lasts for ages and ages. Girls don't stop when they've come. They go straight on, well my girl does. That's why I look wrecked every Friday. I spend all Thursday night squealing."

"You don't look wrecked every Friday, I've never seen anyone such a picture of health--And contentment. Whoever she is, she's doing a grand job on you."

"I do feel wonderful. A good chunk of that is Mr. Carpenter's Plumbing Course. But the rest is down to the workout I'm getting."

"Does your Dad know?"

"Yes. I'm out all night. He would guess. But I told him anyway."

"You told him--Wow--Doesn't he mind?"

"I don't think so. So long as I'm safe and happy. I think that's what he really cares about."

The next day's lessons were such that Karen was never in Lisa's presence without Jet alongside too. The tall brunette fully understood that Lisa would prefer to keep their secret, so never mentioned the matter uppermost in her mind. Lisa solved the problem by coming down to Vocation during her free lesson and waiting patiently to one side until Mr. Carpenter was finished talking to his star student.

"It's a big task, draw each section as a discrete job. Pipe run, parts and cutting list, assembly order and submit it as an assignment. When we're both happy, I'll let you do it all, bit by bit."

"Can I measure up the waste system now?"

"Yes, drop it in next week. Yes, Lisa?"

"Can I see Karen?"

Bill Carpenter turned waving permission as he walked away,

"I told my Dad what yours had done and we got it all sorted, he knows everything, well nearly everything."

"Not that you intend to share yourself out among five boys at Easter?"

Pealle looked sharply their way. Lisa glanced at her, but then replied,

"Hackers no! And anyway it might be six, it would have been six last summer."

"What about Confession?"

"We discussed that too, it's my decision, but he'll support me whichever way I jump. I'll do what I have to do, something I can live with. What do you do?"

"If the wild child has had a ball. But nobody got hurt. I don't do anything. I'll say sorry if I ever think it necessary. If there might be a problem."

After Lisa had left, Karen waited for the probing inquiry from the other girl and waited and waited. It never came. She'd definitely heard, every word, but apparently considered it a private matter.

Good.

* * *

Easter came and went and Karen did to Lisa exactly what she had done to Llew, spoke to her briefly on a neutral topic. She had been searching her mind for one, but when she entered the Common Room, Lisa was unpacking her bag, with her back to the door; the neutral topic waved like a flag, literally.

"Hi Lisa, hold still a second." Karen reached into the back of the shorter girl's neck and tucked the flag down.

"Blouse ticket. Sticking up," she murmured and walked off to her locker. She set her bag down, looked back at Lisa, and raised the eyebrows only enough to show if you had been looking for it. Lisa could choose her interpretation, 'Thanks' would be the ticket, anything else--

Chapter 6

Surfing: Spring 1999

Karen

The smile on Lisa's face was a ghost, there and gone, but all the way up to her eyes, which flicked quickly around the girls. She raised her hands in front of her breasts, her thumbs holding the pinkies into her palms, three fingers on each hand spread, and her eyebrows too twitched, mirroring Karen's. Jet saw nothing unusual, Pealle grinned and Karen silently mouthed 'Oo!' at a point about one metre directly in front of her own knees and turned her attention to her personal chores.

Llew Smith was waiting outside the common room to intercept the Sixth Form engineer,

"It's getting very rough at Tynemouth today, but by tomorrow it will probably be good for surfing."

"Tomorrow night after school?"

"Yes. Bring your gear, I'll stick our canoes on my car, we'll give it a try."

"Okay,"

He waved and turned away.

"That means I'll be late Tuesday as well. This week. Can you come tonight to look at that flow rate problem? We'll leave the electronics for tomorrow."

"Okay," replied Pealle, with shining eyes.

The following evening the wind had abated somewhat, but left an impressive surf running. From the sea road it looked interesting, big but interesting. From the beach it looked huge, Karen viewed it with awe stricken horror.

"It's okay. You can handle that, you'll find it taxing but within your skills. Honest."

Never having worn one in anger before, she twisted and turned and held still to instructions, while Llew checked and adjusted her life jacket. When he was satisfied they embarked at the water's edge among the white soup of spent breakers and turtle-hopped the few metres required to get flotation. Despite the agitated water, she found the larger general purpose outdoor canoe much easier to sit, although much heavier, and more sluggish, than the lively baths ones with their designed-in instability.

"Don't get a shock at how much noise the canoe makes coming down off the back of the wave, it can take it, just sit, let your hips take over, and when you have to lean, lean into the wave."

"Okay."

"Once out there, you can't see somebody about twenty metres away, so I'll follow you out for safety, just behind and to one side, you can handle it, but I'll be there just in case."

"Okay."

"Right, first out past the breaker line. About a hundred, couple of hundred metres or so. Once you're there, ride the swell and watch for me."

"Okay."

You can watch it, and you can be told, but sex is not the only thing in life where nothing prepares you for your first encounter. Punching your canoe through your first breaking wave is another of 'you have to do it, only then will you know'. Obediently Karen put her head down and powered out to sea, the first few she met lifted her prow up a metre or so and crashed her down on the back of the wave. Now she really punched out, knowing the big ones were coming.

Ahead rose a green wall with angry white stallions breaking out of the top.

Punch hard.

The canoe stood on its tail.

The water wall rammed into her chest.

Hooves beat about her head.

She was through,
spitting out salt,
looking along her bow,
straight at the sky.

Then forward and down onto the back of the wave.

The thunderous crash shook her like a jelly.

Karen had no time to react;
the next green wall was upon her.

Power strokes.
Water ram.
Spit out salt,
Crash.
Power strokes.
Water ram.
Spit out salt.
Crash.
Again.
Again and again.

Then suddenly, no ram, no crash, just a pleasant, if big, switchback. She eased down on the power a bit, riding the swell. Llew closed up beside her.

"You okay?"

"Yes."

"Right, it's big, but you can handle it. Remember all you've learned about leaning into the wave, for the rest trust your autonomic skills. When you get to the beach, turn and wait for me, I'll follow you in a few waves behind."

"Okay."

"Turn, paddle gently towards the shore, when the wave catches you, you'll know when it does, lean into it."

"Okay." Karen turned broadside on to the swell, her hips

swinging sensuously to keep her head over the centre of the boat. If a wave was between them, she couldn't see Llew just a few metres away. Then he was behind her and she couldn't see him at all. "Here we go," she murmured to herself and began to paddle towards the beach.

She was pushed gently forward on her nose, then stopped abruptly by an irresistible pull back, as the bow came sharply up again and the wave passed under her.

She paddled forward again.

Exactly the same thing happened.

Puzzled.

Groping for reasons.

Her thoughts were confused,

I must be doing it wrong. She paddled forward, obeying the instructions. *I'm supposed to catch the wave. Not let it go. I'll have to--*

She was thrown up and forward.

A bow-wave forced two huge fans of water out sideways.

The boat sat atop a green cliff,
whilst at the same time
plunging down it.

Later she remembered screaming.

During her next English lesson Karen wrote a poem, but it had been largely composed before she finished the run --

On a Canoeist catching a surfing wave for the first time.

Canoe stands forward on its nose,

Racing down green hill ahead,

Gasping, frightened, can't stop now,

Leaping speed, my boat extend,

Lean in to the steep green glow,

Rushing past my right elbow.
Panic not, be brave my heart,
World is being torn apart.

Boat a roar, wave a thund'ring,
Paddle in the growling jaw,
Angry she bear shielding whelps,
Hidden deep within the pour.
Seeking from my grasp to tear.
World is noise, frantic, warfare.
She bites again. I cannot see,
Hang on in there doggedly.

Spray begins to fall in front,
Wave is breaking over me.
Correct to run more down the hill,
Run on out to open sea.
Turn more back along the wave,
Back inside the tumble cave.
Run in and out, shout with glee,
All just for to pleasure me!

Understanding flooded through her.

You can't be told.

You can only find certain things out for yourself.

So this was why people risk their lives surfing.

Although she might not place it as high as the value of her life, she now understood why some people did.

She ran off the end of the wave into the soup and let her canoe curl around in a wide elegant curve.

Llew flew in low off the end of another wave, over to her left and with shining eyes, she headed back out to sea to have another go.

Half a dozen times the pair paddled out and surfed in, exchanging comments when they could, waves and grins at other times.

Karen discovered that some waves were better than others, the belief about every seventh wave being the biggest is only an old wife's tale if you pedantically insist on seven, it has its existence firmly rooted in solid, factual science.

The disappearance of the sun behind some low cloud reminded them of the time.

"I'll make this my last," called Llew. "You can have another if you want."

"Okay." Karen quickly realised that she'd picked the wrong wave, it was a pusillanimous little troll. She broke to port and ran back up over the top of it, intending to complete the turn and head out for her last time.

Llew was bearing down on her.

Too late she realised.

She'd turned right into his path.

What does it feel like to die?

With a huge spear through you.

He was screaming towards her.

She was looking straight along the canoe.

A fourteen foot,

200lb javelin,

doing fifteen knots.

She prepared to die.

She saw the tiny adjustment he made.

The canoe twitched, passing behind her.

He leaned hard over onto his left ear.

Spun around.

Stopped hip to hip beside her.

Together they wallowed and rolled as the wave passed under them.

Warmth spread about her bottom.

"You okay? You look a little shocked. Saucer eyes."

"I thought you were going to hit me."

"No, but I did need to change course."

"I thought I was going to die. I've wet myself,"

He reached out and held her.

"I'm sorry, but don't worry it--"

"I need fucking. Right now."

"Well--"

"Llew! Now dammit. Now! I'm coming. Coming with fear."

"Can you hold it to the shore?"

"Yes. Just."

"Come on then," he turned and headed for the shore. They beached together and he hauled the boats up out of reach of the greedy waves. Karen unzipped her waistcoat and discarded her monokini on the sand. Her swarthy tummy with its elegant six-pack framed the even darker flush of her pubic hair. Obediently Llew closed with her releasing himself from his own clothes. She slid her arms around his neck and turned her face to him for kissing should he wish to do so. A moment later he was thrusting into her, standing up next to their craft.

"Oh no. I'm going to wet myself again."

"That's okay. Do it. Let it go. While I fuck you. Do it."

"Oh--Oh--Oh" Warm liquid cascaded down their legs as Llew licked and squishy kissed her mouth as he spent into his helplessly jerking girl.

At last she could stand,

"You okay."

"Yes, thank you."

The bark made them both jump. A collie stood next to them, looking up, wagging its tail. Not twenty metres away, a burly police sergeant was approaching.

It's amazing how quickly humans can move when required

to do so; by the time he stopped to talk to them, the lovers were clothed again. Karen could feel gritty sand mixing with the fluids seeping down her legs.

"Good evening Miss, Sir. It's a lovely night for canoe surfing, but it's getting dark. It might save us all a lot of bother, if any reports that come in about surfers doing silly things tonight could be contained by my assurances that they had left the beaches now, so there was no need to call out the coast guard."

"Yes, Sergeant, we were just going."

Karen just had to own up,

"Thank you Sergeant. It wasn't his fault. It was all me. Just to let you know. And thanks again."

"That's okay Miss, just be quick please, there's usually some busybody dialling the station about fun on the beaches. I wish they'd be as quick when it's non sexual crime that's happening."

The canoes and paddles were thrown onto their rack and lashed in place.

"Get in, let's go."

"Your seats'll be ruined." Llew paused, then dived into his boot reappearing with a couple of bivvi bags. They unrolled the bags, threw them across the seats and moments later he had the car moving quickly up the ramp and then away along the sea road.

After a few miles he turned into a country lane and slowed when a high hedge appeared, stopping next to a gate. Karen got out, opened the gate and he tucked his car into the field, behind the hedge, being careful to drive in the tractor tracks. They'd transgressed far enough tonight, an irate farmer as well would be the absolute end.

"I stink. And you will too. Sorry about that."

"It's okay. It was wild, something I'll probably never do again, utterly off limits untamed, but I'm glad I've done it all the same."

She nodded, peeled, and set about cleaning herself up with the wet flannel she'd brought specifically for her face. Never mind, under the circumstances it would do for the other end quite nicely. She dried and dusted. Most of the rest of the sand flaked off with just a stroke of the towel.

"That'll do 'til I get home," she smiled across at her lover.

It was a noble erection.

"Oh--I take it we're not going straight home." She folded her towel and laid it across the warm bonnet of his car, then lay back upon it, thighs spread, arms out in invitation.

"Don't you want to turn around?"

"No. Just do it. I'll hold you. I like that too,"

He closed up and mounted her. She held him and comforted him.

"Oh--Oh--Oh Karen."

"That's right baby--This is what baby wanted--Have a lovely fuck--Come for Mummy,"

He was pounding her, so splendidly helpless, his arms relaxed, she knew that if she did too, he'd fall off her. Hurriedly she cupped his thrusting bottom, taking his weight, her arms like springs, facilitating his withdraw and thrust into her. She held him and comforted him all through the climax, so utterly, completely and wonderfully in control.

He stopped, panting, then his feet stuttered and she felt him take his own weight. She held him and caressed him in silence waiting, presently,

"Thank you," he got off her. "Thanks, that was lovely."

She curled forward and wiped herself down again carefully. There wasn't much of the flannel left cleaner than she was already. She offered it.

"No thanks, I've got tissues."

They dressed in silence, not an easy silence, she had a guess at why.

"It's all right you know. It was nice."

"No it wasn't, I rutted you like an animal."

"You fucked me wetting myself. An hour ago. Wee flowing like Niagara down our legs. You did it for me. You liked it, but you did it for me. That was for you. I liked it. It was for you, but I enjoyed it too." She reached for him, cuddled him into her, and kissed him on the top of his head. "It was okay. It was nice." She waited until his tense body relaxed and he smiled ruefully, before releasing him.

A few minutes later they threw the rolled up bivvi bags back into the boot and, having checked the site for spillages, regained the road as carefully as they had left it.

They returned the canoes to the store and Karen to her home with utmost decorum.

As usual Pealle was sitting chastely, innocently working in the conservatory. The two girls did their electronics homework first. Karen deliberately delayed going to clean up properly, savouring the anticipation of the soothing spray. She grinned to herself.

"Sorry about the pong." She stank of seaweed, it must be very strong because she could even smell it herself. It completely drowned out any lingering odour of her night's other activities.

"It's okay, I quite like it," replied Pealle, herself smelling faintly of shower gel--again.

To her surprise Karen found herself jilling herself in the shower and again in bed, as, in her mind, Llew sped towards her to terminate her life, skewered on the prow of his canoe. On reflection, she wasn't sure that masturbating with those thoughts in her head was entirely healthy, turned over and promptly did it again, screaming into her pillow.

* * *

Being largely deprived of the weekly sexual element of the canoeing sessions hadn't lessened her interest in the sport. Whenever a canoeing article appeared in the sporting magazines, Karen read it avidly and followed closely a story which appeared on the evening television news about two canoeists, Anna Teale and another girl with the most astonishing shade of flame-red hair, rescuing four children from the notorious Blyth-Beach rip. The children had ignored the red flag and swum out from the centre of the beach, within minutes the rip was speeding them towards Norway. Anna and her friend had pursued and caught up with the youngsters and then towed them out of the rip and back around into the next bay in a wide circle. Having tried towing swimmers in the baths, Karen was acutely aware of the skill, and relentless effort, it would have needed for the canoeists to tow two children each, for a distance measured in miles.

Despite their actions leaving the story incomplete, she also sympathised with the attitude of the rescuers who had hurriedly left the scene as the TV camera hove up above the horizon. The girls were obviously unhappy about being filmed, but stood their ground by the side of the road, as their images, viewed from inside a car, grew larger on the screen. Suddenly a dark-red, hot-hatch appeared in shot, carving up the camera car, swung broadside on, rally style, to a halt beside the girls and away with them on board. The stunning blonde driver had kept her drive wheels turning the entire time and was out of sight within seconds.

The TV crew had to content themselves trying to interview the canoeists' backup team as they loaded up the trailer, but who apparently didn't speak English.

"Who were the canoeists?"

"Tahw?"

"Them canoeists the blonde was Anna Teale, who was the redhead?"

"Tahw?"

"Them girls in yon canoes, they've just rescued some bairns, whey was yon, the redhead?"

"Ohw si sith reknolp annaw teb eh t'nseod wonk nehw eht wen muinnellim strats?"

"T'nod' ekam em hgual ll'I evig eht emag yawa."

"Nee gud Clem, these folks is frem Mars."

It all made for a short, and to those in the know, amusing item on the local news. It was inconceivable that no-one back at the Studio knew neither Flame-red Hair nor Stunning Blonde, nor who the backup team were. Karen suspected that the item had been shown uncut because they did know and were frying the talent crispy. When the backup team leader had taught Karen Science, his English had been excellent, for a born and bred Geordie; his partner was Llew's boss and taught in the room next to him. For an English teacher, she also spoke perfectly understandable Geordie, although her accent did suffer from a childhood spent near the Home Counties, but no-one would ever have guessed any of this from their Manuel from Barcelona impressions. Flame-Red Hair and Stunning Blonde were the pair interviewed by the girl who presented the sailing dinghy programme under the section, 'Things You Can Do From Boats: Fishing. The boat building presenter had probably chosen them primarily because they too were TV Natural Earth Programme presenters.

Having had the name drawn to her attention, Karen then became aware of it cropping up in the canoeing press again and again. Anna Teale regularly led expeditions to explore unmapped rivers and gave freely of her time to canoe in charity events and accompany handicapped kids, but Media hype was shunned. Occasionally a scene-setting photograph would show in the background, a girl with flame-red hair and/or a stunning blonde.

Karen added Anna Teale to her Heroines Hall of Fame and, on reflection, her fellow rescuer and their getaway driver, Jennifer and Sylvie Jackson joined her.

* * *

The Head of the Technology Department had known for years that he had an unusual student studying under him. Just how unusual only became apparent when she no longer had to wade through the chores necessary to acquire the skills she craved; properties of materials; tool care; tool usage; and the like; and could concentrate on her true love, pipes and what you can do with them.

"I know it's early days yet."

Karen only knew she was being addressed because Bill Carpenter was looking directly at her, his voice was pitched so low it only just carried,

"But can I ask, have you got a job?"

She replied in kind, shaking her head,

"No. Pealle and me, similar problems."

"Would you like a temporary job, while you're looking? Mike D'Illion's a friend of mine, he needs some expertise in his warehouse. Somebody to answer queries about plumbing. You're exactly what he needs, just he can't afford to pay you plumber's union rates. He'll pay you well for a warehouseman, when you live up to my hype, but you'd earn more as a plumber."

"I earn nowt as a plumber Mr. Carpenter. At the minute. And mostly they're firing not hiring. So that's not going to change. Where do I find this Mike D'Illion?"

"At the Works."

"Sea Road?"

"Yes, just along from Crossers, go tonight, he's expecting you."

"You knew I'd say yes."

"The arrangement was I'd call him if you said no."

The Severed Head
Part Five

The astronomical profit on the first, modest, tools-and-spares order, paid off the loan and funded a second, larger order, with no need for financial assistance. Subsequent orders began to generate income on a scale for which no plans had been made.

"Have you decided what you are going to do with the money?"

"It's weighing down the bank at the minute, have you?"

"To start with yes, in the long term, not yet."

Not everything had gone smoothly, however, mostly they were merely the usual little niggles of quantities and specifications, but a whole case of bolts had mysteriously disappeared from the previous month's order and in addition,

"You need to get onto our supplier, his last load was a day late. I had to drive on, straight past the lorry park, timing is everything."

"I'll do it tonight."

Karen

The interview with Mike D'Illion was more like a cosy chat with a group of friends. A good looking girl in a smart little red suit with white shirt and grey tie met Karen at the door and introduced herself with a handshake as,

"Stacey, Senior PA."

From there Karen was taken into a comfortable office and introduced to her boss to be, Paul, foreman of the warehouse, and Mike D'Illion the founder's son and reincarnation of the old block. Bill Carpenter had obviously mentioned the canoeing because they talked about that first which put her at ease for when the probing questions started. When they got down to the crunch, they did so gently,

"The job is to be a Saturday Girl alongside Paul, working skeleton staff service mainly for doctors and drivers and secretaries and the like."

"Saturday DIY Home Engineers?"

"We're not going for the mass market, just those who need that bit more specialist advice and expertise, for that bit less outlay, than the local Hypermarket provides."

"Despite its much vaunted claims on television." Put in Stacey, revealing a festering sore.

"Sounds good."

"Bill says you can provide it."

Karen tipped her head.

"Why do you want to be a warehouseman?"

"I don't. I want to be a plumber. But needs must."

Mike D'Illion obviously already knew,

"So how long will you be staying?"

"Well at least the year. And on until plumbers start hiring again. At least. I may like it enough to stay. If I still feel as welcome after one year as I did after one minute."

"Some of the items we lift are very heavy."

The statement was left hanging. Karen smiled, stood up and proffered her hand to Paul.

"Give me your left-wrist."

He did so and a moment later he was across her shoulder in a fireman's lift.

"Open the door." She strode through the doorway and ran up the flight of stairs outside, then back down again and returned him to his chair, Paul was puffing, Karen wasn't.

"A year ago I couldn't do that. Or the job. But I can now. The strength bit is the easiest part. It's the acceptance."

"Equal opportunities?"

"Yeah." Nodding at the girl. She turned back to the men. "If I was a man. And you a girl. Nobody would have twitched. At what I've just done. But you two are shocked. Stacey isn't. But you are. Because I'm a girl. I want to change all that."

"When can you start?"

So when the October week holiday came around, more than a year on from losing Seth, the new warehouseman had lots to tell him.

Chapter 7

Facing Realities: October 1999

Karen

Karen returned to Scotland to say goodbye to her cousin, unemotionally, but with flowers of course. She sat at his graveside all morning, telling him about her Dad and Pealle; Lisa and Siew Mui; Llew and canoeing. She told him about her Saturday job and the intensive plumbing course, targeted specifically at students who could be crammed.

"It's only short on experience. But I make up for most of that by reading the trade journals. So your cousin is a whiz at plumbing theory."

She dusted the vase and reset it on its plinth.

"And Mr. Carpenter is trying to get me the experience. By letting me re-pipe the craft room. Cope with seized joints. Painted over joints. Imperial measurements."

She arranged the flowers more artistically.

"Lead pipes, iron pipes, copper pipes. It's a mind bending mix. And he's letting me sort it out, all by myself. Item by item. We've drawn the plans up like assignments. And the work itself. I've done the waste pipes. And the supplies to the sinks. I got 'A's for both of them. Next it's the biggie, the heating. It's twin four inch iron, gravity fed. I'm changing it to copper and radiators, pumped. I'm having a ball. A complete ball."

She waited until she was ready to leave before mentioning the last and most important item.

"There's one other thing."

She walked around and stood at the foot of the plot, hands clasped loosely in front of her.

"Thank you for my freedom. It's my most cherished possession. That's what I've called Rockhopper. To remind me always."

Pealle

Later the same day, back in Novochester, Dennis was gently chivvying Pealle.

"You need to get ready to go to Trevor's Eighteenth."

"I'll go and see who's there, if it's just Trevor, Craig and me, I'm out of there."

"Okay." Dennis dropped Pealle off at the Falcon's Rest and waited, the blonde reappeared almost at once,

"It's okay, most all of those who said they were coming are here. Come back for me at 10.15."

When she learned that Pealle had a future stepson in the business the chef, Kent Thomus, was eager to talk with her about her job. They were concentrating so much on the food talk that they only became aware that Trevor had conned Jet into trying to down the half a yard of ale in one, only a second or two before the airlock broke. The acknowledged down in one champ was un-warned and unprepared for the resultant tidal wave.

Soaked, one down to Trevor and her reputation as a sink not quite in tatters, but badly dented, Jet stormed off to ring for a taxi whilst aggressively refusing all offers of help. Outside, having successfully discarded her peers, she began to repulse another offer,

"Come on, I'll take you home."

"No I can manage by--"

"Please? An olive branch?"

"Oh, sorry, didn't see it was you. Okay, an olive branch,"

He guided her across towards his car,

"I'm surprised that the Queen of the Dunk didn't know about the half yard of ale." It was meant kindly as he pointed out later, but at the time it was the flaring match into her powder keg.

Jet went skywards, a jagged lightning flash, fizzing as she went. Before he was able to form any sort of defensive reply she'd covered several topics of sexist behaviour, sports where you were wet, cold and frightened simultaneously and his inability to make the correct choice when faced with only two options. She stopped, eyes, blazing.

"So what did you do?" he replied equally angry. "Did you fight, or did you quit? You crawled away beaten by someone who didn't even know she was competing with you. Didn't even mean to compete with you." The justice of the accusation did nothing to cool the exchange, rather the reverse,

"Why her? Not me?"

"No reason." He was now shouting as loudly as she was.

"What's wrong with me?"

"You weren't there!"

"I hate you."

"I hate you back." They stopped, the silence after their shouting, strange, eerie, punctuating a cusp moment. "No I don't," he continued softly. "I think you're lovely."

By the time Pealle came to check up on Jet, she was nowhere to be seen. A bystander told her, erroneously, that her friend had gone off in a minicab.

Jet didn't make it home that night.

Stacey

The same day, but several miles to the East, another conversation was producing warm feelings within the group.

A middle aged man in shirt sleeves was talking with a second man wearing a coverall over his more casual clothes and a younger woman dressed in a trim and elegant red suit.

"It's the smile that I've noticed," said the boss.

"And the way she runs up the stairs." Added his PA as she handed out the coffees. "How do you find her?"

The blue-collar worker sat down whilst he composed his answer.

"It's difficult to be objective, she's so good I'm in serious danger of gushing. Her knowledge of pipe-work and plumbing is phenomenal, much deeper than mine. She's ferociously strong, well you knew that, and super fit and no job's too onerous. She's eager and willing and friendly."

"How do you think the Saturday service is progressing?" The girl consulted her clipboard. "Financially I mean."

"Well, we must be doing all right, we're busy all day, run off our feet, it's the shortest day of the week."

"It's no longer a service." The boss was well satisfied. "It's a necessity, you broke even on week three, you've been in significant profit ever since."

"That's not exactly a surprise."

"I asked the computer how many of our new customers since we opened on Saturday, actually traded with us for the first time on Saturdays."

"And --"

Stacey hadn't briefed her boss on this,

"Too many."

The men sat silent, digesting the news.

"And over ninety percent of them have traded on weekdays since--at lunchtime and just before closing."

"We were aware of that too."

"So, we hire her permanently?"

"I'll be writing a very serious letter if you don't." Paul was smiling, but nevertheless serious.

"Can't say fairer than that, would you get all the documents organised ready?"

The girl nodded and made a note on her clipboard. "She's coming for her second interview next week, let's hope she says yes."

Karen

As usual Dennis met his daughter at the station.

"Have you seen Pealle while I've been away?"

"Yes."

It was too inviting, she couldn't resist it,

"Did she stay over? I told her to. If she wanted."

"Yes. She spent a couple of days at school, logged on, got loads of stuff off the net about the business project."

"Did she get copies for me?"

"Yes, loads, you'll need to lead an expedition to find your desk."

"Great." *Nice one Dad, but don't worry, I'm not going to ask, you'll tell me when it becomes serious, until then give her a good time. Besides which, I'm enjoying watching you squirm.*

"She went to Trevor's Eighteenth, on Tuesday. He's not a nice boy that one. Apparently he played a trick on Jet, soaked her with beer and ruined her night and probably her dress too, she had to go home in a taxi."

"Look out Trevor."

"Mmm."

His secret mistress hadn't seen Llew on the Monday and didn't see him on Tuesday. Then on Wednesday she bumped into him unexpectedly, right outside the Sixth Form Common Room. The meeting was awkward and strained,

"Hello."

"Hello."

An explosion of violent invective from inside the Common Room interrupted the conversation, Melanie was castigating Maggie,

"Some Men! Not Men! If all men were like that the human race would have followed the dinosaurs long since."

"Invigilating, must dash. Bye." He'd gone.

Melanie flew past blushing fiercely, the eyes, full of unshed tears. Behind her, Melanie's friends told Maggie to shut up, then followed the distressed girl down the corridor into the toilet.

At end of school Karen went to Llew's room to sort their problem out. Again he was agitated, she didn't need two guesses.

"Spit it out Llew. There's something on your mind. All day. Am I dumped?"

"You know when you were away in Scotland last week, at your aunt's farm?"

"At Bencaillie. Yes."

"I went out and met somebody."

"I'm dumped."

"Karen."

"It's okay. It was bound to happen sometime. D'Illion have asked me back for a second interview. So if I pass the course. Which looks likely. I'll be leaving in the summer. Decisions would have to be made. They've been made for us."

"You said it yourself, that you don't think of me as your boyfriend. My new friend definitely does."

"It's okay Llew. We only ever were just good friends."

"I would like to part as friends, because I loved every second of our time together."

Karen grinned, from deep inside,

"So did I. I had a good time. Okay. Friends who used to fuck. Thanks for teaching me. Canoeing and sex."

"Thanks for letting me. You taught me as much as I taught you, about both of them. But there's something else. I have to tell you who my girlfriend is, because it's someone you know." He was fiddling with his keys and dropped them.

Who could it be that would make you this nervous Llew? Of course, another sixth former!

"Who is it?" *Who would I like it to be?* "Melanie?--Not Maggie?" Her eyes, were alight with delighted mischief.

"You only just missed. Juliana Euphemia Tissue."

Karen's grin became open laughter.

"How come? You don't like each other--Didn't like each other."

"You're quite right, we didn't like each other. We fancied each other something rotten, but we didn't like each other. We'd had a row about the Victorian idea of women being men's possessions, well not a row exactly, but a stupid disagreement, when fundamentally we were in agreement, proudly overstating our cases and refusing to compromise, neither of us told you I gather."

"No you didn't. I just knew you were off Jet's team."

"Yeah, well I was in the Falcon's Rest with a couple of friends, we were going on to town after our meal and nearly all your class were in, celebrating Trevor's Eighteenth."

"I heard. He conned Jet into trying to down the half a yard of ale. When the airlock broke, she got it all down her front. She had to take a taxi home."

"She went to ring for the taxi. But I took her home instead and we got everything sorted out."

"She'd be cross and upset. Trevor getting one over on her."

"And about the misunderstanding over the homework and because canoeing didn't come up to expectations."

"And you comforted her?"

"Not immediately. We started with a blazing row in the car-park."

"Starting where you left off in July. And your hidden feelings for each other surfaced. In the middle of 'I never want to see you again'. Stamping of feet. Gurning of face?"

"Yes, at the height of the row. We were just about to come to blows and then suddenly we weren't trading punches but kisses. All my clothes were wet through with beer seeped across from hers because the kisses had been accompanied by very tight cuddles."

"Jet's parents are away. What time did you get home Llew?"

"I went straight home."

"Did I ask the wrong question? What time did Jet get home?"

"Juliana hasn't been home, other than to pick up some clothes."

Karen grinned, the sense of mischief intensifying,

"Is that why she's not here? Is she at Coquetdale Halt? In a railway carriage? Playing house?"

"You know full well she's on Work Experience all this month."

"That's not a 'No'."

"We play house at night and before you ask. Yes, Mummies and Daddies too."

"Congratulations. And the very best of luck to both of you."

"Did you know that she knew about us?"

That was a stunner.

"No."

"The weekly disappearance on a Friday hadn't gone unnoticed and was matched up with the day out during the Christmas Holiday. That's what the row was really about, but neither of us had admitted it, not even to ourselves. Juliana was mad at me for choosing you, I was mad at her for giving me up without a fight. Neither of us blamed you. We didn't want to hurt you over it. It nearly sunk our relationship before it started, you know that moment about three seconds after you first touch each other, when you realise that you both want to take the other to bed."

Karen thought of Siew Mui,

"Yes."

"Suddenly she said 'Llew, what about Karen?' It was only the fact that I am merely one of your lovers that saved the day. I am, merely one of your lovers, aren't I?"

"Yes. I try not to actually lie, Llew. Even if sometimes I intentionally mislead. We agreed you are not my boyfriend. And you are--you **were** not my only lover."

"You have some tight mouthed people as friends, Lisa and Sid know too, Juliana tells me they've kept it secret between the three of them."

"Pealle probably knows as well. She's never said. But that's nowt fresh."

* * *

Karen went visiting the Wilkinson Hotel, specifically to see the best chef in the district,

"My eighteenth. I want it at home. I know it's months away. I'm just at the planning stage."

"Can I do a spread?"

"Of course. That's what I hoped. What?"

"Traditional English Fare. Whole roast suckling pig with roast potatoes. Rack of Lamb with redcurrant jelly, Yorkshire puddings and mint sauce, Whole Roast Ox--"

"Len my birthday's in August!" He frowned at her, continuing the gentle wind up,

“Yes, but August on the Tyne--”

“And I’ve booked a heat wave!”

He came clean grinning,

“Rockhopper Salads, a wide selection of cold meats, pâtés, pigs in blankets, eggs, pickles, a seafood platter, ethnic platters and soft buns. Cakes and mousse and fruit.”

“And hot Chinese chicken legs and baby new potatoes.”

“You said you’d booked a heat wave.”

“Chinese not curried! Hot as in degrees Celsius not small chilli peppers.”

“Of course you can, you can have anything you like. Up to and including me.”

“We might have a talk about that. I’ve just been dumped. It was done gently, but I need seeing to.”

“I was joking.”

“I wasn’t.”

Len reacted.

“You look just like Lara Croft looks. You know if she lets a Xian catch up with her. On the Floating Islands in Tomb Raider II. The words ‘My On Petard Hoist Own’ occur. Shuffled about a bit. In your mind.”

“Hmmm, while we’re talking about incest, how’s Dad?”

Karen ostentatiously consulted her watch.

“I should think, there’s a very good chance. Right at this minute. That he’s up to his workman’s huts in one of my best friends.”

“Really?”

“Well she’s probably my best friend now.”

“Not Jet then?”

“No Jet’s got her hands full of somebody else.”

“Well I’m glad about that. Jet is beautiful, but was often hard work, high maintenance. Is Dad’s girl nice?”

“Provided she’s not playing tennis, yes. Really nice. She’s lovely. Kind, self effacing. Caring and supportive. She moves like a panther. Controlled, silent, smoothly. Unhurried, unfussy, elegant. Don’t say anything Len. They haven’t told me. It’s funny really. I come home and she’s sitting there. All prim and proper.

But she's obviously straight out of the shower. I mean, straight out."

"How do you know?"

"She's got long hair. Can't get it all under the shower cap. And we sit there all night. Pretending she's just my friend. Then Dad takes her home. It's a twenty minute round trip, tops. But he's gone an hour. When I'm away, she sleeps over."

"Are you mad at her?"

"Telemarks no. They're having a ball. Dad's really settled. I giggle about it all the time. I have this overwhelming desire to tease. Sometimes I cannot resist it."

Len grinned shaking his head,

"Our Dad corrupting the younger generation. What's she like playing tennis?"

"Exocet missile. Only one objective, total kill. And, she hasn't missed for over three years."

He turned and, linking her, walked into his kitchen. "I'd like to do a dry run for your party, for my twenty-first. At home."

"Sounds good."

"Invite your close friends, most of mine have moved away, lots of them are abroad. Fortnight on Saturday?"

"Okay."

During her next Vocation Lesson,

"Mr. Carpenter, can I make some steel frames? For a welding project? Just two."

"What are they for?"

Karen told him.

"I've sketched out this design. What d'y'think?"

"How heavy are the twins?"

"About twenty kilogrammes each. Say twenty-five with the frames."

"Will you manage fifty kilogrammes?"

She nodded grinning broadly.

"I can chin-up one handed."

"They should do the job fine then."

Pealle

Pealle opened her front door for him as Dennis walked up the front path.

"Are you okay?"she asked. "You don't look good."

"Opening night nerves. You'd think having done it once I'd be alright, know the score so to speak, but it doesn't get any easier."

"I'll try to make sure you never have to do it again. They're waiting for us in the lounge, they've guessed what's up, I'm pretty sure."

Dennis took his coat off and methodically hung it up, Pealle produced the little cube shaped box and let him open it and adorn her.

"Come on, they're not going to say no now, are they?"

Felicity and Fergus Tumpkins had guessed correctly and smoothed the way as much as possible.

After the congratulations, they smoothed the even more difficult event too.

"So when are you moving out? Today?"

"Not really out, but most weekends I'll be away and some mid-weeks, if that's okay?"

"Yes, of course it is darling, put it on the calendar if you know in advance, but do let us know if you're supposed to be in, but you change your mind."

"I will Mum. Thanks."

"Have you told Karen?"

"Tomorrow night. And, that I'm really nervous about."

"Has she ever asked, about boyfriends or --"

"No."

"No hints, no vibes? Never asked where you sleep when she's away?"

"Nothing."

"She'll know then, it won't be a problem, she'll probably be relieved you've told her at last."

Karen

Len's twenty-first was a success and the buffet was particularly praised. Some of the guests were his own, but Karen's friends, as expected, provided the vast majority. Len drew his sister aside,

"One of your mates is well gone, she's sprayed herself up the front of every boy in the room, including Dad, during the last hour."

"You're quite wrong. She's happy and sober. If she was drunk she'd have handcuffed herself to me. To protect herself from her own excesses."

Len held her close and whispered,

"I'm lime green jealous."

"If I've guessed why, you're wrong again."

"Well I take it she's the one?"

"You take it wrong. Pealle is the white mouse in glasses. The girl trying hard not to usurp my position as the hostess. Dad went straight over and apologised when Lisa put him back down."

"Oh. I assumed--never looked past the dish being friendly to everyone. But now you come to mention it, I've seen mice like her in glasses before, scratch the surface and you find orange and black stripes."

"Exactly. You should see her on court. Ruthless serial-killer."

"So who's the ultra friendly dish?"

"The Lisa."

"Oh, Lisa, as in seven at one go?"

"Six. Seven was the little tailor. But at one go yes."

"She looks like a nice girl."

"She is nice. So am I. But liberated. Just like I think it's okay to at least think about having my brother. She thinks it's okay to enjoy herself."

"Amazing, she looks lovely and-"

"She is. But she's single at the moment. Probably holding auditions. And she chose to miss three boys out. Two because she knows they're courting. The other one. Well, we all choose to miss him out."

"You reckon she's nice?"

"Nice yes. Virgin no, like both you and me. Nice with cream on top."

"Introduce me."

Karen towed him over to intercept her promiscuous friend, before she managed to arouse someone to a reaction.

"Lisa, this is my brother Len. He fancies himself as a cook. He'll tell you he took a week to prepare that spread. He didn't. He knocked it up last night at work. He's just a lying tow rag, who wants to prise you out of your knickers.

"Karen!"

"But he'll bring you an edible breakfast in bed the next morning."

"Lisa I'm not--"

"It's okay Len, your sister and I are good friends, take me for a walk around the garden and entertain me. I have to be in bed by," she looked at her watch. "Ten, or I'm going home--Len, you've got less than 100 minutes, start prising."

"Hi Mel. Can I get you another drink?"

"You could show me around the table, I've never seen such beautiful food and it tastes even better than it looks."

"That's a Rockhopper salad. The chef created it specially. For somebody who likes sweet and sour. The new potatoes are buttered. Boiled with mint and buttered--The meats are all strong flavoured cuts. Brisket and such --You want to be a chef?"

"I'd love to be able to create all this; the texture of that chicken, it's hard to believe it's chicken."

"Chinese chefs taught him that." She waved around. "Nearly as good as gentle sex. This lot."

Melanie looked up, eager, searching,

"Would you tell me what that's all about? I'm utterly confused, with Maggie ranting on about men abusing us and then Lisa flowing willingly from boy to boy, like trying on clothes."

"I'm more in Lisa's camp. Than Maggie's. I'd give you a biased opinion."

"Everyone gives biased opinions, the rarity is someone who knows they do. Would you tell me, show me what's up. The only thing I know about sex is why stinkhorns were destroyed during the last century," She gave Karen the eyes. "And that only because you jumped in to save my blushes, I know nowt."

"I could tell you. And you'd still know nowt."

"Could you show me then?" Melanie had barely paused before asking the question.

"I could. Wouldn't you prefer a boy to do it?"

"No I would not, I've tried that route, I let Craig walk me home after the open evening. I was nervous and scared, but so was he, so I was determined to be friendly and co-operative. I thought together we might explore a bit, learn a bit. Make another date to learn a bit more, have some gentle fun finding out what all the fuss is about, then he grabbed me. Suddenly, just grabbed me."

Karen cuddled the shorter girl in and stroked her back.

"Oh Mel."

"I've still got the bruises on my tits. They're yellowing but I've still got them. I had to fight him off. Just suddenly out of nowhere he grabbed me, it wasn't nice Karen, I had to hit him. He apologised and ran away. I never told anybody, but you, now; he apologised again the next day, he seemed. Well, scared of me."

"You picked a frightened little boy. Who probably didn't know what to do. I bet he was working to instructions. From somebody else who doesn't know what to do. What you really need is an older man. Somebody who knows what he's doing."

"You could pretend you're a boy, show me what a boy would do, so I'll know when I go to Uni., so I'll know what to expect when I find my older man."

"Imagine being snogged while jilling. But a hundred times nicer."

"But I don't know what that's like either."

"Which?"

"Both. I was all tooled up to snog Craig when--And I've never done the other."

"Telemarks! What's Susan playing at? And Jane?"

"I told them I did, it's not their fault. I've tried, but--well I've never got any joy out of it; you could show me, people go on and on about it--I've tried, I get sore and wet the bed--You have no idea how often I've cried myself to sleep."

"Mel if I were to show you--I'm bisexual. I like girls too. I'd end up snogging you. For real. Shagging you if you didn't stop me. You'd be fighting me off too."

Melanie was obviously shocked and reeling, exactly as Karen had intended, but also adept at fancy footwork, the tall girl watched with mounting excitement as she regrouped,

"No. I wouldn't, that's okay, I don't mind, I could live with that, payment for services rendered if you like, it's the not knowing that's driving me potty. Please Karen I'm in real danger of cracking up. Blasting Maggie that day was only the tip, I'm sure I'm right and she's wrong, in spite of Craig, but there's a huge explosion bottled-up waiting."

"Come on." They slid away upstairs into Karen's bedroom. She locked the door.

"Are you sure this is what you want?"

The shorter girl nodded.

Reluctant, excited, sure there was a better solution for Melanie, if not for herself, Karen closed in.

"Don't say you weren't warned." She gently cupped her friend's face in both hands, touched noses, and slid in to kiss. The lips that she kissed were shut and flat; a window dresser's mannequin would have given more response.

"That was like kissing a Statue. That's the sort of kiss I'd give Trevor." She tenderly caressed Melanie's cheek with her fingertips. "Soften up. Your shoulders are stiff and square. Shake your arms. And hands. Like this. Shake all that stiffness away. Loosen the shoulders. Swing your hips. Think loose. Think fun. Think I am going to like this." Karen performed to match her words, after a moment Melanie copied her.

"I'm going to kiss you like a lover. Then you can choose after. To go on with it or not. Okay?"

"Okay."

"Just stay floppy. And don't pull away if I do something you don't like. Stay with it. Try to like it. Tell me after how it feels. If you don't like it we'll stop. But you've got to do it the once properly. To know you don't like it."

Melanie nodded and this time slid her arms up around the tall girl's neck as she closed with her. Karen kissed her eyes and nibbled her throat and on downwards, feather soft kisses on the swell of her breasts above the neckline of the dress, the faint smell of exotic perfume drifted up from the cleavage. Then when she finally returned and closed on the other girl's lips, she found them soft and plump. She slid her tongue in teasing against the other's teeth. There was a moment's pause and then the gap between the two girls melted away,

"Oh Karen, do it again."

This time she included a gentle smooch of the other girl's ear in her tour.

"What have you done to my toes?"

"Strange isn't it? Like dialling long-distance. Ears calling toes. Ears calling toes, do you read me? Get ready to curl up. Go!"

Melanie pulled her in again and got her toes curled for a second time.

"Want to go on?"

"Yes, please."

"How far? It gets better. A lot better, but you need to keep on fully joining in. To get the best out of it. How much do you want?"

"Everything, show me it, all of it."

"There's much more than just kissing."

"Yes, all of it."

"Mel, last warning. I am going to enjoy this. I can't help it."

"I know."

"Okay. I'm going to strip you. Make love to you. Make you come. Make us come."

Melanie stood quite still as Karen toured her, touching bare skin with tingling caresses, watching as Karen wriggled out of her party dress and then revelling in the sensations as her friend's hands gently peeled her of hers.

"There's one other thing. I'll probably murmur endearments. Tell you I'm loving doing things to you. Possibly even that I love you. It's to help things along. Don't get up tight about it."

"I won't--Darling."

When Karen reached behind herself to pop her bra, Melanie mirrored her actions.

"No. Let me. Just let me." Sequentially, the bras slid down arms and onto the floor, unheeded. Karen lifted the small breasts up and kissed the bruises and then the nipples. Melanie's eyes, closed. Karen reached down and gently slid her friend's wispy tangas down her hips, by the time she released her, the smaller girl was wriggling out of the knickers, a moment later the second pair also hit the carpet. Now Karen slid her arm around Melanie's waist as her other hand glided down her tummy and in between her thighs. Melanie gasped, her thighs parted, head back, mouth open in shock. Karen kissed her, filling her with tongue and fingers simultaneously and pulling her hard to her. Melanie grew heavy in her arms and Karen guided them over towards the bed. Presently she had her friend nicely snuggled on it. She gently increased the lip suckling, ear tonguing, nipple nibbling, fondling and frigging as Melanie's passion mounted,

"Darling Mel. Is it true you've never come?" she whispered.

"I don't think so." Breathy and panting. "I don't know."

"You haven't then. Believe me. You wouldn't answer 'don't know', if you had. I'm going to make you come. Don't get scared darling, it gets very intense. You'll think you've died and gone to heaven. Everyone does. The first time. Just stay with it. You'll come back eventually."

Melanie nodded, she was probably well past the stage of making decisions.

"Come on. Kneel up. On the bed. On all fours. Just go with it."

"Hike hiss?" Karen adjusted her until she was exactly right, caressing her girl's breasts. Gently she explored her cunny, Melanie wasn't exactly dry, but far from ready.

"Think the sexiest thoughts. Sexiest you can think. Naughtiest, sexiest thoughts. I won't ask you what they are. Think anything you like. They help to juice you up. Get you ready." Suddenly Melanie was all gooshy. "That's it. Now you're getting there."

"Hot's at?"

"Ssh. Sexy thoughts. Think that naughty, squishy, sexy thought again." The cunny she was caressing gushed its response.

"Oh--Oh!"

"Don't worry about falling down. When you need to, just fall. You won't hurt yourself. I'll not drop you." Melanie fell face down, star-fished on the bed, squealing and jerking as Karen pleasured her. The tall girl waited as long as she could, as multiple orgasms crashed their way through her friend's body, then mounted the humping bottom and, whilst maintaining the caresses on her friend's clitty, fucked energetically against her. She licked her girl's cheek; the moist face came around offering the lips and, whilst calling endearments to her lover over and over, she exploded.

It was several minutes of caressing, snuffling and suckling later, after Melanie had turned back over and was able to repeat her question.

"What was that in me?"

"My thumb. I chose to do that to you because you can't do it to yourself. Only someone else can do it to you. Thumb on your G spot. Fingers playing your clit. Orgasm guaranteed. Just about."

"G spot?"

"Yes, well--"

"Maggie says there's no such thing."

"Well, for her maybe there's not. There's blind people. Deaf people. There may be G spot inactive people. But, I know not in my case. And, I think not in yours."

"No! That was--It was --"

"Shh. Yes, Melanie dear, I know. I was there remember? I lived it with you. Show me how you tried to jill yourself."

Melanie steepled four fingers tucking her thumb into the centre and Karen grabbed them instantly.

"Little wonder you got sore! Flatten your hand. Gently caress all over. No outside. Find where it feels nicest." She gently pulled her friends hand from between her thighs. "Probably up a bit, yes, there."

"Oh--Oh."

"Speed up if you want to." The vibrating fingers became a blur. "Some girls even like it smacked. **Gently**." Melanie smacked her clitty twice and screamed, Karen muffled her friend's lewd and explicit instructions with kisses, as she slid her fingers into her to help, and only managed to keep her in place by holding her hard down on the bed. Presently keeping her in place became so difficult that complying with the constant stream of lewd instructions was suddenly a much more effective and attractive alternative. She mounted the other girl between her spread thighs and pressed in vibrating against her sensuously. Her world softened, melted and all its problems washed away in waves of pleasure.

After quite some time of relaxed inactivity, Melanie spoke softly,

"Did I shout what I think I shouted?"

"Yeah probably. I don't take much notice. Not of orgasmic squealing. The brain's not connected to the larynx. But remember in future. What you squeal. What you ask your lover to do to you. When you're with a boy, he might take it as an invite. And justifiably so."

Melanie was more ruefully pleased than slightly embarrassed,

"Did you? Take it as an invite I mean?"

"Yes."

"Oh--Did you accept?"

"Yes. I snogged you. And tribbed you pussy to pussy. And it was lovely. Thank you."

"No Karen, thank you. I'm back together, I've had a lovely time and I've made a decision. Thank you!"

The clothes in the mirror were fine, Karen decided she'd do and waited for Melanie to finish her final adjustments.

"When you're jilling yourself to sleep tonight. As you crest the peak. When you start to come. Slide a finger inside. Or two. Teach your vagina she has a job too. But just a couple of fingers. Not your whole hand!" Melanie slid her arms up around the taller girl's neck and kissed her slow and deep,

"Thank you."

"You're welcome. My pleasure in fact."

When the birthday boy's sister re-appeared, the first person she saw was Lisa.

"Oh. I rather hoped you'd be in bed by now."

"Len persuaded me to curb my impatience, on the promise of an edible breakfast in it tomorrow. And where the hell have you been anyway? People are leaving."

"Teaching a nice girl new tricks. I've been in a bit of a sex desert. Got some catching up to do."

"Melanie?"

"Does it matter who?"

"Well somebody had to do it, I trust that you gave her a good time, she deserves it. Go and say goodnight to the guests. Len and I will wait to the end."

Eventually there were only the three Robinsons and Lisa to be seen, standing bunched together in the hallway.

"This can't go on any longer Sis, I know it's a source of endless amusement to you, but --"

"Okay."

"So where is she Dad?"

"Where's who?"

"The tigress with the glasses, pretending to be a white mouse, the Siren in the Miss-Butter-Wouldn't-Melt outfit."

"Pealleovbelles Tumpkins," put in Lisa and added to Karen's amazement. "We've known for months she must have a man, just, until tonight, nobody knew who he was."

"Pealle," called Dennis looking up. His eyes, softened as he saw her peeping over the ornate balustrade that edged the wrap-around landing. "You might as well come out darling, we're blocked."

The ex-mouse in glasses came half way down the stairs, all pretence discarded, long hair down, black, see-through and too-short nightie, marginally more lewd than nakedness, the tigress at the centre of her territory, tail twitching, on full sexual display. She made no attempt to hide anything.

"How long have you known?" The question was aimed straight at Karen's eyes.

"Since the first night Dad took you home. Well, before in fact."

"I've been worrying--And you knew all along--You rotten--You miserable--You--Stepdaughter you!"

Karen held her arms out and the other girl ran into the hug. The outfit matching, balls of fluff on her otherwise bare feet, clicking on the parquet flooring.

"I'm sorry. But, you never said anything. And, it struck me as funny. And, you've got to admit, I kept out of your way. Smoothed the way even. Paid for my fun."

Pealle put up her face,

"You're forgiven," she said and pulled her stepdaughter to be, in to kiss. "We were going to tell you tonight." She shyly withdrew her left hand from her friend's neck. "Both of you." Bridging the entire width of the third finger, three diamonds blazed in a neat line. "But I'm glad you knew already and that you don't mind." Pealle was hugged and kissed and passed around for loving,

"There's nothing to mind." Karen included the others with a wave. "We're really pleased."

"There are two people newly engaged here. Don't I get ravished too?"

Melanie

At school, a few days later, Melanie saw her chance and grabbed it.

"Sid could you guard the door for me please?"

"Erm--Well yes, I suppose so."

"Thanks."

She slid past him into the Sixth Form Boys' Toilets. They weren't as fresh as the girls', but no worse than many public wash-rooms in town. She pushed the door as far as it would go, which, being a council door in a post World War Two school, was far from firmly shut.

Her quarry gawped at her,

"What are you doing here?"

"Cornering you. We can talk here in private, Sid's guarding the door, or in the common room in public. Your choice, which?"

"Talk about wha-'

"Which?"

"Here."

"I want to show you something." A moment later she had popped her top, the expression of surprise on his face, already high, soared. "They should be this colour all over, except for the nipples of course, these yellow splodges are the remains of the painful bruises you gave me last week."

For a moment he just stood silent, shocked. Then,

"I'm sorry, I didn't know, I didn't mean--I'm sorry."

"I want to know was this your idea, or were you working to instructions?"

"I--Well I-"

"The truth!"

"I was working to instructions," he replied with total resignation. "But I thought they were right. I thought that's what you had to do, I was scared in case I got it wrong, so I followed the instructions even though --"

"Even though what?"

"Even though I didn't like hav----I -- I thought that's what you did."

"Even though you didn't like having to what?"

"Roughly grab, squeeze."

"Your instructions were dog vomit, this was assault and my guess is that was only the beginning, the end product was to be a full blown rape." His eyes, went down in shame; he wasn't even looking at her naked breasts any longer.

"I'm sorry. I'm--I'm sorry, I know I can't undo it, but I want to make it up to you, I'm really sorry." The eyes, looking straight into hers had bypassed her breasts. She covered them slowly, his gaze never wavered.

"Right. There's a candle lit Carol Singing at the Church at the Big Lamp on Saturday. Rangers have organised a nosebag and snogging party in the Scout Hut afterwards, bangers in buns, Pepsi 'n that. You can make it up to me by taking me and being nice and gentlemanly to me, on my terms. You get scrubbed from head to toe, nails, teeth and tail, dressed in your trendiest party gear and you pick me up at six. You escort me, never leaving my side and we do exactly as I say, when I say it and how I say it. Take it or leave it."

"I take it!"

She plucked two pieces of card out of a pocket,

"Our tickets, we'll need them to get in."

"Yes, I understand."

She nodded, turned and opened the door a crack, Sid nodded to her,

"All clear."

"Thanks." She slid out quickly, seconds later all three had dispersed.

Craig found Trevor in the common room, being a prat, so Karen would be close by.

"Trevor, if you ever give me advice on how to run my life again, I will beat you to a pulp."

"I never-"

"Another word and I'll do it now." The look in the irate boy's eyes, commanded silence. Craig then picked out the engineering girls, edged over to them and spoke quite low. "How much is a ticket to the Rangers' party on Saturday?"

"£7.50 and good behaviour,"

He gave Pealle a pursed mouth look, but made no comment.

"It's for charity. Hence the high tariff. At least £5 will go to Pudsey. Off each ticket. The more that come. The higher the take."

"Ah. Right, thanks."

* * *

Pealle drove Dennis, Karen and Lisa to the Carol Singing in the Church at the Big Lamp. On the corner opposite the Church, a group of working girls were talking to a reincarnation of King Kong and a barely less-big, sandy haired man. Kisses were being exchanged under mistletoe.

Chapter 8
Celebrations: December 1999
Karen

Karen's thoughts had her hiding a smile,

If I fail at being at Plumber, I could always try that and get paid for doing something I'm good at.

Pealle found a parking place and the group moved into the Church. A few minutes later the working girls also joined the congregation; one of them detached herself and moved across to the Robinson group.

"Hello, I thought it was you driving in."

"Hello--"

"Maisie when I'm dressed like this," interrupted the other girl quickly.

"Oh. Maisie. Maisie this is Dennis, he's Karen's dad."

"So you're himself are you? Pleased to meet you at last."

"How do you do," said Dennis, colouring slightly, but the way he proffered his hand to shake was warm, outgoing and friendly.

"We saw your minders. Those are two seriously impressive guys," said Lisa.

"They aren't minders, I won't ever work for a pimp, they're friends. They do take care of the girls though, good friends."

Presently Maisie rejoined her friends as people began to settle for the singing.

"She really sounded as if she was telling the truth. About those gorillas. Not being minders. Just good friends."

"She was," said Pealle "Those three are Monta's boys, I know that for a fact because the kids play tennis, the Thompson twins."

"Three?"

"Stone, Flint and Jack, Jack's the little redhead, just sitting down now, next to the big biker that's just come in, I know she's a girl but they call themselves "The Boys', she's the twins' Mum, her real name is Mrs. Janie Thompson. The biker's her husband, she's a biker too, fastest thing on two wheels in Novochester, so they say."

"Those working girls really liked Monta's boys. You could see it in their eyes. And the way they were talking. Their body language."

"Yes, they're lovely, hard but nice, ruthless but fair."

"Like a certain blonde bombshell not a thousand miles from here," said Dennis. Pealle gave him the eyes and opened her mouth to protest, but he cut her off. "That dodgy match point last week, Novochester and District Indoor Challenge Cup; Championship Point which you had won when Sun-chi smashed out, until you called it in, you had to play two more games for that."

"I called it in, because it was in. Hey up, we're on."

Dennis and Pealle accompanied Lisa and Karen to the Rangers' party and they spent a pleasant evening in each other's company in the Scout Hut, dancing, gossiping and munching tasty titbits. Melanie was accompanied by a solemnly attentive, uncharacteristically quiet Craig.

When the couple reappeared just before the close up, after an absence in excess of an hour, that the time had been successfully spent, was obvious in two pairs of eyes, shining with orgasmic echoes. It was a different, mature Craig and blissfully happy Melanie who danced the remaining minutes of the night, before leaving, tightly cuddled together.

"Where to Lisa?"

"I'm expected at The Wilkinson later, you could drop me

there please."

"At the--Who are--"

"Shut up Dad!" and

"That's enough Dennis," said Karen and Pealle together.

* * *

The telephone was answered on the fourth ring,

"Hello."

"It's Karen, Aunt Morag."

"Oh, hello dear, how are you, no problems I hope?"

"No. Everything's fine, we're looking forward to seeing you. I'm ringing to ask a favour. Did you know Dad has a girlfriend? Well a fiancée really. Ring and everything."

"No. The scallywag, he's never said tweet. Who is she? How long--"

"It's my best friend. She's called Pealleovbelles Tumpkins, just Pealle to her friends. She lives more with us than with her parents now. I was--"

"Wanting to bring her up for Hogmanay?"

"Yes. It's an awful cheek I know. But--"

"It's fine, it's wonderful, I'm so pleased, Dennis has been alone for far too long, of course you must bring her, is it a modern, double-bed girlfriend, relationship?"

"It is down here."

"That's no problem Karen; it's the best news I've had this year, bring her with you, I'll sit on my curiosity until I can quiz the girl herself. Tell her to be ready to spill her life story."

"Okay Aunt Morag. Thanks. We'll see you on the Thirtieth."

"Okay, bye."

"Bye." Karen replaced the receiver on its rest and watched the display reset. "All done, invitation, bed the lot. I told you there'd be no problem. Aunt Morag's chuffed to stoppers. But you are going to be grilled for your life story. I did warn you." The blonde pulled her in to kiss,

"Thanks daughter dear, I'll have to think up some amusing diversions, the truth's too dull to live through."

"Talk about tennis. About who's shagging whom, on tour. Those two that had to break off. To play the match. That finished off afterwards in the shower."

"I can't tell them about that."

"See your life's not dull. You're already having to edit it. You'll be fine. You could do your party trick. I've never seen it. Just heard about it."

"It needs a hard ceiling."

"It's an ancient farmhouse. Pine boards held up by beams."

"Square section beams?"

Karen nodded.

"How wide are they?"

"Thirty, thirty-five centimetres."

"And how tall, how far off the floor?"

Karen stood up, extended her arm and mimed forcing her hand flat to a ceiling.

"About half a metre beyond that." Pealle looked thoughtfully at the height,

"Hmm," she said.

* * *

Christmas Dinner was by invitation in The Wilkinson.

Although a bit of a clippie's holiday for the Chef and his staff, at least they did get to sit down to eat it with their families. During the meal, Monta's Boys, and the fact that several weren't, came up in conversation.

"I knew from several sources, not just the tennis. I wanted to be one, but Dad works for St Paul's Harbour. So despite Monta being keen, they were the only company that was interested in a female sparks, I decided against it."

Dennis continued eating, the rest of her audience were confused.

"When I left home I wanted to cut the apron strings, not replace them with welds." She looked around the questioning faces. "St Paul's Harbour is a wholly owned subsidiary of Monta Industries, they bought it when it went bust in the eighties. Dad works for Monta."

"It would be hard in this burgh to find someone who doesn't work for either them, or Stybes or Kroffts. I know they don't broadcast it, like 'A MONTA COMPANY' in bigger print than the message, but when you see official documents, like their post, as often as I do, you'd be amazed how many companies sport the flying M, or Stybes' Fishtail Mountain Peak, or Kroffts' Circle-K tucked away in a corner somewhere."

Pealle added a detail,

"Just them or Kroffts, Stybes' CEO is Anna Monta, as in daughter of John, CEO of Monta Industries and the late Margaret née Stybes. She owns it outright."

That grenade, that two of the biggest local conglomerates were actually one, had everyone else poised, eating irons frozen, gazing at the blonde.

"This is integration gone mad. Next you'll be telling me you work for her Len. That Stybes owns The Wilkinson," exclaimed Karen.

Len snorted and looked at his sister.

"Oh Telemarks! You do. Don't you?"

"No I wouldn't dream of telling you that. Of course I don't work for Anna Monta. Stybes don't own The Wilkinson--I work for her sister. It's a wholly owned subsidiary of Monta Industries, just like the Harbour. It was Shirley Monta that interviewed me for this job, I mean there were a dozen on the panel, but it was obvious within seconds that only the curvaceous crumpet sitting next to the Chair was of any consequence, it was she who asked the searching questions, the ones where the answer mattered."

* * *

The Hogmanay celebrations of December 1998 had been devastated by the absence of Seth; Karen was determined that he be remembered with joy the following year. She briefed her family and they agreed to help.

The short Scottish winter-daylight was already a memory when the girls were getting ready,

"I brought a posh frock, but the party trick looks best with a short skirt and I couldn't do it in a tight dress anyway."

"Top and skirt to start with. Change later." Pealle nodded and went off to get ready. A few minutes later,

"Karen, can you help me please?"

She joined her friend in the big double guest room.

"Please put my plaits in for me." Karen separated three strands, stopping in astonishment at what she found embedded in the blonde's hair.

"This is wire."

"Yes, it's for the party trick; I only wear wire for the party trick."

"You only wear wire?"

"And a fig leaf, of course."

"The lengths some people go to for a laugh."

"I know, what next? Tuning their bodies up with exercises I shouldn't wonder."

Giggles.

The party slowly got under way, the Robinsons gently chivvying people to get ready and assemble in the farmhouse kitchen.

"Has everyone got a glass, with something in it--Yes,--Because my daughter has something to say."

"Last year was blighted by the loss of a son. Brother. Cousin and, for many of us, our best friend." Jo and Duncan met Karen's gaze unflinchingly. "It's right to mourn him and I do. I loved him. And not merely as my cousin. I had very long-term plans. I don't know if he knew." She shrugged. "We've lost him, but our lives are richer. And always will be the richer. For having known him. So now I smile for him. All raise your glasses please--To one of the joys of my life--To Seth."

"To Seth." Dennis set his glass back down and led a round of applause.

"Now then. Let the celebrations begin. First. These little scallywags need tossing about." Karen handed the twins the frames. "Assume the position." They curled up around the steel, either side of her feet and she checked quickly that they were holding tight. "Aunt Morag. You've been feeding them meat again. I'll not be able to do this next year." She snatched the children up above her shoulders and whilst swinging her hips voluptuously, alternating first one hand then the other, pressed them repeatedly to the ceiling. For a few seconds she became a sexy cheerleader playing with her pompoms. The twins screamed and yelled in mock fear, but their eyes, were alight and much of the noise was giggles. Karen lowered them down again, swayed and sank coiled into a chair.

"That's me finished," she said. "For the night. Ply me with drink and oatcakes. I need building up."

"Have you got a party trick Pealle?"

"I can do something daft with tennis balls."

"She does something mad with tennis balls," corrected Karen. "I've never seen it, but I'm told it's impossible, fantastic and funny. Come on girl. Get 'em out for the lads. I've been looking forward to this for months."

Pealle pulled her little knapsack over and spilled out her trainers and tennis balls.

"Get a camera," continued the taller girl. "You'll want a camera."

The blonde exchanged her stilettos for the trainers, as she replied,

"I'll crack the lens; don't say I didn't warn you." She reached a tennis ball up towards the centre of a beam and dropped it, noting where it hit the floor and took up position two baby steps in front of that point.

"Ready?" Uncle Hamish raised the camera.

"Yep."

Pealle curled her plaits up into a pair of comical horns, lobbed a ball over her shoulder and back heeled it hard against the beam, the second ball went over her other shoulder being kicked as the first was rebounding, as she found her rhythm she waved her arms outwards and flicked her head from side to side, Gurning cross eyed with her tongue up inside her top lip. The balls, now being back-heeled hard and fast, thudded noisily against the ceiling beam in an urgent, jungle beat, Pealle's feet were blurred with speed, the overall effect was of a Dutch milkmaid marionette clowning about while suspended up off the floor. She held it for about twenty seconds while her entire audience roared with laughter and then softly flicked the balls forward over her shoulders and caught them. She curtseyed gracefully to the applause.

"Wow, that's control."

"No, it's nothing compared with what Ray Lindwall, the great

Australian fast bowler could do. He would ask a batsman where he wanted the first scuff mark on the new ball, bowl it, and put the first mark exactly where nominated. That's control!"

It was some time later that Duncan managed to cut Karen out of the herd.

"I thought you might like to know, I think Seth might have had the same thoughts as you. He didn't date, turned down some genuine crumpet in his time. He used to say he already had someone special, I'm sure he meant you."

"Oh. Thanks. I didn't know. Thank you, you've no idea how much better that's made me feel."

Duncan nodded, smiling, and then waved at the discarded steel frames,

"How do you do that? Is it a trick, a technique?"

"Muscles. I'm sure there will be a trick method. But mine's canoeing muscles. And timing."

"You haven't got any muscles, not that sort of muscles anyway."

"I have. A loose top hides the proverbial multitude." She whipped the top off, Duncan's eyes, popped. "When you get around to taking your eyes, off the tits. You'll see the muscles."

"Oh. S-s-sorry K-K-Karen, you're s-s-so direct, but even s-s-so, you're not m-m-muscled, like m-m-muscles on your m-m-muscles. I couldn't p-p-pick the k-k-kids up, I t-t-tried."

"The strength of a muscle bears no relation to its size. Or t-other way up, if necessary. So I'm told." His obvious level of stress, which was anything but distress, triggered the recognition of possibilities and desires. "Have you got a girlfriend at the minute?"

"No, not at the m-m-minute, not ever. I go t-t-to t-t-talk t-t-to a girl I l-l-like and t-t-this happens." Karen smiled gently, reached out and caressed his face.

"And if a friend flashes her bra at you. It has the same effect,"

He dragged his eyes, away from her breasts again, tried to speak, struggled and gave up.

"Would you like a friendly feel? Not a fuck, please Duncan. But I'm well up for some seriously heavy petting. Squealing and grunting heavy." Again the words failed to materialise, but the eyes, said it all. "Meet me in the barn. Next to the loft ladder. Five minutes."

Karen sorted through her little case murmuring to herself,

"KY Jelly. Tissues. Little towel. Pen torch. That should do--Karen you ninny. Travel rug."

When she got to the barn Duncan was waiting outside, his agitated manner and gestures told all, there was somebody else there already.

"Of course there is. Haven't you noticed? Jo and your kid sister haven't been around for a while. They're at the front. They've left the back for us. For me. And you. If you said yes." His face, dim in the weak light, was a study. "Have you done anything like this before?"

This time he managed a word, "Nothing."

"Okay. Don't be scared. Don't worry. It's not an exam. You're not going to flunk the course. Just two friends having some gentle fun. The most exciting time of your life. So far. With luck." She led the way into the inky blackness of the barn and then guided them up the ladder and to the back of the hayloft with the beam from her penlight.

"Help me lay the rug out. Now kneel down on it. Back in the dark I'm afraid. From now on we feel." She put her hand over his mouth to stop the ineffectual attempts to speak. "Just go with the flow Duncan dear. Do it slow. Do it gentle. And we'll be fine. Follow my lead. Clothes first. Feel and kiss anything new you uncover, if you want to. Put the clothes in a pile all together. Then you won't lose anything. I won't have to climb up to my bedroom window naked." The giggle was accompanied by a noticeable relaxation of his neck muscles.

"That's right. That's lovely. Swap you skirt for trousers. Knickers for boxers." She assertively encouraged him to lie down beside her and guided his face towards a nipple. "Nurse. Like a baby. Let mummy feed baby. Oh baby that's nice. Wet your fingers. Now slide two around and in. Nurse. Don't stop. Oh--Don't stop--Oh--Oh." Karen jerked and kicked, but kept tight hold of her boy to prevent him from mounting her, not that he tried. Presently she had her fill, for the moment, and gently uncoupled from his caressing fingers.

"Thank you Duncan. That was lovely. Now you." A squirt of KY jelly on her hands allowed her to masturbate him using the twist over the top of the penis technique, he only lasted seconds, before jerking and grunting against her, sucking hard and squishing her firmly. She slowed and released him when she felt his hands touch hers.

"Oh, Karen--Oh my."

"Better than jacking yourself off any day. Isn't it?"

"Oh dear--Karen--Oh."

"Did you enjoy that?"

"Beyond words."

"Are you going to thank me?"

"Yes, of course, sorry I should have done it already." There was a long silent pause. "Oh. T-T-Thank you K-K-Karen that was lovely."

"Duncan, remember this instruction and obey it all your life."

"T-T-To t-t-thank a girl after s-s-sex?"

"Up to and including your wife. Every time. Society considers it okay for you to notch your bedpost. Macho man. A bit of a lad. But degrading for a girl to be a notch on anyone's bedpost. It's viciously, hypocritically, wrong. Like the intellectual rape of one half of humanity. But a fact of life, so thank her. She has risked her reputation to please you. At the very least, thank her."[1]

"S-S-Sorry. I never thought about it that way." He felt for her face in the darkness, took it into his hands and kissed her tenderly. "Thank you."

"Okay just relax, lie still." She wiped and mopped with tissues and the little towel, using her penlight to guide her. "I'm going to stroke your tummy. And suck a response out of your nipples. And later you can do something else. When himself is ready."

"He'll never be ready again, I've died, I'm a husk, a sucked dry shell. They'll find me years from now, shrivelled, discarded, ecstatically dead."

"Silly boy. You're going to have my bum cheeks. In a few

1 I apologise if this offends feminists today, but when I was young the 'risk to reputation' was a potent force in society. You can take the girl out of the prejudice, but not the memory of the prejudice out of the girl. P.C

minutes. And ecstatically dead people don't hump and grunt. Like you will be. Trust me, I'm a canoeist."

The unmistakable sound of a slap and squeal punctuated her words.

"What was that?" he whispered. Another slap and squeal.

"One of the girls is getting spanked. She might have been naughty." Slap and squeal. "I'm not that keen. But you might be. Turn over, see if you like your butt paddled--And ecstatically dead people can't spin over like that." She sensuously caressed his bum, with her other hand under him, monitoring the state of arousal of his penis. Within seconds it was obvious that she didn't need to paddle him, the mere thought of being spanked was enough. Duncan was erect, hard and ready. She hurriedly smeared some KY jelly between her cheeks.

"Climb on me like the ram tupping the ewe."

"Like this?"..

"That's nice. Now hump me--You can have--my tits--if--Oh--Oh--Ooh."

Karen came to lying squashed and satiated under Duncan, who was also stirring from his post orgasmic relaxation.

"Thank you, Karen, that was really lovely."

"Thank you, Duncan dear. I really enjoyed it too."

They got dressed and slipped quietly out of the barn while muted squeals and gasps drifted down from above their heads.

"They're still at it."

"I could be. Girls take a lot of warming up. But once we're there, some of us can go all night. Come with me to my bedroom. I want to show you something. Help you I hope."

The pair slid through the party, with Karen keeping their end up, whilst hoping that Duncan's, 'I've just had a mind blowing experience' flag, sticking out of the top of his head, would be put down to his speech impediment induced shyness. "Lock the door." When he turned to face her again she took her top off and stood square on in front of him as she pulled her bra from her pocket and discarded both garments on the bed. He looked, smiled then transferred his gaze straight into her eyes.

"Say after me. 'I have kissed and sucked those two tits'. Say it now."

"I have kissed and sucked those two terrific tits and it was perfectly marvellous and thank you and I do know why you wanted me to say it."

"Any girl that's worth it. Worthy of your attention, Duncan dear. Will wait while you get it out. So walk straight up to her and say what you want to say to her. Her reaction will tell you all you need to know. To begin with anyway."

* * *

The four inch iron heating pipes in Mr. Carpenter's Craft room, had huge jutting out clamp around supports that were responsible for a couple of seriously damaged ankles a year, on average, and numerous lesser injuries. They ran around three sides of the room, taking up a vast area of floor and on through the rest of the block. A pair of blanked off two-inch spurs, routed directly from the boiler, that had been the intended primary feed before several rooms were added to the building between foundations and official opening, were still live. The authority had insisted that only they reroute the feed pipes, but had graciously condescended to allow Karen to connect her system up to the live spurs and back into the cool return, through specially inserted connectors. Not that they knew it was a student, and High Telemarks, a girl, that was doing it. This had saved a lot of face at County Hall, as had they not agreed, Bill Carpenter would have done it anyway, just not told them.

When the ambient temperature finally went up to bearable in early June, he slipped the leash on his star pupil,

"Your last vocational Exam is next Monday, have you got any others after that?"

"No. Freedom beckons. I'll have to crawl to it on my knees. But I'll get there."

"When would you like to start on the heating?"

"Tuesday. But I know that might not suit."

"When you can do it suits, Karen. Tuesday will do just fine."

For the rest of the following week Bill Carpenter competed for his classes' attention with an attractive, busty brunette in a boiler suit, scrabbling about the perimeter of his room, whilst watching with steadily increasing satisfaction as she removed the ankle smashing impedimenta and simultaneously brought many square metres of floor space into use. The controllable high powered heating system that she installed had service fittings, drain plug and pump that were not only up to the job, but also discretely tucked away, yet accessible.

Karen had to cut up the waste iron pipes. She chose to do it during a lesson when she would be un-worshipped by an admiring audience of youngsters, thus ensuring the safety of their eyes.

Sid was helping her, turning them over when she'd cut half way through, so that she could finish slicing a section off and then slinging the section off the loading dock into a skip. He chose this slack time to ask the question he'd puzzled over for two years,

"What made you want to be a plumber?"

"Which of our books taught you the most?"

"Bollard and Towser."

"Who are they?"

Under her persistent questioning it soon became apparent that Sid's interest in Bollard and Towser stopped at them being authors of their best textbook.

"Rebecca Towser is Reader in Fluid Dynamics at The University of Midolander. Wins beauty competitions in her spare time. Stevie Bollard is a working plumber. Writes crosswords. Designs specialist work clothes." She plucked meaningfully at her boiler suit. "Stars in her own productions of sex educational films. They're hot porn too. She is my Heroine Number One."

"You're serious, aren't you?"

"I know all the theory of cunnilingus and fellatio, courtesy of Stevie Bollard."

"Who?" If Bill Carpenter was not sure whether to be irate or deaf, he had compromised on interested.

"Stevie Bollard. 'Better Sex for Girls, Volume 2, Oral.' Lots of the tips are aimed at men. Men who want to do better for their girls."

"Oh right."

"You can buy them from sex shops. Or mail order of course."

Man and girl turned back to their jobs and continued

working.

Sid pinched himself, winced and looked mildly surprised, as if he hadn't expected it to hurt.

Then Trevor appeared. He had been sauntering home from his Maths exam, seen the activity and come over to investigate. The sight of a girl that everyone knew he fancied but was scared of, wielding an oxy-acetylene torch, cutting up iron as if it were bread, was most probably what forced him to start teasing and taking the Mickey. His spiel was interrupted after only a few words,

"Don't look my way Trevor. This baby burns your eyes."

"Don't look that way Trevor, it's UV--"

Trevor tore his eyes, away,

"I know, I'm not stupid," he walked over to a curved bit of pipe sat in the curve and started fooling around, rocking, spinning. Sid took the latest piece out and skipped it.

"Trevor, you're in my way. Move please. More please." Karen set about her last cut. Meanwhile Sid returned for the curved section. Despite his instructions to vacate it, so that he could skip it, Trevor stayed sat in the curve, swinging, teasing and enjoying himself. Sid was beginning to get miffed when the last section clanged to the ground.

"Hold the door please Sid." Karen plopped the torch off and laid it down carefully in its rest, while she discarded her anti UV mask. She then plucked the curved pipe up and waddled out with it. Sid held the door wide open, when she reached the edge of the dock she dropped the pipe straight into the skip. She and Sid returned and carried the last two cut sections out. Trevor was stood up in the skip shouting abuse, complaining that his ankle was broke. Then he saw the pipes and the ankle recovered enough to help jump him out of one side of the skip, as the pipes fell in the other.

"How many press-ups do you do a day for your canoeing?" Sid might have been asking the time.

"A hundred. And chin-ups, sit-ups. Squat-thrusts and that."

"You're mad, not fit, not safe," shouted Trevor and walked away. He seemed uncertain which leg needed to limp. The plumbers returned to Mr. Carpenter's room to sweep up.

"But it's every other day. Well, four times a week. And some weights and running and stuff."

"Is it a hundred of each?"

"Yes."

"I couldn't do fifty."

"I couldn't do twenty. When I started. It took over a year to work myself up to a hundred."

It is an historical fact that the following winter the authority took direct control of the heating through its own central computer serviced by sensors in all schools. The sensors were built down to a price and installed by labour whose primary interest was to get the job done. It was of little significance that a sensor for an entire suite of rooms was in a draft, or a sun-trap, faulty or even unconnected. Moreover the contractors removed many of the existing electro-mechanical thermostats from the classroom walls, disconnected them by cutting the wires out and then carefully replaced them, without telling anyone in the school that they were doing it. The thermostats looked untouched, and okay, they even clicked reassuringly if their settings were adjusted, but most of them controlled precisely nothing. Consequently when the new system boiled a quarter of the school, whilst freezing the rest, there was no way of changing the situation.[2]

The torrent of complaints was dealt with in the LEA's usual way. Ignore the first lot, deny the next, and then reply that the sensors proved the complainers were wrong, finally, when summer comes, take a look.

Why public authorities treat their employees in this cavalier manner is unclear. It is surely not that with a bit of luck all action can be postponed at least one financial year, possibly two and the heating in County Hall, four miles away, is fine and the same computer controls it, so there's no problem anyway?

No, that would make an eighteenth century redneck plantation owner's treatment of his slaves look okay, so it can't be that.

Throughout this entire time, Bill Carpenter was able to relax

2 Think that one through, Dear Reader. The mindset that gave the order to do that defies credibility; but I didn't make it up, that's what they did, it's true! *P.C.*

in his pleasantly warm corner.

* * *

One Saturday morning, with the supermarket shopping about to be done, Pealle led the way and almost walked into Sid on the doorstep.

"I came to see Karen."

"We'll do the shopping, you see to your guest."

Karen waved her parents off and drew Sid inside.

"Coffee?"

"Erm, thanks, it was --"

"Just say it Sid. It's never as hard to say as it seems."

"You know that day you dropped Trevor into the skip?"

Karen tipped her head and walked away, obediently Sid followed her through the house and up the stairs to her room. She waved at the video collection, cutting directly to the chase,

"Which one do you want to borrow?"

"Well--All of them, not all at once obviously, eventually."

She plucked one out of the rack and gave it to him.

"Start with that one. It's less educational. But more erotically exciting. I like Stevie, but you'll probably go for the girl made up like Queen Cleopatra. Don't expect to get through it without jacking off. You won't. Especially not the scene where the maid puts her Queen to bed. You've been warned."

"Oh--You're so--I don't know how you do it."

"By refusing to let them inherit the Earth. Meek is not spelled P-R-U-D-E!"

"If I--If there's bits--If I'm not sure --"

"If there's bits you're not sure about. Can you what? Just say it Sid. The answer's probably yes. But I don't know the question yet."

"Would you show me?"

"Would I make like a real live dolly? While you practice on me. What as? Girlfriend? Friend? Obedient slave?"

"Friend. I've got a scholarship to South Berkshire starting in October, four years BEd course, PE and Craft. We might never meet again after this holiday."

"And you'd rather not travel south a virgin?"

"The exact opposite; I intend to travel south a virgin, but when I find my love, I'd rather not trample on her orchids through ignorance. I held the door for Melanie, when she straightened Craig out, in the boys' loo. I heard what she said, couldn't help hearing."

Karen nodded.

"She must be the most forgiving girl around, I'd like to think that the girl I fall for will be as forgiving."

"But you don't want to make it necessary. Not gratuitously anyway."

"Exactly."

"Where do you draw the virginity line?"

"Him inside you."

"Even only one push?"

"Yes."

"Fingers?"

"Fingers are okay."

"Okay, I'll make like a life sized dolly for you. If necessary."

She drew him back downstairs and made coffee.

"Erm--How did your boys ask you, when you--you know? How did you know what was going down?"

"Mostly they'd been there before. With somebody else. So did things they pretty well knew I'd like. When I didn't object they moved up the gears. My virgin asked my help, very like you did. But, to cure her virginity. Not merely pave the way."

"Her--I mean--Sorry."

"Yes, her. Does that shock you?"

"Yes. Erm. No, I mean yes and it shouldn't."

"Do you know of any heterosexual boys that held still for other boys when they were younger?"

"Yes."

"So do I."

"Sorry Karen, you're absolutely right. Your own business, equality 'n everything, it's wrong to grant myself the privilege of being shocked."

"Don't forget, your love might also have a past. Possibly murky. She might consider it entirely her own business."

"I'll think about that, get used to it. What could I do that I know she would like?"

"Kiss her goodbye. Walk her home from something utterly mundane. Lecture. Tutorial or such. Say goodbye and wait. If she waits too, she's waiting to be kissed. Close up smooth but slow. Give her time to confirm. But unless you've read things badly wrong, she'll meet you half way."

"Okay. I can do that."

"Invite her for tea. In your room."

"I can do that too. It's the rest that's the problem."

"Okay. You've met your girl. You think she's wonderful. Last night you kissed her goodnight. The heavens reeled around you. Today she's coming to your room. So she has decided to give you a clear shot at her. Could be as long as eight hours."

"How do I know I've got the clear shot?"

"By the way she agreed to come to your room--

'Will you come to my room for tea tomorrow?'

'What is it like?'

'Just a typical student's room, a bit chaotic.'

'Oh like mine then.'

'We won't be disturbed. We could get to know each other.'

'That sounds nice.'

'Come in the afternoon, two o'clock. I'll bring you home at ten.'

'All right'

--You've clearly stated your intention. To try to pop her out of her knickers. And reserved enough time to carry it out. She's said 'Okay you can try.' And promised not to fight you. She might even help. Provided you don't scare her off."

"And what if she said no?"

"How badly do you want her? Badly enough to woo her? Badly enough to buy her flowers?"

"Flowers?"

"Exactly. If not. Try another girl. Try the girl who smiles and says 'Hello' to you. Specifically to you. In the coffee bar. Or tutorial. But be aware that she might have long-term plans in place already. Plans that include you."

"Okay, I've got her lying here beside me, how do I avoid scaring her off?"

"Kisses are more intimate than sex. Eyes, jaw lines, throats, ear lobes all need kissing sometime. Suck her lower lip, gently. Never suck hard. Anywhere, unless she asks you to. Leaves hickeys. She'll almost certainly kiss you back. Slide your hand firmly onto her bum and pull her gently onto your erection. You're inviting her to choose. You can even ask. Is this okay? Or whatever. A gentle press against you is "Yes." Don't go for her tits. Fondle her bum. Up her skirt, down her jeans, whatever. Bum first then her cunny. When she spreads her thighs to let you in, take her knickers off."

"You make it sound like a training manual."

"Sorry. It is, but I didn't mean to. The theme is firm, gentle. Not fast, but not slow either. Steady. Kisses, bum, cunny, not tits. Within that you have complete freedom of expression. Let her give you her tits. When she does. Tell her they're lovely."

"They will be, never seen any that weren't--you know Page 3 and that," he finished lamely.

"You've probably never seen any that weren't a source of concern to their owner. At some time. Tell her they're lovely. Make a point of it. Most girls are worried about their tits. Too big. Too small. Too high. Too low. Ugly, misshapen, wrong."

"How? I mean--Why? I mean --?"

"How do **you** feel about himself?" Karen pointed at the straining front of his trousers.

"Oh."

* * *

When Karen graduated from Saturday-Girl to Full Time Staff on leaving West Novochester, Foreman Paul took her into the warehouse and introduced her to her work colleagues, several assorted youths and men, of which four caught her attention, a slow-moving, mountain of a young man called Pete, his older, white haired, and barely-smaller friend, Snowy, and two scumbags, sniggering over something.

She didn't have long to wait before she found out what.

Part Two:
D'Illion Hardware
Chapter 1
Snowy and Pete: July 2000
Karen

"We've heard about you," said Pete.

"And seen where you've been," added Snowy. "It is always unusually tidy, my dear."

Karen saw it coming from Sheffield, Nichol and Blakey were still sniggering at each other,

"Karen go down to the loading bay and get me a snap-on sky-hook, with a long-stand."

"No."

The sheer effrontery took the bullies totally by surprise.

"Hey youngster, you don't walk into a works and refuse orders. Do it."

"No, I'm here to work, not pander to bullies massaging their egos."

"You stuck up little--"

"I'm your co-warehouseman, not your skivvy. And, the sky-hook with a long-stand errand was in our course at school. With striped-paint. Reversed-flanges. And idle, bullying, chauvinist work mates."

"Well now," drawled Foreman Paul, wooden-faced. "I think that about covers everything, shall we all go back to work now?"

Later,

"Are you having lunch in the canteen?"

"Yes, I meant to."

"Pete and I will go down with you, answer any questions you might have."

"Thanks. I'll happily go with you, but I don't need an escort you know."

"You do! Trust me, my dear, this morning you bested two nasty people, not that I'm saying you were wrong to do so, quite the reverse, but watch your back."

"Thanks."

The canteen, although for all workers, was café rather than restaurant, tiled floor, melamine tables. A line of fruit machines stood out from an oddly angled wall, helping to square the room up. Karen paid for her meal and led the way towards the tables. Nichol and Blakey were at the end of the counter engrossed in the display; she would have to pass too close, she stopped.

"My coffee is black but also scalding. If a foot comes out to trip me. I'll make sure it goes down your front. So choose. Graciously move out of the way. Let a lady through. Or blisters on your dick." Then she just simply waited, utterly ignoring such comments as,

"Where's the lady?"

Presently the two were forced to move on down the counter to get their own meal, by the sheer force of her expectation that they should.

The white-collar worker, in her smart red suit, white shirt and grey tie, clutching a clipboard, who was engaged in administration with the chef behind the counter, watched this exchange ironically. As the pair moved off her eyebrows twitched but she said nothing about the incident.

"You obviously don't need an escort as much as I thought you would, my dear, but do always watch your back with them, won't you?" Snowy was serious.

"Yes."

Karen ate politely and Snowy fastidiously, while Pete worked steadily from one side of his loaded plate to the other, as if it was merely another task that needed completion. During lunch Karen watched the fruit machines separate several squaddies from some money.

"I'm not sure about fruit machines at work."

"Yes, it is a complicated one. I sometimes go on, spend one pound and off."

"He'll get the jackpot, he always does." Pete had barely paused in his feeding, to offer his entire contribution to the lunchtime conversation.

"I'm not going on, there's not a jackpot ready." He turned back to Karen. "There are regulars on every day, but several people have been counselled over it. The problem is that the meals are thirty percent cheaper than they would be without them."

"I had noticed, just not linked the two. Thank you fruit machines."

The following morning when she walked into the rest-room Karen caught the vibes clearly, the bullies were sniggering again; there was a nasty waiting for her somewhere. Snowy followed her in and Pete closed straight up to him.

"What's a jackoff?" he whispered. "They said to ask Karen for it."

She walked straight over to her new friends and leaned between them, an arm around each.

"They're trying to trick you into being rude to me Pete. Just ignore them."

Pete turned to the other two furious; they left the rest-room sniggering uncontrollably.

"It's okay Pete. I know you wouldn't be rude to me. I'll explain what a jackoff is at lunchtime." She finished quietly.

"Are you sure that's wise my dear?"

"Well, are you going to do it?"

"Point taken."

Snowy led them over to a lonely table at lunchtime and Karen waded straight in.

"A jackoff, Pete. You know when you play with the little guy. Down there. And he goes hard."

Pete had coloured from hair to toes.

"Well it's got lots of names. But jacking off is one of them."

"Mum said not to."

"But, Mum isn't always obeyed?"

There was a pause; Pete's eyes, were right down in shame,

"Not since--"

"You need to know that Pete's mum died last year."

"Mum meant not too often Pete."

"Oh."

"And keep quiet about it. Don't talk about it, unless it's safe. With your best friends. Nicest friends."

"Not them."

"No. Definitely not them."

They settled to eat their meal, presently the big boy plucked up the necessary courage,

"Is it okay, like, sometimes?"

"Yes, everybody does it. You, me, Snowy."

Pete looked at his friend who nodded slowly.

"When we need to. Them. They'll lie. Say they don't. But they do!"

"They tell lies, I know."

In gentle accord the meal continued.

"Have you got a girlfriend?"

"No, girls don't like me."

"Yes, they do. Some do. Have you ever had a girlfriend?"

"No."

"Have you ever let a girl stroke him, the little guy?"

Pete sat up wide-eyed,

"No."

"Would you like to? If the girl was willing?"

Pete just sat quite still and silent. Karen had her answer. They finished their meal and stacked the dishes away, Karen held Snowy back a little.

"If you can think of a safe place. I'll do it for him. I feel so sorry for him."

"The safe place is no problem, we will go to my place, it's eminently suitable, the question is what about afterwards?"

"If he likes it enough to pay for it. There's plenty working girls who need the money."

Snowy nodded, his head tipped in agreement,

"There's no chance of you feeling sorry for his old grey haired friend too, is there my dear?"

Karen grinned,

"You never know your luck in a big city."

Snowy's house, in an older, upmarket part of town, stood in its own grounds surrounded by mature trees. Next door a similar building had been converted into a private school, the one on the other side had become a Consulate. Inside, Snowy's place was palatial, but just like the outside, restrained and classy. The huge entrance hallway, which rose the full height of the building, had a polished wooden floor. On the left a staircase climbed up the side and back of the hallway.

Centrally placed, a single, elegant, human-life-size, bronze reclining-nude-mermaid commanded the space. To one side a neat little plaque on a metre high marble plinth announced it had been presented to Amos Joshua Snowdon-Lynes for being Salesman of the Year 1990.

Not merely because of the white hair after all, she thought, with understanding and sympathy. She also knew with absolute certainty that despite the apparent juxtaposition, the award and the statue were not connected.

"Through here," said Snowy; he led the way to a side room and ushered them inside, Karen's feet sank into the carpet.

Pete, transformed, his persona filling the huge room, strode over to the French windows.

"He should have been a gardener, not a warehouseman, but he couldn't read the application form," Snowy murmured to Karen as they followed.

The garden was in keeping and scale with the rest of the house. To the left the size of the pergola-shaded patio was only betrayed by the sturdy teak table, chairs and swing-bench set occupying barely half of it. Ahead the vast lawn merged into the mature trees, heavy with an immature crop of nuts, beech mast, acorns and conkers. Over to the right, a line of short thick trunks, supporting even shorter, incongruously thin branches, dripped with cherries, plums and apples.

The confident, mature man, that until that moment Karen had been unaware existed, surveyed the scene.

"They're doing well, you've thinned them properly, most people stop far too quick, keep them well watered and fed. They're not in the clear yet. You're making them work very hard you know." Secure and authoritative, Pete was speaking from a position of knowledge and looking at the fruit trees.

"I know, I've been obeying your instructions to the letter. I didn't want to lose any; I can't afford to wait 20 years for crops. I haven't got 20 years most probably."

"You won't need to wait 20 days for the cherries and the rest will be close behind."

The confident authority figure had vanished as fast as he had appeared, a nervous little boy, lost in a big man's body, sat at the edge of Snowy's sofa, taut and strained. Karen, kneeling beside him, knew the cause and the cure.

"Pete, I'm shy. Can I cover your trousers? Before the little guy comes out to play."

"Yes." Full of relief.

"We'll use the paper. Then when I'm happy, it can fall off."

"Yes." Snowy covered him with the evening paper and Karen caressed his trousers. Pete might be painfully shy, but his penis wasn't. She had been a little concerned about the size of his member, in case it matched the rest of his body. Her defence of Melanie against Trevor's childish bullying had been a plumb centre gold, but she'd loosed the arrow with her eyes, shut. She was relieved to discover, when she freed him from the underwear, that he was no bigger than Llew had been. Fine, this she could manage. She stroked and teased and fondled, gently encouraging the paper to slide slowly off the big boy's lap.

"Oh Pete. He's lovely, so pretty. He's so nice." The throbbing penis in her hand swelled up dramatically, she changed to long slow caresses. Pete pulled his top up and spurted up his tummy in thick jets. Karen continued caressing,

"Just say. When you want me to stop."

"Now please."

"Was that nice?"

"Yes, thank you." Snowy handed the younger man a hand towel and he began to mop and clean.

"Come on you, my dear, your turn." She shuffled backwards, creating space next to his mopping friend and opened up her second set of flies of the evening. Snowy was slightly larger than Pete and uncircumcised which contrasted with his name. She looked up at him,

"How do you like it?"

"When you do me, grip much tighter and do it much harder than you did Pete please, my--sorry."

"It's okay, I was only teasing. In your mouth it's fine, not patronising at all. Like this?"

"Oh yes. Look out! I'm there!" Snowy too spurted up his tummy.

"Pete, there's four kinds of girls. Put four fingers up."

"Four fingers."

"First kind won't jack you off. That's most of the girls you meet. Married girls. Girls with partners. Young girls. It's wrong to ask. Do you understand?"

"Yes, why I was cross, with them."

"Good lad! We'll fold a finger down, there." Karen held the next finger. "These girls will do it for money. Working girls. Some people call them prostitutes. It's insulting. I always say working girls." She nodded at Snowy. "We will take you and find you one."

"Okay."

"It's not cheap. You can't do it often. Too expensive."

Pete was nodding; the girl understood that he accepted that something that good carried a hefty price tag. Karen folded the second finger down.

"This is me. Girls who do it for friends. It's okay to ask. It's not easy to ask."

"I know, I want to aks, I can't."

"This last finger is your girl. The girl who does it only for

you. She does anything for you. She wants you to do things for her. Do you understand?"

"Yes."

"When you find her. You don't need these other girls. Do you understand?"

"Yes."

"Is there a girl? A girl you want as your girl."

"Yes, Deanne."

"And that's where we leave it for today, trust me my dear, leave it there. Pete you go home to Aunty Cath, Karen has to go home now."

"Don't grin too broadly Pete. People will guess."

"I'll say I'm happy, I can be happy if I want, I don't have to say why." He left, waving goodbye and grinning broadly.

"So who is Deanne?"

"It's so nice to meet somebody who can do the sums, and get the right answer, without having to resort to taking their shoes and socks off. Why are you working as a warehouseman?"

"Why are you?"

"I tried the Rat Race, it cost me my marriage, my kids and almost my life. I took a long hard look at the remaining options and ended up in D'Illion's warehouse. The money is dreadful, but I've got my kids back and my ex-wife and I now meet every Thursday at five for coffee and enjoy it so much we are considering a lunch soon."

"Value, price and cost and the difference between them and all that."

"The cost was too high."

"Deanne?"

"Deanne is my cleaner. She's about ten years older than Pete, a plain comfortable woman, who is now available, since she was widowed last year. You're the wrong sex for Cupid my dear, now answer my question."

"But I can see, cancels things out. Okay, I love pipes. They are so simple, yet you can make the most mind-bending things out of them. From a Klein bottle up. I have pictures of ICI on my bedroom wall. My friend has Tom Cruise."

"You are an incredible lady, could you feel sorry for me again next week?"

"I could, it's not impossible."

"Can I do anything for you in return my dear, today I took and gave nothing back."

"I don't agree. I enjoyed jacking you off. I was in control. Girls often aren't, our fun is at the whim of someone else. I've been lucky. I've had a boy who let me help him get me off. And didn't challenge me over it. He didn't even mention it."

"Would you tell me?"

She looked him straight in the eye while she told him, "He had me from behind. Let me frig myself while he did it, I came. I hadn't got there face to face. Your trousers seem to have swelled."

"He would love to do that and he has no shame, so he flaunts it; I would love to do it too, but I do have shame, so I apologise, for him and me."

Karen cast her eyes down. There was a pause, not long, she'd been hoping he would ask and he had.

"You can if you want. I don't mind. Unless your ex-wife --"

"My ex-wife married my ex-best friend. That is not going to change and yes, my dear, I do want, now if I may?"

Karen stood up facing him and smoothly, unhurried, undid the belt on her jeans and pulled them down around her knees, her knickers followed almost as far. She turned, flicked two cushions onto the floor and knelt on them supporting herself by lying forward on the seat of the easy chair, offering her pert and shapely bottom. She slid two fingers in and out over her engorged clitty,

"I'm ready, do me please."

Snowy knelt behind her covering her like a big stallion with his favourite mare. He rubbed her with his leaking penis, her little cunny gushed her response.

"No need to pull out, I'm protected."

Gently he pushed in; Karen included his invading manhood in her caresses.

"Oh yes!--Do it--Yes, now!" She collapsed forward onto the chair, squealing, jerking, the hands holding her hips had to grip firmly so as not to lose her. She lay bumping gently backwards and forwards her fingers at her clitty caressing without conscious instructions from a brain, totally engrossed in giving up for fucking, the body it controlled.

* * *

In late July, Dennis asked his daughter,

"What do you want for your eighteenth?"

"What I want and what I can have, are different things."

Her dad just waited, knowing that if he didn't force her, she'd tell him truthfully. "I want a car. I know I can't have it. And don't tell me different. Pealle and I do the books remember. Buy me a little surprise. I've started saving for the car. At work. I've set up a savings get first bite scheme."

"Okay."

On the morning of her eighteenth Karen bounced through to the master bedroom. Pealle was already awake and nudged Dennis over to make room as Karen climbed in beside her. The girls kissed,

"Happy birthday, darling daughter."

"Humph!" Exclaimed Karen, but grinning as she did so. Dennis was rummaging on the floor at the other side of the bed, then leaned past Pealle and kissed his daughter,

"Happy birthday," he said and presented her with her card which had a plump little packet taped to it. Inside the card was a promissory note.

Buy the best car you can find for your money.

We will tax and insure it for you.

Meanwhile all we ask is that you don't run off with ours, without checking that we don't need it.

Happy Birthday,

Love,

Mum, Mum and Dad.

Inside the packet was a spare set of keys to the car.

The morning's post produced a good crop of cards for the birthday girl and a slim brown envelope for Pealle.

"That's really nice of everyone. Especially Llew and Jet, from holiday. Very thoughtful. What was yours?"

"Mason Construction."

"Well--Pealle!"

"Fast track apprenticeship, starts Monday." The two girls hugged and danced, whooping around the room.

* * *

On Thursday Karen was hurrying through town when she saw Snowy in The Coffee Café, writing in his notebook.

That must be the 'Coffee with the ex' place. She glanced at her watch, the ex was late. Oh dear.

Instructions to leave it notwithstanding, Karen made it her business to identify Deanne and then contrive to bump into her in the supermarket.

"You're Snowy's cleaner aren't you?"

The buxom young matron was apprehensive, defensive,

"Yes. Why? What's Wrong?"

"Nothing. I work with him. I was just admiring the towels you got him. Would you tell me where you got them?"

Towels were obviously okay, Deanne was much more relaxed,

"Matalan, in the sale."

"Pete was really taken with them too."

"That big teddy bear, I feel so sorry for him. He's a bit deaf you know and it wasn't spotted at school. He was thought to be a dunce and left without learning to read," She became quite assertive. "But he's not a dunce, he's a good gardener. It was him moved all those fruit trees from Snowy's flat to the new house, last autumn, never lost one, he'll even get a small crop off them this year. He prepared them properly, before the move."

"Which fruit trees?"

"The cordons, all trunk and no branches."

"They've been moved? Recently?"

"Last November, a month after Snowy moved from the flat."

"They shouldn't have made it. None of them. They're mature trees, too old."

"As I said, he's a seriously good gardener."

"Do you like him? I mean, like him?"

"I do, a lot, you could do a lot worse. He's a huge, strong, ox of a boy and as gentle and thoughtful as can be. Treat him nicely, you could do a lot worse."

"I'm not on his shopping list. But, you are. He fancies you something rotten."

The look in Deanne's eyes, was unmistakable, despite her urging of Karen to take the big boy on, she was glad the younger girl didn't want him. Pete was definitely on Deanne's shopping list, the most likely reason for her not having measured him for curtains already was-

"I'm older than he is, nearly ten years older."

"Of no importance to Pete. I doubt if it ever crosses his mind. He fancies you, not your age. As you said, you could do a lot worse. Get him to see to your garden. Take it from there."

The cleaner was seriously considering it.

"He's going to the Cornwell Allotments' Show tonight. In the scout hut? Next to the allotments?"

Deanne nodded.

"Ideal place to bump into somebody. And arrange a meeting for later."

"Yes, nearly as good as a supermarket."

"Guilty as charged. See ya Deanne. Eight o'clock tonight, scout hut. Bye."

"Bye--Thanks!" Already several feet away, Karen waved without turning around.

When she got home Karen asked Pealle,

"How was your first day?"

"Okay. My workmates are nice enough, we're based in our own schoolroom, with an instructor, most of the day. When I go into the works; I'm with a little ball of a granddad called Charlie for six months. He's lovely, but the management relations are dreadful. Nobody comes down out of their ivory tower to talk to the squaddies. All communication is by paper, the company calls it a daily broadsheet, the squaddies call it the daily broadside."

"Oh dear."

"And it is a bit, lists of complaints about timekeeping, time off, underproduction, lateness, losses, exhortations to greater effort. I compared some, I think they have a template made up, even the same typo appears. It says coulkd, twice in the third paragraph, you'd think somebody upstairs would have noticed, if a first day apprentice did."

"What does your foreman say?"

"'That? Huh! Never read it.'"

"And he doesn't get rollicked for it?"

"No darling, he doesn't, I don't think he's talked to his line manager this year. I go on site a fortnight on Wednesday, perhaps it'll be better there."

The following Thursday Snowy was in The Coffee Café again after work and again the ex was late.

* * *

Nichol and Blakey had tended to leave Karen alone after the first two days, but Snowy told her not to be complacent. They always gave little Jamie a hard time, mimicking his stammer and sniggering; during a slack time one morning Karen found them in the rest-room, they had the elderly man cornered,

"C-C-Customers P-P-Paul," Blakey shaking his face about, right in little Jamie's.

"C-C-Customers--" Nichol had taken up the chant, Karen barged between them and plucked the little guy out of the corner into dodging space.

"Jamie. I need to talk to a brain. As you're the only one handy. How would you feel about reorganising the warehouse?" She had pointedly turned her back on the bullies and continued outlining her ideas straight through the invective and abuse coming from behind her as if they were alone in the room. Little Jamie heard her out nodding.

"I nu-nu-know what you're on about, b-b-but I don't think it'll go down well. We'll be more efficient, so l-l-less workers needed, jobs will go," he escorted her outside. "Mind I c-c-could suggest where the c-c-cuts c-c-could be p-p-placed."

"You should complain to Paul."

"Just l-l-leave it B-B-Big Kay. I don't hear it. I didn't used to stammer, it was the stroke, b-b-but I revel in it, it shows I'm nu-nu-not dead. I retire soon, it's nu-nu-no b-b-big deal, it's their p-p-problem nu-nu-not mine."

At lunch Karen mentioned the scene and little Jamie's indifference.

"He's handling it correctly," Snowy replied. "I should have said before, it's the one other serious aspect about those two, Blakey's brother is in security. He's good at his job but blood ties are very important to him, he would support the brother rather than the truth. He's done it before; he doesn't accept that by doing so he's making his brother even nastier. There's no way Jamie could take them out and he'd have security on his back if he found a way. And so would you, don't drop your guard my dear."

"I won't."

The door to the canteen was about half way along a corridor with emergency fire exits at each end. From the side opposite the canteen, passages from various places like the Showroom and Maintenance entered the corridor.

The three friends left after lunch and turned into the one for the Warehouse and Lorry Dock. The open plan warehouse stairs were several metres down the passage and directly opposite the Female Wash-room. Snowy and Pete went straight ahead up the stairs while Karen peeled off into the wash-room.

Two girls in the corner sprang apart; the taller one hurriedly stuffed her glistening naked breast back into her top. The warehouseman recognised the other one as a lorry driver, who drove one of D'Illion's few liveried rigs, the taller girl was a stranger.

"Hi Jill, Hi," called Karen cheerfully as she ducked into a cubicle. That was a shame, she quite liked Jill, she was sorry to have interrupted her pleasure. When she came back out the driver was waiting for her.

"What are you going to do?"

"Wash my hands."

"About me and Joy."

"Nothing. Well, apologise for interrupting." The other girl's eyes, were full of pain. "Jill--Nothing." She pointed at the door. "Joy will be wanting to know. Nothing. It's your business not mine. Go."

The lorry driver left slowly, indecisively.

It was nearly a fortnight before the tall girl saw them together again.

Chapter 2
Joy and Jill: September 2000
Karen

Karen excused herself from Snowy and Pete and took her lunch over to the lorry driver's table.

"Hi Joy, I'm Karen. We never got properly introduced." The girl shook the proffered hand. "So what do you do?"

"I'm a driver too."

"Ah right. That's why I rarely see you. How did you get to be a driver?"

"Same as me, learned in the Army, but she managed to stay the whole course."

"Thanks, for not, you know."

"It's much easier if you come out," said Karen as she accepted the proffered seat. "Then there's nothing to, 'you know'."

"Just get fired."

"Do you know gay men drivers?"

"Yes."

"Who are out?"

"Sort of out."

The tall girl spread her hands, shoulders hunched,

"Sex equality. If they fire you, they have to fire them too."

"Didn't work in the Army. My Colonel caught me in bed with his wife and his secretary, she was a Captain, his wife a Major, somebody had to go. Somehow it became Sergeant Jill Peezon, I never did quite work that one out."

Karen laughed,

"It's never the expected outcome."

"I'd like to come out, stop hiding, be myself, say 'This is me,' face the world."

"They probably already know. I did as soon as I saw you. You could test the bath. Stick your elbow in."

"Karen are you gay?"

"I'm bi. If it moves, I start panting. Well, nearly."

* * *

Snowy was sitting in his secluded booth drinking coffee,

Drinking coffee so it's Thursday, thought Karen in an atrocious American accent and suppressed a giggle. She would have gone in to join him but she'd arranged to pick Pealle up from work, the traffic had made her short of time and anyway this was meeting with the ex time, she shouldn't intrude. She took a detour through the car sales forecourt. Other people seemed to be able to pick up clean, low mileage cars cheap, but they'd all gone when she was looking. She was obviously looking in the wrong place. Twenty minutes later when she passed him again Snowy was engrossed in writing in his notebook, she hurried on to catch her meter and collect her Mum.

"Have you been waiting long?"

"No, but hurry darling, I'm bursting."

"So it wasn't a one off?"

"No I checked this morning when I got in, they were the same, filthy, filthy and stinking, full of yesterday's broadside, everywhere, used and everywhere. By now they'll probably be full of today's broadside, I went to the pub at lunchtime, with the other sparks, I don't know anyone that goes into them, but somebody must."

At lunch the following day,

"How did you get back to your wife?" Snowy glanced at Pete,

who was slicing up his cake into face-shove-able sized pieces, oblivious,

"The feeling of betrayal took a lot of getting over, until I realised who was to blame. I had been trying to forgive them, in my mind, but failing, then I forgave myself, after that it was easier." He drew the notebook out of his pocket, glanced at it and replaced it. "We talked about the lunch yesterday, it's not fixed yet, but getting nearer. I'm going to squander a pound," he rose and wandered over to a recently vacated fruit machine.

Pete paused in his feeding,

"You watch, he--told you!" The bandit was vomiting coinage all over the floor accompanying its payout by a light show and sirens, not quite drowned out by the shouts and cat calls of the rest of D'Illion's work force scattered around the room."

"Not again!"

"That bloody Snowy!"

"Now there's a surprise!"

The win neatly closed the topic of Snowy's wife, which Karen had regretted raising the moment he had begun to reply. She guessed that she already knew the real story and that Snowy lived with the disappointment by pretending, noting down the imagined conversation in detail, perhaps even embellishing it later. Such a shame.

"Don't Karen!" She warned herself aloud later. "It's entirely their business and you've only heard one side. It's not the same as tipping Deanne off. Don't meddle."

The Severed Head
Part Six

The businessman had been unable to contact his supplier, there had been people around and then the lines had been down for forty hours. Together the problems had put him in a foul mood for days, a fact that went totally unnoticed. Now he was alone and the telephone was at least ringing at the other end.

"Oui," said the familiar voice of his supplier's secretary.

"It's Buyer."

The girl switched to her excellent English.

"Hold the line, I'll put you through."

"Hello, Seller."

"Your man Gantel was late, again!"

"There are problems."

"I don't pay for excuses, I pay for goods delivered on time. If your camel-shagging peasants can't do that, I know some who can."

"No abuse with me, the matter finished, you not see him again."

"You are so right."

"The next load is today and I replace you bolt that you lost carelessly --"

"It wasn't me that--"

"No excuses with me. The bolt are replaced, same price, put him on you next order, we must keep the paperwork. That all?"

"Make sure it's on time."

"Oui." The man who described himself as Seller put down the telephone, intentionally cutting off any further exchange. "Customers!" he snarled in his own tongue. "But I don't need this aggro," he addressed his partner. "When is Gantel due in?"

"Tomorrow night. The reception committee is already waiting. The story will be that he never got off the boat, we had to retrieve his lorry ourselves." Seller nodded and moved on to other business.

Karen

Karen was giving a customer his invoice when she became aware of an altercation at the next section of counter. A plump, middle-aged lady, with a smaller agitated male in tow was giving little Jamie a hard time.

"I just want it replaced under warranty. No excuses. No prevarication. Just a replacement." She drifted nearer and Jamie began his cry for help,

"B-B-Big K-K-K--"

She addressed the customer.

"Can I help?"

"If you know where the central heating pumps are, this lump doesn't--"

"Doris--" The protest may have been weak, but it was at least sincere.

"Shut up!" She hadn't even glanced at him, only his reaction betrayed who was being addressed. "You can replace this one. We bought it last week, there's the receipt and it's bust."

"They do that occasionally Madam. May I see it please?" She took the Grundfos pump, shutting her ears against the tirade aimed at D'Illion's lousy after sales service.

Jamie, not trusting himself to be able to say it, held the sales invoice with his finger pointing to the code number, between Karen's face and her hands wielding a power driver, cracking the pump open like a Macaw with a Brazil nut. She glanced at him and nodded, laid the water chamber down neatly, with its four Allen bolts upright in their respective positions, turned the pump over and unscrewed the vent bolt. A single sharp hammer blow on a copper drift and the impeller mechanism was lying in her hand. She carefully wiped the spindle and its housing clean of the Africa shaped map of green grunge coating three parts of it. Then neatly cleaned the green debris out from clogging up the impeller blades. Within a minute the unit was re-assembled and she plugged it into the mains. She showed a couple of seconds glimpse of the spinning spindle to the little man hovering in the background, before switching it off again.

"There, that should do it," she said, as she replaced the vent plug. "They need regular cleaning. I recommend monthly. Six weeks maximum. When you use it as a pond pump." She folded the invoice and handed it back to the fuming woman, ignoring and interrupting the protests that it wasn't a pond pump. "And that isn't the pump on this invoice Madame. But no charge for the service, or the errors." She tugged Jamie away, continuing to ignore the words aimed at her. "Come on we've got customers."

A few minutes later, her attention was distracted by waving from behind the client she was serving currently; the little man, now alone, was holding the pump up,

"Thank you," he mouthed. "Sorry, it won't happen again."

Karen smiled, nodded and continued her work.

When he got a chance Jamie thanked her and,

"How did you know?"

"I don't smoke."

"You c-c-could smell the weed before you opened it?"

She nodded.

"I c-c-could once it was open, but you obviously knew it was there already. I didn't know you c-c-could use them as p-p-pond p-p-pumps."

"It's the running costs that's the attraction. Much more expensive to set up the pipe work. And difficult. With the pump having to be below water level. But dry. But then the cheapest metre-head-litre per buck around. By far."

"And easy to replace if necessary, there must be twenty p-places within a mile of here that stock them."

"And precisely one that stocks submersible pond pumps. Giving half the output. At twice the purchase price. And several times the running costs. And that's assuming he has the one you want in stock."

The call floated along the aisle,

"Customers."

The chatting couple had already begun to step forward towards the counter,

"C-C-Coming P-P-Paul."

* * *

Somebody had left the pipe racks in a mess. Karen went for her gloves and returned, alone, to sort matters. There was never anyone around when pipes had to be moved, they were everyone's bête noir, with a lorry-load holding top place.

All the hair on the back of her neck went up.

Suddenly dizzy, she sat down like a toddler, straight legged, directly to the floor.

How had that happened?

Everything went black.

The scenes enacted around her, involving her. Nothing worked, arms flopped, legs heavy and hurting as they were lugged about, just the recorder in her brain relentlessly documenting who was doing what and that she couldn't stop them. The recorder stopped when the unwelcome activity did.

She came to with a splitting headache and goo running out of her.

She had drifted in and out of consciousness, while they used her for fucking.

As well as feeling nauseous.

And impotent.

She was mortified.

When the call to arms had come, she'd been caught unready.

The chagrin was almost unbearable.

She'd let the Sisterhood down.

She struggled to her feet, dizzy and swaying, and lurched her way to the wash-room, holding onto anything handy as she went. If any proof of the unwelcome activity was required it was running down her thighs. She wanted to be sick, but rinsed her mouth and the urge subsided. It made her feel better, as if being sick would have been a further indignity. Doggedly she stripped off, cleaned herself and freshened up. Her strength seeped back, welcome, like water to roots, after the drought breaks. The headache was under analgesic control by the time she came out, but the side of her head was very tender. She had been gone forty minutes but nobody seemed to have missed her. There was nobody around to complain about her absence or hear her justification.

Well if they can do without me for that long, another thirty or so, until lunchtime, is an entitlement when you've just been raped.

She took the permanent marker pen from the pipe bench and two spanners from the tool stack. She hefted the spanners, too short, far too short to get the leverage and power she needed, she tested several, eventually settling for two pair of 24 inch Stillsons that she could hear whoosh as she swept them through the air. With the pen and both wrenches securely out of sight, she made her way down to the canteen, flexing and exercising her arms to make sure they were working perfectly, then stood in wait, opposite the wash-room, under the warehouse stairs into the passage, just off the corridor to the canteen. Several pairs of legs came down to lunch carrying assorted fitters, drivers and warehousemen, then the two she wanted.

"-- have you seen her?"

"Probably still lying there, stupid bitch."

"I'll go to check after."

"No you won't, we know nowt about it. Right!"

"Right."

She slid out from under the stairs and stepped quickly after them, any lingering doubts as to whether she should change her mind, and merely report the incident, had gone with Blakey's callous description of her. The wrenches made giant circles out sideways and then down, forward and up, straight up between the men's legs and crashed to a halt between their testicles. Like a good boxer, she'd aimed beyond the actual point of contact; Karen's arms jarred to her heels with the effort.

One wrench buried itself into the bigger, more thickset man. Nichol was lifted clear of the floor.

She stepped over the silent, jack-knifed bodies, snapped first one, then the other head back by the hair and wrote RAPIST, with her left hand, on each forehead. She slung the pen aside and sauntered into the canteen.

Joy joined her before she reached the counter.

Jill had peeled off to use the internal telephone.

She hadn't noticed them outside the canteen, but they must have had to step over the two men on their way in, the two fire exits from the corridor were exit only and none of the other passages went near the lorry dock.

It was only seconds later that Jill finished her conversation.

She joined Karen drifting along the counter selecting her lunch and finding somewhere to sit, while the lorry drivers chatted to her quite normally.

Sundry other people from the offices and showroom joined the queue behind them and settled for their meal.

Unreal.

Surreal.

“Have you had any luck with changing the system yet?”

“I haven’t asked officially yet. Some of the warehousemen don’t like it.” The trio made their way to a table and sat down. “They think it’ll cost jobs. They might be right. If it does, it’ll never change.”

“Everyone stay exactly where you are. Two of the lads have been attacked. We want statements.”

Blakey’s brother.

Karen had forgotten the security connection.

And she’d made another mistake.

Telemarks!

She went to rise, to own up, hands held her firmly in her seat.

“You came in with us--from the wash-room.”

“My prints are all over the pen-”

“No they’re not.”

“I remembered to wipe the wrenches-”

“We wiped the pen. You came in with us from the wash-room. The corridor was empty. We were talking about changing the system. You didn’t think that you were going to achieve it. You were in a cubicle, someone said ‘Oh Shit.’ You thought it was me speaking. Don’t elaborate, keep it simple. Above all, admit nothing, it’s all sorted, taken care of.”

“Honest Karen it’s sorted, keep it cool, it won’t be for long.”

“Then the heat’ll be off. We know nothing. We went into the loo together, we came out together.”

“Why are you doing this?”

“Tell you later.”

Despite the graffiti on their foreheads, such an effective and devastating attack on a big, thickset bully-boy and his mate, with weapons that required an effort to lift, never mind wield, had to have been carried out by at least two strong men. So initially the girls were left alone, giving the warehouseman time to organise her thoughts.

Keep it simple. That's easy, tell the truth, just not all of the whole truth. It was mid afternoon when it was realised that the last people to come from the important corridor, before the discovery of the badly injured men, were Karen, Jill and Joy. They got to Karen last.

"I went into the wash-room. Cleaned up. Came out again."

"Who else was in the wash-room?"

"Jill and Joy went from there to the canteen. I didn't see anybody else in there."

"Somebody came in and went out again."

"I didn't see anyone."

"She said something to Jill."

"I was busy, I didn't see anyone or hear anyone. I'm not saying they weren't there, only that I didn't know about it."

Later that night Karen reviewed the day. She didn't want to burden her dad and Pealle with the knowledge and nobody else was offering themselves. Llew and Jet would have wanted her to go to the Police, Len was winning a cake making competition in Berlin, with Lisa mopping his brow, Siew Mui's new man decidedly wouldn't want a distraught, round-eyes-lesbian-ex around his girl, eventually she took her mum's picture from the master bedroom, knelt down at her bedside and confessed the incident.

"I didn't lie. But I set out to deceive. It'll be a sin. I'm sorry Mum. But I will do it again, if necessary. Please show me a better way."

It's the same answer to the impossible conundrum; if you want to go there, don't start from here; once the attack starts, the better ways are none options; you must learn to avoid. How's your confidence, are you going to be okay?

"The confidence is fine. But I'll check dark alleys more carefully in future. I'll be fine when I get over the other."

I love you darling; Pealle will hug you for me without asking why; if you need it.

Karen needed it and Pealle didn't ask why.

The investigation petered out later the same day; somebody looking across from Administration thought they had seen men running from one of the fire exits. The search switched focus and died. A few days later Karen met the drivers in the car park,

"Well?" she asked.

"You beat us to it. Five girls in two years. Then they got careless, did little Sandra, the blonde fork lift driver?"

Karen nodded.

"She had to have an abortion. They didn't knock her out completely. It took her months to face the facts, but eventually she remembered who."

"All their victims, except Sandra, were gay. All but one of them were heterosexual virgins, before."

"We were going to do them next week. Had it all planned."

"Alibi the lot."

"You just brought it forward a few days."

"Hurried us, for a few moments."

The tall girl nodded as the pieces clicked into place,

"Ah, yes. The telephone call."

"Stacey had to know when the attackers would be fleeing from where."

"So that somebody could see them, it was neither the planned place nor the planned time, as I said, you hurried us."

"But it was worth it, with cream on top."

"We will cherish for ever, the sight of those Stillsons buried where natural justice demanded they go."

"You did a super job Karen and we know it. Thanks."

"I did it for me. Nobody else. I didn't know about anybody else."

"Oh--We didn't know--Sorry. When?"

"An hour or so before I did them. They were careless with me too. Why didn't anyone complain?"

"Why didn't you?"

Karen looked down, around and didn't reply.

"Yes, everyone has a good reason not to. The strongest one

being that you probably won't get a conviction."

"It was shame. I was ashamed."

The lovers enfolded her and hugged her, loved her silently, that was a pit Karen had to climb out of herself.

"We went visiting yesterday and told them when they got out we were going to put them straight back in again."

"But we were going to finish the job, do the other half, eunuchs this time."

"Do you think they'll run?"

"Dunno. But if they do, we'll find them. It might take a week, but some trucker somewhere will spot the car and then --"

The Severed Head
Part Seven

Buyer sitting in his car in a secluded corner, watched as his latest consignment was processed without a hitch,

"That's better, that's how it should be," he muttered grimly. "Upstarts need a good kick to get them nicely back in line." As usual the emotional buzz produced an overtly sexual reaction. He re-checked around before releasing his erection from his trousers and relieving himself into some tissues, then drove off. The nearer he got to home, the less like a dog with a hard on and the more like a beaten cur with its tail between its legs he became.

By the time he turned into his drive the transformation was complete.

The following evening the shipment, including the crate of bolts, had gone, already several hundred miles nearer its eventual several destinations and Buyer as usual relieved the dog of its hard on, before he too headed off to his.

Karen

Nichol and Blakey never did return to work. The rumour was that they left the district, but Karen's level of interest in the matter was that she neither knew nor cared. Apart from a visit to the Genital and Urinary Medicine clinic to reassure herself about disease, she tried to consider that the incident had never happened. This didn't work, so she thought it through very thoroughly and accepted that she'd lost a battle, but won the war, which at last gave her inner peace.

The paperwork associated with the administration of the warehouse, by the warehousemen themselves, was minimal, most of it was done automatically on the computer when items were logged as sold. However breakages, inaccurate storage, the occasional theft, and other mistakes and losses meant that the stock list was never quite right. This situation was at its least offensive just after stock takes, but seriously annoying immediately before, when the computer might claim that there were a dozen, three-clawed bath wrenches in stock, but the docket contained five, two-pronged slurry-stirrers, three of which were broken. It was Paul's job to keep on top of this and the reasonably acceptable level of inconvenience was due entirely to his efforts.

Karen knew that she could improve it.

The warehouse aisles led off at right angles to the service counter. A couple of metres down the central one, some shelving on the right hand side had collapsed. It had not been repaired, because the subsequent hole was such a handy place to discard wrappers, swarf, breakages and other rubbish. The Hole only got cleaned out when its contents spilled into the way far enough seriously to hamper progress.

Karen coveted that space more than her neighbour's ox.

She spent a week drawing up her ideas as a specification list, brainstorming with Pealle and her dad and then sorting, sifting and honing the ideas down to a solid core office specification and a few rogue possibles.

She researched her ideas meticulously with Stacey.

"Supposing I wanted an office computer. Product library.

Database type research centre. Would the company fund it?"

"Where, here or at home?"

"Here. In the warehouse. Just a PC. Not a biggie like the company computer. Not like Bertha. And the manufacturer's data sheets as paper records."

"If you put together an attractive package and you could persuade Paul to part with the cash, Mike would okay it on my say so."

Karen produced her sheet.

"Would this qualify? For an attractive package?"

Stacey read the sheet carefully twice.

"I could recommend most of this easily, but there's one item you won't get, even if I recommend that you do, which I won't."

"The link to the company hardware?"

"Yes, you've got it down only as a possible, did you have reservations too?"

"I didn't know what safeguards were in place. Whether I could accidentally change something? Without realising it. For example."

"The safeguard is you will not be granted the link."

"That's fair enough. But that means I could be online. The Internet hacking ungodly couldn't get at Bertha through me."

"Yeah, no problem, but make sure your own defences are substantial and kept up to date. You do know to decide on the software first, don't you?"

"Oh yes. That was drummed into us at school. Find the software that does what you want. Then, and only then, look for the computer that will run it for you."

"We have Site Licences for lots of useful programmes."

"I know."

"At least you'll be starting from scratch, you won't need to sort the bugs out of your paper office first."

"Just get Paul to agree to the money."

"Snowy could do that in a couple of days, my guess is you won't need a couple of minutes. Get the submission to me, I'll put it to the boss but we'll not release it into the public domain until you've seen Paul--In the meantime, I know you've been on a couple of courses on hardware."

Karen nodded.

"There's a one coming up shortly in The Wilkinson that might appeal, but Management this time, watch out for it."

During a slack period a few mornings later,

"Paul," she drew the foreman along to the rubbish pile, avalanching out of the Hole into the way, even more spectacularly than usual. "If I organised a bin for rubbish. Cleaned the Hole out. Can I have it? Make up an office. Get on top of our shortages."

"Are you after my job Karen Robinson?"

"Yes. But not this week."

Paul looked into the wide innocent eyes, laughed and gave his consent,

"But no money out of my budget."

"Next to nothing. Just a thousand pounds."

"Slimy stopcocks! No!"

"A thousand from budget's nothing to you. Contented workers. Less hassle from bosses."

"Three hundred."

That's shelves and a basic, used computer.

"Satisfied customers. Nine-fifty."

"Five hundred."

Now we've got the printer, some reference books and access to the net.

"Less work for you. Nine hundred."

"Oh Bollocks."

Gently does it Big Kay, time to wheedle.

"Just nine hundred. I'll put the rest in myself."

"All right nine hundred pounds! Devious, manipulative baggage, but I want it up and running by Friday."

"Overtime? You're a hard man Paul F'Ostergill. Okay, you win, I'll do it."

"You know full well I didn't mean overtime!"

Karen looked at him all hurt and contrite.

"Oh Double Bollocks! Itchy ones! All right, overtime. Now can I have my job back while there's still enough to call a job?"

Karen hugged him and kissed him on the cheek,

"You're so sexy when you're being masterful," she murmured

breathily in his ear, released him and wandered off looking for Pete.

"Pete please help me lug these bins along to the Hole."

"I tumbled the rubbish out, like you aksed me, it's a mess, Paul'll go apeshit."

"He was okay about it. We'll clean it up now."

Together they stripped Karen's new office site of its old clutter, and swept the place out, clean down to its underwear. The flat-bed trolley, with its two empty rubbish bins, stole back barely a quarter of the space. Karen could see the rest clearly in her mind. Her research had left her several options. She had only dared hope for the grant of £500 which would have got her the small pre-used office. The additional funds might stretch to new gear, bearing in mind that a requisition, put through the D'Illion books officially, with the company retaining ownership, might qualify for discount and something off the VAT. It definitely would provide the most important of all in her eyes, although by no means everyone's, racks and racks of manufacturers' data sheets on their products, neatly catalogued and maybe even the odd luxury, like a chair! The one thing on her shopping list that she had been assured she wouldn't get, hook-up to the company computer network, she had deleted from the submission. As this had as many drawbacks as advantages, she wasn't too fussed; besides which, with no electronic connection to the company hardware, she could safely have her little box on line and that was in the submission and had been authorised, a big plus.

"Now what do you do about the rubbish bins?"

Pete took a deep breath and repeated his instructions from memory, like a mantra.

"I empty them every night. And, during the day if they get full. But, every night even if there's only a little in."

"How do you empty them?"

"I can carry them if they're light. But I must use the trolley if they're heavy."

"And if you're not sure about anything?"

"I aks you. Or Paul. Or somebody."

"Thank you Pete. How's Deanne?"

"Wonderful." Then quietly, looking around furtively. "She's

teaching me to read, with books we bought, and magazines with pretty ladies in them with no clothes on, and they make the little guy go hard when we read them, and we get excited and it's nice, we have a nice time. I can read some of them myself now." He grinned, nodding as he spoke. "And the gardening pages and I don't need the other girls." He stuck four fingers up and then folded three of them down, now grinning broadly. "I've got my own girl."

Motivation is a wonderful thing, mused Karen. If wanting to be able to read badly enough so that you could read your soft porn books yourself, and glean tips to try out on your lover, meant you learned to read, who should be allowed to complain.

Two weeks later a small discreet notice from the senior PA appeared under the banner trailing the Conference on Managerial Skills, in The Hotel Wilkinson, now less than two weeks away. Karen was intrigued.

Chapter 3

Conferences: November 2000

Karen

She pointed the notice out to Snowy.

"'There are still a small number of vacancies for typists and secretaries to enjoy a weekend in romantic surroundings, with just a few hours work during the day.' Have I read the missing section correctly? And another few hours during the night. Something like?"

"You read it correctly, they are short of female heads for the Training Weekend, there is no work during the day, the girls are escorts for the evening. They will accompany their partner to dinner and to the dance with him later. You don't have to go to bed with him, but you will be tacitly expected to and you can if you want."

"I detect some censure. More than I was expecting."

"It's not your thing, my dear, not the sort of thing in which you should get involved. Steer clear, dangerous waters."

"It sounds exactly my thing." Karen had been seriously considering going on the course anyway, now all doubts had gone. "I would be in control. I don't have to fuck him. If he's nice and friendly and I want to. I should be allowed to."

"Something about Geese and Sauce?"

"Precisely. There's Stacey now. I don't even have to trek up to the Admin Suite." Karen stood not quite directly in the way of 'the girl in red carrying a clip board,' as she thought of her, looking at her whilst pointing at the notice.

"It appeals, you can put me on the list. The product specification skills are probably much better than the secretarial ones."

"Karen! My dear."

"It is alright Stacey, I know the real score."

The Senior PA consulted a sheet deep among those on her clipboard and wrote an entry.

"How's your dancing?"

"More fair than middling. Quite like it, but not really my scene. I can follow a lead."

"That means it will probably be better than your partner. Any preference for or against colour, it's a Commonwealth Conference, there'll be everything but green."

"Dammit, I'm into green. No, no prejudices that I know of."

"There's a Maori, ex-rugby player, international, but just not quite a full cap All Black, more than a bit of a radical, you'll probably be on the fringe of some pretty hot policy arguments, rather than avoiding being trodden on, if you'd really prefer not to dance."

"Sounds fine. You pair us up before we go?"

"When I can, if there's an obvious fit. He is John Smith, his real name is something I can't get my tongue around, but he answers to John Smith, at conferences anyway, I think you'll find the two of you will get on. What name do you want on your nameplate? Many of the girls use a convenience name."

"Rockhopper."

"CK and double P?"

"Yes, just like the penguin."

Stacey made some more entries, nodded and walked off, after two steps she turned again,

"Sorry, prospectus and all that in the internal post on Monday. If you haven't got it by Tuesday, get on to me fast."

"You won't be told will you? One of these days, my dear, it

will be the death of you."

"Don't be a grouse. Who knows? I might find my man. A Maori rugby player. Sounds exciting enough to give it a whirl. Be happy for me."

Reluctantly Snowy forced a smile to his lips, although it failed to reach his eyes.

"You didn't have to think about the convenience name, it just came straight out, tends to make a body think."

"It was my pet name. My favourite cousin's name for me. We were to be each other's first, we discussed it, agreed on it." She turned away to hide the pain. "My next visit. Then the big C got him." The tears welled up; she forced them back, blinking. "Twenty days, from not feeling all that well, to the end." Snowy cuddled her in, drawing her out of sight behind the fruit machines. "He didn't last three rubbishy weeks." She straightened up looking at him through the blur. "We dashed to his side. Took us most of the night. But we didn't make it. I never even said goodbye."

"And now you fuck anyone that asks, in case they never get another chance."

"Do I? Is that what it is? I've never said no, not in the whole of my life. Not that I've had that many offers, but I never say no. You'll be right, yes." The threatening tears were bowing to her control. "That's one reason why I don't like smoothies. I like to negotiate up front. Yes, or No, like we did."

"Start getting ready to say "No' my dear, the smoothies are just about ready to make their moves on you. It is your choice entirely, but if you let them into your knickers, your street cred will take a hiding."

"Would you mind being used as cover?"

"Not at all, I'll wear your favour with pride. It is only cover, isn't it?"

"Yes, despite how much I like you."

"Fine." But again the smile failed to reach the eyes. "But you are making an error going to the conference, allow me to dissuade you my dear."

"No."

"What happened to my compliant little girl that is so rewardingly sorry for me from time to time?"

"She got gang raped. Girls have had their lives ruined. Their whole life. Not me! This one hit back. But your compliant little girl died among the pipe racks. Four weeks ago."

"Nichol and Blakey? I did wonder ..... one of these days you won't have time to swing a wrench." Karen disengaged from his embrace.

"I will still be nice to you. Whenever you like. But the compliant girl's dead. And I miss her too. Don't ask for her back, she's dead. Thanks for the hug. I needed it."

The Severed Head
Part Eight

That weekend, a consignment of spares and parts arrived in a busy tropical market.

The joy that the arrival of such a consignment generates in a third world market would come as a shock to anyone who has run out of screws on a Sunday lunchtime and is used to dashing to their local DIY Warehouse Hypermarket, where they expect to be faced with a choice of several dozen different fasteners, all more or less suitable.

Many customers in that particular market hadn't seen a threaded piece of metal for sale for three years.

The swarm of locusts descended, paid up and departed with their booty.

The most prized items among the poorest people, were the splintered pieces of packing case with their reinforcing wire and staples attached; with these, arrow heads, spears, fish hooks and consequently tomorrow's lunch, were only time and effort away. Within an hour, nothing was left, no stock, neither vendors, nor purchasers, not even a stain on the ground.

In due course, a shipyard, discreetly tucked away out of the main stream of nautical business, took delivery of a crate of high tensile steel bolts.

Karen

The prospectus had arrived obediently on Monday. Karen and her friends pored over it at lunch.

“There’s an afternoon tea session. Before check in.”

“To size up your partner my dear, during tea the pair of you decide whether it is a double, two singles adjoining, or in two different buildings.”

“Oh.”

“I take it that he will have to be King Kong before you consider either options two or three?”

“Are you going to the pictures? Can I come?”

“No. It’s a bosses’ meeting. I’m going to tell them what they do wrong.”

“Oh. I’ll not bother then.”

“And he’d have to be Godzilla. I always felt sorry for Kong. When he picked at her bather, I’d have taken it off.”

“Hmm, follow that one through, get the story straight in your mind and tell me next week. Mr. John Smith is going to have the sort of weekend adolescent boys have wet dreams about.”

“I’ll ask him at the end.”

“Have you got two ball gowns?”

“What?”

“Friday, formal dinner 7.00pm, Saturday, formal dinner dance 7.00pm. You will get away with a decent cocktail dress on Friday, but Saturday, you’ll need to splash out a bit.”

The telephone had been ringing for a while, but Karen knew not to hang up, there were a dozen or more reasons why--

“Hello.”

“Lisa it’s Karen. Sorry. Catch you at an awkward moment?”

“Bath time.”

Oh dear, important pair bonding activity interrupted.

“Can Len ring me back?”

“Half an hour?”

“Fine.”

It was a good hour later before Len rang her back and the details of two meals were discussed,

"Friday, surf and turf with baby new potatoes and a Rockhopper salad-'

"And cook the potatoes-"

"I always do."

"But your vegetable chef always doesn't. I want them cooked. I do not want to be able to break windows with them."

"She's much better now, the greens crunchy, the roots soft. Can I tempt you with fish 'n chips on Saturday? I've been promised some decent Nadines."

"Crumb-coating to die for, parsley sauce?"

"Karen!"

"Sorry. I'm not treading on your Art honest. Okay. Cod if possible, or Haddock. And If the promised Nadines and hence the best chips in the world don't materialise. I'll settle for new potatoes again. If you have to swerve suddenly on the day."

When Karen presented herself at The Wilkinson on Friday evening, the foyer was full of freshly arrived luggage. In the accompanying throng there were a sprinkling of familiar faces. Her cases were taken from her and stored to one side, then she was ushered into a waiting area and issued with a little green and gold nameplate, which said,

Rockhopper

nestling in a cradle of laurel leaves. Stacey drew her over to a group of men and girls at the bar,

"John this is Rockhopper, would you kindly escort her for the evening?"

"Certainly ma'am. What is your pleasure Rockhopper? It's a teetotal bar until after dinner."

"Pepsi please, no ice, twist of lemon."

John Smith was chunky rather than tall, barely topping Karen in her trainers. He had short dark hair, greying at the temples and his sweater and slacks matched her own grey top, blue denim bolero and jeans perfectly. He had a craggy, lived in face,

By a rugby boot occasionally, thought Karen, stifling a grin, but his voice was low and gravelly, warm and reassuring. John gave her her drink and guided her over to sit at a table.

"Now then Rockhopper, who are you and, more importantly, why are you here?"

"The who is a warehouseman at D'Illion. I love pipes and what you can do with them. Traded not much money for greater happiness. Got the best deal available at the time. Your turn. Who are you?"

John cleared his throat,

"That is my name in my own tongue, I export tree ferns from ecologically managed forests, mainly Dicksonia Species; in my country they are firewood, by the time I get them over here, they are green gold. The only problem is they aren't fully hardy in Britain. Why?"

"You first. I did who first."

"I don't know, I really don't know. I'm hoping that will become clear during the weekend."

"My why I think we are about to agree."

"Agree?--I expected to have to negotiate."

"A friend of mine told me about negotiations. Mostly they are froth. Stinging. Smelly. But unimportant. State your preferred outcome. Let's see if we can agree on it."

"I would like the full facilities, close personal attendance from nine 'til five but also from five 'til nine."

"That will require a double room."

"-- Yes."

"Okay."

"I'd prefer a double bed too."

"So would I--Utter silence. Is that the end of our negotiations?"

"Rockhopper, what are you getting out of all this?"

"A mini break on the edge of the countryside. They say a change is as good as a rest. I'm going to be living in the knickers of a man who has seen parts of the world about which I can only dream. Will that do for now? There's more. But I might tell you that later."

"This weekend was potentially a bore, but not any more."

"I don't know if this helps your 'why'. But--I gathered that

I wouldn't be doing much dancing, but I would be listening to heated arguments."

"That explains a lot young Rockhopper, thank you, my 'why' is very much clearer."

"It's after five, can we check in? I would like plenty of time to get settled."

Their room was a small suite, bed sitting room with mini bar, bathroom with shower over the bath and tiny kitchen. Many small bulbs and reflectors provided the lighting, except around the dresser mirror where three small fluorescents provided intense but non-dazzling illumination, for perfect face application. The themed colour scheme was calmly pleasing shades of peach and apricot. Through some French windows, overlooking the bypass and the hills to the North, there was a balcony, complete with pot plants, a sage green patio table and, as Karen quickly discovered, surprisingly comfy matching chairs. When she had finished checking out the furnishings and appraising the view, she leaned back against the balcony rail and grinned at her companion as he followed her through the French windows.

"It's lovely." Her eyes, were shining.

"It's barely two star, but they say that the food is good."

"It had better be, or the chef will get a slagging."

"You slag chefs?"

"Only this one. But he's good. The food is good."

"The loveliest thing about the whole deal is my escort. I choose to see it through her eyes. It is lovely--May I hold you?"

"Yes, anything you want, I'm in Wonderland. Explore it with me."

He closed up to her and held her, she slid her arms around his neck and gently snuggled, moulding herself around his erection, looking down to get it right. He kissed her eyes and her neck, when she could get to it, she kissed his mouth.

"If you want to take me to bed before dinner. Do it now, before my shower. Then after dinner. Tonight. I'll dance for you before bed. If you'd like that."

"I would love it," he gathered her up, carried her into the room and laid her on the bed. He was getting lost in the ramifications of her outfit; although he'd managed to bare enough of her for fucking, good foreplay was still several items of clothing away and she could sense that he was very eager.

"Just do it John. Now. We'll take our time later. Have me for yourself now. That's right. That's better. That's nice, push up hard when you come. Yes. Do it. Do it to me. Do me," and thrust her tongue into his mouth.

She held him and caressed him and made sure that he had a lovely climax. She got almost as much pleasure from that as from coming herself. It was a very different type of pleasure, but nearly as rewarding.

He obviously knew she hadn't had an orgasm,

"Thank you, sorry it was no good for you-"

She had stopped his mouth with her hand.

"It was lovely. I like giving, I enjoyed it. You can make me come later; I'm looking forward to it. But that was lovely. In a different way, but still lovely."

"How?"

"It's about control. When I come, I'm helpless, it's wonderful and I love it and I will surrender to you later. But you are in control, not me. I have just been in control. I love that too, it's different, but still lovely."

"You are an amazing person."

"Thank you kind sir."

They took turns in the shower, their conversation ranged over a number of topics, finances being one of them.

"You know how you criticised this room. For being barely two star."

"Not really a criticism, more an observation, it's quite nice really."

"I'd like to earn enough money. To acquire the experience. To consider this room barely anything."

"It's no different you know--It's just degrees."

"Show me."

"Like when you're a kid, and you've got fifty eight pence, and that'll buy you a Budget yo-yo, with change. It's a shame to settle for the Budget when for seventy pence you can have the Super. Then Granny gives you thirty pence, now it's a shame to settle for the Super when for a mere eighteen pence more you can have the Deluxe. It's no different when you're thinking in thousands. The secret is to decide what you can be happy with and strive for that. When you achieve it, you'll be happy."

"Settling for the best you can get. Gives genuine happiness?"

"Striving to achieve the best you can, then settling for it. But, don't be afraid to fail. If you never fail, you can never be sure that you have achieved the best you could do. Tonight, I would also like you to do something else for me, stick to me like toffee paper."

"What?"

"Decline invitations to dance with other people, to anything with other people."

"Equal shares Mr. Smith. Me first, last and everywhere in between. When you are taken away for a meeting. I'm on your lap throughout."

"Physically on my lap?"

"That would be nice."

"Rockhopper, you have a deal."

Dinner was way out of the league of the relatively simply furnished room and John and Karen enjoyed it very much.

"I'll have the fruit juice and the rack of lamb and for Mademoiselle fruit juice and surf and turf, rare, with a Rockhopper Salad."

The waiter paused, confused,

"Speak to the chef. He will have the salad ready. Just ask for it for me."

"Very good Mademoiselle," he went off obviously unconvinced, but giving Karen the benefit of sanity. It was a waitress that served them the juices, but when the waiter returned with the main courses, he did so pushing a trolley and served them with reverence.

John's rack of lamb looked luscious with its row of little chef's hats on the bones and the crisp vegetables, in their little piles, among the baby new potatoes. It was Karen's salad however that drew the attention of the populace. It was served on a huge clamshell. Four large Buttercrunch lettuce leaves, their midribs nicked through to allow them to lie flat, were fanned out as a base. Mustard seedlings cushioned two rare fillet steaks set in a frame of baby new potatoes, side by side at the base of the leaves, each with three King Prawn tails spiralled off it. Circular nests of thinly grated raw carrot and swede contained clutches of dark seedless sultanas, pale plump raisins, grapes and Silverskin onions. The hard-boiled egg had been sliced in half lengthways to display its double yolk status and the Gardener's Delight tomatoes nestled in threes, each with a single Chinese leaf rising out like a spear point. Rose cut radishes and other more varied leaves formed a little posy to one side.

"Now I understand, I take it you know the chef?"

"Intimately. Slept with him for years." Nearby heads turned sharply towards them. John's expression was comical.

"An ex who still likes you enough to serve up something like that."

"Still loves me. Not an ex. A current."

The comical expression was becoming tinged with horror, whilst the nearby interest level soared, she came clean giggling.

"He's my brother."

"Oh, more beguiling nooks and interesting corners to explore. What culinary delight awaits you tomorrow night?"

"Fish 'n chips."

"You have got to be kidding!"

"It is to a chippy wrap what this is to a beef burger with leaves and mayo."

"Ah."

"Succulent fish. Which could be anything. In crunchy crumb-coating. Long, fat, waxy chips, golden brown skins that detach from the flesh like tissue when you cut into them. Sweet. Not everyone's cup of tea. Some deprived souls like Maris Piper. But give me Nadine any day. And parsley sauce of course."

During the meal she learned a lot about tree ferns and hot springs and international, but not quite full cap, rugby.

{'That was my failure, I repeatedly never got a full cap, I did the best I could and settled for that.'}

He learned a little about pipes and bends and Mobiüs strips that have only one face and one edge and strange structures like

Klein bottles that can only be fully realised in four dimensions. Following on from that, they argued, gazing deeply into each other's eyes, like lovers, over what a four dimensional universe would comprise.

The coffee and mints were finished when a man with bushy hair tapped John on the shoulder and said,

"Conference suite, Room C." The man patrolled on, selecting his team.

"Who's that?"

"Paul Crossers, your biggest competitor."

They stood up and followed him down a corridor,

"More like Sylvester to our Tweety Pie."

John nodded sagely and resumed their discussion.

"How close could someone, removed from you in the fourth dimension, be to you, but still hidden?"

"Right next to you. Close enough to reach out and touch. With shorter arms than mine." She extended their arms with a step sideways. "Nearer than we are now. But not between us of course."

"No that would have to be at zero in the fourth dimension and we could see him, or would we? What if--"

The security guard on the door interrupted,

"This is a private meeting, er --" He bent forward and read her name. "Rockhopper. Wait over there with the other girls."

Karen ignored the calculated insult, but politely stood her ground,

"I'm with him."

The guard restrained her turn away.

"Be a good girl and don't give me any grief. Over there with the other girls."

"I'm with him."

"She's with me--" John murmured,

"The girls are in the bar John," said bushy hair. "Come on through."

"Do you want me in on this discussion?" he had called without taking his eyes, off the security guard,

"Of course."

This time even more softly, straight at the guard's face,

"She's with me." He turned and towed Karen with him. Behind her she heard the next delegate say 'She's with me.' The little conference room contained only men when they entered, but by the time the door shut there were two other girls present as well as Karen.

"Restrict the alcohol intake." Whispered right in her ear.

"Check." She murmured back. "What can I get you?"

"Wave the vodka bottle about, but serve me pure pineapple."

Karen brought their drinks over and joined her man on his lap in a huge easy chair. He indicated her near opaque grey liquid with cherries resting in the bottom of it,

"What on earth is that?"

"You have vodka and pineapple, I have vodka, bitter lemon and maraschino cherries." She offered him a sip; the vodka content was as imaginary as in his drink.

The chairs were arranged in an oval with a flip chart centrally placed midway down one side, thus ensuring that it was out of view of many of those present. Karen was just about to draw John's attention to this when,

"Take notes then." A large, and, for some reason not obviously apparent, angry man was thrusting a clipboard and writing materials at Karen's hand. That the female present was automatically the scribe, coffee maker and general dogsbody, to be ordered about as and when, was as alien to her as the sky-hook and long stand.

"No, I'll quote you flow rates through pipes. Head equivalents of bends. Suggest the best pumps for a given purpose." She pointed at the little blonde on a knee two along. "She'll recommend which fork lift to use. For which pallet weight. Advise on safety procedures." Indicating the third girl, she continued the protest. "She'll tell you the problems you create working late. And she can't vacuum through. We all know why we were invited. We are comfortable with that. We have specialist skills and knowledge we will share with you." The pleasant, bustling lilt took on a hard edge, as she looked him straight in the eye. "Taking notes is extra." For a moment she thought she'd killed him, he went puce, all over, including his balding bullet head.

"Stipulated that you are here as an expert in fluid dynamics and because we want us both here, would you take notes for us, as a favour to me? If you won't, I'll be quite happy to take them myself," said John.

Now that was a whole new can of beans,

"Certainly." Karen plucked her reading glasses from her handbag, headed the page "Conference Room C' and quickly sketched a two column table. She wrote Name in the first column and Occupation/Company in the second and drew a line underneath. Rockhopper, Warehouseman/D'Illion went into the top space and John Smith, Director/Greengold Tree Ferns joined them forming the beginnings of a list. She passed the clipboard on. "Please sign in, legibly, in order." The board made it's way slowly around the group. Bullethead ostentatiously read the top name, looked hard at Karen, and pointedly passed it on without signing.

"Leave a space," commanded Karen to the young man cuddling the pneumatic little cleaner, who was next in line. When the clipboard finally got back to her she wrote 'Bullethead' in the space.

"Dispatch Clerk/Crossers Hardware, he likes to think of himself as a manager, but he isn't, he's a senior clerk. Clerk will seriously annoy him if he ever sees it," murmured John in her ear and Karen obediently added the entry, stifling a grin.

"Ready when you are everyone," she announced.

The meeting was about Management Skills, Styles and Effectiveness, and took the form of a brainstorming session followed by discussion of the various issues raised. The little blonde forklift driver, sporting a badge that claimed she was 'Detroit', offered to write up the brainstorming on the flip chart if nobody criticised her spelling.

"We won't do that. Had you been born in your name. And rich. You could have been Vice President by now." It took a moment or two for the reference to sink in, but then most of the room chuckled at Karen's observation. Detroit immediately organised an exchange of position of the flip chart and the chair at the end of the oval, where everyone could see it, and pushed the adjacent chairs out slightly so that the oval became a U facing her.

The discussion dichotomised into two camps, Management by Agreement and Management by Dictation.

Karen was quietly chortling inside. By taking on the flip chart, and rearranging the chairs, Detroit had created a pivotal role for herself, and made full use of it, tally marking how often items were covered and drawing attention to those being neglected.

The argument raged like a hard fought cup-tie, with the well-known pros and cons of both systems being thoroughly explored. Although most of the neutrals who eventually chose, did so on the side of Agreement; the more entrenched views on the opposing sides were as far apart as ever. John had argued strongly, persuasively and occasionally quite vehemently in favour of Agreement, but hadn't been able to waver Bullethead, by as much as wishes become horses for beggars to ride.

The big man summed up his case oozing arrogance,

"As has been said before, if you've got them by the balls, their hearts and minds will follow."

Karen jumped in hard.

"Wrong. If you've got them by the balls all that happens is they wait. If it takes decades. Even centuries. You have to let go eventually. They just wait. They wait patiently until you have to let go. Then they take you down into a cellar. Or out into the garden. And shoot you. Ladies and gentlemen it is late. I have a lot of notes to write up. This meeting is now closed." She stood up and waited for John to join her. The little cleaner and several of the men followed her lead, Detroit tore her sheets off the flip chart, with a flourish. Bullethead was turning puce again,

"Hang on-"

John interrupted him,

"We are already fifteen minutes over time. The meeting has been closed. After you folks." He was pointing at the door. People began to stream through it.

"My meeting can't be closed by a blue collar! A female! A dame de voya-'

"Well, she just did," interrupted Detroit stepping past him, holding her rolled up flip sheets in one hand and her date in the other.

"Would you like a nightcap?"

"Not really, take me to bed. Well, take me up. And then to bed in a few minutes. I need to tidy up these notes first. Before I forget."

They did their rounds and then went up to their room. Karen set about ordering and tidying the notes from the meeting, while John got undressed. He came over and gently kissed her neck and her shoulders, she felt the zip of her dress give down her back. She paused and spoke over her shoulder,

"Do you want me to dance for you?"

"I do, but I can't wait to get at you again, can we give it a miss until tomorrow? I've had a hard-on, on and off for well over an hour."

"I had noticed. Okay, strip me while I finish this." She found it very arousing to be undressed by someone whilst needing all her concentration on the job in hand, she didn't want to be thinking 'The forecast was excellent' but write 'The foreplay was excellent' even though it was.

At some stage in the proceedings Detroit put her head around the door and called,

"Here's the flip charts." The little fork-lift driver, dress loose to the waist, leant into the room to prop the paper roll up inside the door. A moment later she glanced back over her shoulder giggling, as she was plucked backwards out of the room by her bare tits.

Karen had to transcribe the last few pages standing, bending forward to write, with her lover sensuously fondling her breasts, whilst standing proudly erect between her cheeks. Eventually she was finished.

"Do you want me to come on you?"

"Yes, of course."

"Would you do me like this then. And let me help. I can almost guarantee the outcome."

"Like this?" His hands gently pummelling her breasts, were darker against the comparative paleness of her golden brown, his cock was nuzzling between, gently, gently, finding his way into her.

"Yes. That's lovely," she murmured as she slid her hand down to tease her clitty.

He readjusted his grip to accommodate her.

"Hold me lover, I'm going."

She was picked up and carried to the bed, where a controlled sideways crash got them onto it. As the energetic thrusting resumed she began to build again from the slight dip induced by the cessation of activities. He pushed her over, star fished, onto her tummy, and then pounded her roughly into the mattress. Her flickering fingers fell still through lack of need, she was over the hump, screaming down the slide and into her pillow.

He let her ease out from under him until they were lying in the spoons position, then he retrieved the duvet and covered them, managing to do so, still coupled together and without releasing her,

"Goodnight little Rockhopper."

"Squawk." His chuckle was the last thing she heard, and a twitch of his penis inside her the last thing she felt, before sleep claimed her.

Karen stretched luxuriously and turned over to cuddle her companion. He wasn't there,

"John?"

"Awake at last I hear, if you dive in the shower and throw a face on, I would be honoured to escort you to breakfast." His half shaved face was looking at her from a body leaning backwards out of the shower cubicle.

"When did you get up?"

"Nearly two hours ago. I've been for my run; Hexham's lovely at this time of year."

"You ran to Hexham?"

"I think I took a wrong turning on the way back, but that stone arched bridge at Berwick is beautiful lit by the rising sun."

"You --"

John swerved away from the lunge,

"You may hug and kiss but not tickle--Not tickle--NO!"

Together they walked sedately down to breakfast.

"So what will your brother have laid out for our delight this morning?"

"Choice of fruit in syrup. Or fresh. Choice of cereal. Croissants beurre and coffee. Any combination of fried egg, bacon, sausage, kidneys, cutlets, tomatoes, mushrooms, baked beans, toast and tea. Craster kipper, smoked mackerel--Then for the main course --"

He firmly smacked and squished her pert bottom up her short skirt.

"You've got no knickers on."

"Yes, I have. Sort of. They're just a bit skimpy. This lecture you're giving on Marketing. I'd like to assist. Turn your pages. Mop your brow."

"I'd like that, we can rehearse af--Goodness me!" The dining hall was crammed, tables spilled across the vestibule, a steady stream of customers were entering by the main door and joining a shuffling line of assorted breakfasters: business executives, secretaries, lorry drivers, children, collecting meals from an extended counter, negotiating additional portions and paying at the tills. Another stream flowed out of the door, wiping mouths and dusting paunches.

"Impressive isn't it? Len tells me that they break even at fifty. Hit the serious profits at five hundred."

"There must be close to that today."

"It's a bad day when they drop below a thousand. Plus the guests of course. This way." She towed him towards the lounge where the hotel guests were having waitress service breakfast. "They were doing it when he got the job. In a small way. He realised the potential. Canvassed the locals. Set it up big. Now Avant-garde run a bus service from the lorry park. Six 'til nine, every morning."

The lecture on Marketing was packed to the doors. With John as the action on screen and Karen as the unobtrusive, complimentary musical score, they made the ideal double act. Fifty minutes of superbly crafted presentation, to a rapt audience, was followed by questions, the first few of which John deftly dealt with, then a small, thin man, with grey hair and moustache, and a tired, haggard look, spoke up,

"Culp Mason: Mason Construction. What you say is fine, but what do you do when you research your market, produce the product they want, at a price they're prepared to pay, then your well paid workers go on strike for more money?"

"Can I?"

John waved her forward.

"They didn't Mr. Mason. That's what was said. But, it was not about money. It was to do with not being people. Merely Company work units. It was revenge being taken. On an uncaring company. With uncaring management. And, because the toilets smell."

Shooting him dead might have produced a less shocked silence.

"All those may be false. Or, gross distortions of the facts. But it's what your workers believe. So to them it's true. When did you last check your broadsheet? To make sure it said something worth reading? And wasn't just last month's complaints rehashed. Or, not even rehashed, reprinted. Misprints included. Do you walk through the works? Talk to labourers? Apprentices? What's the name of the latest baby born into your workforce? When did you last visit the squaddies on a site? Take a leak in one of their toilets? And, check for yourself. And, if you don't do it, your management won't."

She stepped right up to him.

"You're quite right. You pay your workers well Mr. Mason. But, they hate working for you. So they dodge and weave. Skive and steal. Bleed you white to make it bearable. That's the real problem. And, that buck stops right in your lap."

He tried several times to reply.

"Proof is less than ten minutes away. Your nearest construction site. Go and check. If I'm wrong. I'll hold still for you to tell me so. And, I'll apologise. In public."

Two hours later Stacey joined Karen, John and Mike D'Illion for lunch carrying a beautiful bouquet of flowers.

"Aren't these really something?" she lovingly stroked the cellophane. "Of course they're from Jean Bullivant's so you'd expect them to be nice, but still."

"They're lovely. But you deserve them. For organising such a wonderful course."

"Yes, I do, don't I?" she looked mischievously at her boss. "So I'll expect something like on Monday, meanwhile I'll pass these on to their owner shall I?"

"I always say thank you--All right, watch this space on Monday, pass them over." He stood and reached out for the bouquet. She passed it over and he read the card,

"Oh! Yes, I heard that the two of you had had words, I think he must have listened. He's checked out, said he suddenly had a lot of work to do," and presented the flowers to Karen.

Speechless with shock she read the card,

Miss Rockhopper,

No apology required,

Culp Mason.

* * *

The fact that the bath was designed to take two only became fully apparent when they snuggled together into it. John lay on his back with Karen lying back on top of him. He played languorously with her body, whilst kissing the face lying on his shoulder, which she had turned towards him to facilitate access.

"What are your immediate goals?"

"I'm saving for a car. I would really like a family hatch. That's not true. I'd really like a repmobile. But I'll probably have to settle for a compact."

"And in the longer term?"

"Husband, house, kids. Investment in the future."

"Thirty years from now?"

"Rockhopper Hardware. The size of Crossers, but caring like D'Illion."

"Are you good at business?"

"No. Rockhopper, how good a businesswoman are you?--Erm, well; I'm a fair fuck."

He plunged her under the water, she surfaced smiling and

sprayed his face with a mouthful of water.

"Don't lie! If you're ever asked that question the answer is 'I'm a fantastic fuck'." She wiped the water out of her eyes and snuggled back into him.

"Are there other family Smith members?"

"A daughter who is the light of my life, with a most appropriate name: Sunrise. And I think there is a wife somewhere, Sunrise and I get cards erratically, birthday, Christmas."

This decidedly was not what Karen had wanted to hear, but it was her own fault, she had asked.

"Oh. I thought that position might be vacant."

"She left to go to the market, September 1 1997, the day after Princess Diana died, and never came back. A while later we got a letter from Australia, with a photograph. She was holding a paper so we could see the headline about Diana's funeral, about all those flowers, she just said sorry but she had to go. When a card arrives we know she's still alive, but we've never seen her since. I miss her, but Sunrise misses her dreadfully." John stroked her hair and kissed her forehead. "So there's nobody in that docket, but it's not vacant either. Has that changed things?"

"No. A wife at home. That might have changed something. But one away on the loose. Not divorced because she might return someday. With her head sorted out. That's okay."

"She's got through a series of lovers since she left. She telephoned me and asked for my consent. I don't think for one-second that the outcome depended on my permission, but it was really nice to know that even if we never meet again, I matter enough at least to be consulted. I said 'Yes' of course, no other answer would have been reasonable, but that means that I consider myself free to love you, emotionally and physically, but I'm not free to marry you."

"I think that's fair. Also I have a good idea how you and Sunrise feel. My Mum died when I was six." They broke off the conversation for a few minutes to strengthen the pair bond with kisses.

"You know when you said you'd slept with Len for years, was it just a shock tactic or did you mean in the same bed?"

"In the same bed. Mum died and I had to cope. The night of

wiggled it at Karen on the rare occasions when the youngster's ardour failed her. John, apparently, was also aroused by the idea of Karen waiting to be enjoyed, whilst draped only in a towel specifically placed to allow free access to her bottom and breasts. He sensuously washed the beautiful globes, Karen imagined she could see them standing out even further, firmer, as her nipples erected, once more, under his caresses.

"And your dad?"

"I tried to give my dad my cherry when Len left. I was fourteen. And again when I was coming up to sixteen. But he wouldn't have it. He wouldn't even pet me. Have a wank off me. Because he wouldn't stop at once."

"No, it never stops at once."

"You and Sunrise? The control slip occasionally?"

"Yes, I'm not as strong as your dad. Weak, took advantage of a lost daughter."

"I know she'll still love you. Does she still like you? Give herself to you willingly?"

"That's not the poin-'

"Does she?"

"Yes. Sometimes we just hold each other, sometimes we make love and sometimes it's --"

"So you solved the problem differently. Not strong, or weak. Different."

"I wish I could see it that way."

"We all do what we have to do. Most of us do what doesn't hurt others. Even if it does hurt ourselves. I have a friend called Lisa. Devout Catholic. Loves being gang banged. Takes the boys on in half dozens. And not just once each either."

Between her cheeks John's penis bounced its appreciation of her story. The idea of a girl encouraging her friends to take turns fucking her, again and again, was one he found exciting. She snuggled against it, enjoying, savouring the anticipation.

"Then she prays for forgiveness. I don't agree that she needs to be forgiven. But she does it anyway. She's in a stable relationship now. I don't know if she's faithful. Or if she's allowed to be naughty sometimes. She's very happy, so's he."

More gentle smooching and lazy kisses followed, then John

asked about her name.

"Why specifically Rockhopper? Is there a story behind it, or do you just like penguins or what?"

"I looked like one. When I was very little. I had short legs and was very stiff. I waddled about on my heels. Jumped up and down off kerbs, two footed. And my cousin said I was his darling little Rockhopper."

"Didn't you mind having your name messed with?"

"My cousin was my favourite person in the whole world. After my family. He could do no wrong. I looked them up in a bird book. And I liked what I saw. They looked funny. With their crests stuck out like bunches and I liked that."

"So you did your hair in bunches?"

"Yes. With pale ribbons with long tails. I pulled the sleeves of my jumper in. And I waddled about with my arms down inside. And my hands stuck out sideways. And he called me Rockhopper from then on." The sudden desire to cry was successfully repulsed with a strongly clenched jaw and went apparently unnoticed by her companion.

"Did you really have short legs as a kid?"

"Yes." She lazily stretched one out; it reached half way to the ceiling. "Hard to believe now. But I did. I've got photographs to prove it." The incidental invitation to extend his caresses was accepted and shortly afterwards, the penguin, with the incredibly long legs, was encouraging her companion to do what his penis had been urging for some time, to mate with her, yet again.

* * *

The following Monday while Karen's fingers were flying over her keyboard, hands rested on her shoulders, she turned her head and looked straight into little Sandra's eyes.

"Thank you," said the blonde fork-lift driver. "I've been to several of those weekends, but never managed to get into a meeting before. Now I know how it's done, I'll never be left out again."

"You grabbed the chance with both hands. Chaired the meeting from the floor. And your spelling's fine."

She was kissed full on the mouth,

“Thanks again. Bye.”

* * *

“How was your day?” asked Pealle her eyes, shining with delight. The other two could both see she was bursting with news, savouring it, allowing them first bite.

“Fine. Both Sandra and Doris came to see me. About crashing the Management Meeting. Worth it all round.”

“My bosses are chasing their tails agonising over changing the name; I mean it did nothing for Calder Hall/Windscale/Sellafield’s problems, so how is it going to help ours? I can see by your eyes, that yours was eventful.”

“Massive, no broadside, the site manager toured the site, there were two visits from Head Office, the second of which was unannounced and proper toilet paper in clean sweet-smelling toilets.”

“Are we talking to a trainee sparks crackling with happiness then?”

“You are. I can’t get over the Head Office visits, the first one was to tell us some company news but the second, nobody knew he was there. He arrived right on the hooter, but when the Site Manager saw him, he shot across to escort him, greased ferret job and was shooed away, so it was somebody really important. Little guy, thin, grey moustache, he looked really ill. He spoke to Charlie, so no doubt I’ll be told tomorrow. Small beginnings, but --”

Karen held up her hands with her fingers crossed and did some pirouettes.

“Just an acorn. From which a forest giant may grow. Hopefully one day?”

The blonde grinned broadly, nodding.

The Severed Head
Part Nine

The small ex-navy frigate limped into dry dock. Her engines would have eagerly thrust her more forcibly, but her decrepit hull would have been weakened still further. She had had several lives already; smuggler, gunrunner and pirate were only three of the later ones. She was about to return to smuggling, but people this time. She needed a refit, the kind of refit she wouldn't get several thousand miles away, at Swan Hunter.

Whilst tucked away out of the main stream of nautical business, her cabins and holds were stripped out and open-plan, horizontal shelves replaced them.

Eager workers swarmed all over her, around the clock. The ageing and now slightly buckled plates of her deck and hull had enough of their missing rivets replaced, using any fixings handy, to staunch the worst of the leaks, whilst oakum and other rammed fibres stemmed the most enthusiastic of the rest. A coat of paint conferred upon her the new official title of ferry, whilst her revised interior provided packing space for many more cargo than was officially claimed.

Chapter 4

Consequences: Summer 2001

Karen

The success, on so many fronts, of her sortie into temporary 'company call-girl' status prompted Karen to stop dithering and try her luck at reforming the structure of the warehouse, despite the universally cool reception from the chosen few she had consulted about it.

Nominally; all manufacturer's 15mm pipe fittings should fit all manufacturer's 15mm pipe and any half inch Imperial pipe encountered whilst renovating old buildings. The reality was slightly different. But, the differences became quite dramatic when you drifted away from copper, or up the sizes, until rather than expecting one manufacturer's fittings to be suitable for another's pipe, eventually you reached combinations that Karen could guarantee wouldn't fit.

A typical example was when Foreman Paul had called her over to examine a failed joint.

"It's just not good enough! I bought those in good faith." The customer was irate beyond any level of justice.

Karen examined the joint. The Carruthers' metric curve and Mainwaring's Imperial pipe section, neither of which were vinyl, had been vinyl welded together and consequently sprung a bad leak.

"But not here. You didn't buy them here Sir."

"Of course I did!"

"This little crown motif on the pipe. Means it's Imperial, two inch. It won't go into the curve. That's metric, 50mm. Somebody had to pare it down. To get it in." She pointed to the tell-tale flat crescent, peeping out from the join. "See. There's one trace there."

"Well I shouldn't have been sold it."

"I agree. But we don't stock Mainwaring's Imperial range. For that very reason." She waved at the disaster. "You didn't buy it here. But we can sell you the correct pieces. Pieces that will fit, if you want. And the correct glue."

A few minutes later the still disgruntled, but now accepting-his-fate customer sloped off to pay for his correct pieces.

"Thanks Karen, I was close to telling the lying little git to piss off!"

"I do it inside my head!"

But lying customers, and genuine mistakes, notwithstanding, it all made nonsense of having all the pipes here and all the connectors there, with all the tees somewhere else in their own sets of racks, when Blooggs' Bends and Carruthers' Curves were not interchangeable, yet stored in dockets side by side.

"Paul. The way we've got the warehouse set up is counter productive. Can I draw up a plan for you? For a rethink. Would you look at it?"

"Is it going to cost me another grand?"

"No. And the last one didn't cost you that much."

"With your overtime it was slightly more, I didn't mention it before because I got a good deal. How much is this one going to cost me?"

Karen had to release the grin, even though she'd worked hard and quickly, and not clocked in some of the over-time due, the final bill had been well over the thousand and Paul hadn't complained.

"Okay, I plead guilty. But can I do it? At the minute we're working inefficiently."

"I'm agreeing to look at it, nothing else."

That night, on her way home, the young warehouseman bought a 200-sheet notepad, B grade drawing pencils and draughtsman's eraser, and shut herself away after dinner, seriously to set about her plans for reform.

* * *

A few days later Karen saw Bullethead again, this time the centre of a truly vicious attack. She was in an accessories concessionaire choosing a scarf and scarf ring to go with her cocktail dress, when Bullethead's voice cut through her thoughts, but high pitched, wailing with hatred,

"It's black. How dare you give me black? You worthless, spineless boy. It's black."

Karen peeped around the display. A small grey woman in a wheelchair was holding a pink scarf by the designer tag, flicking it away from her as if she wanted to lose it, but still gripping it tightly,

"I want pink." It was Bullethead that was being flicked at.

"It is pink Mother, that's just the washing--"

"It's black, worthless, spineless boy. I want pink. Pink d'y'hear? Pink!" The flicking got more and more agitated. "Worthless, spineless, just like your father. I want pink. Pink!" The scarf slid untended to the floor, while the old woman propelled herself in ungainly jerks out of the shop.

"I'm sorry Sir, but--" the young Saturday girl, verbal salve at the ready and anxious to please, had got it completely wrong. The apology unleashed a tirade of vicious abuse at her, her hair, her makeup, her manners and deportment, somewhere in the tirade Bullethead produced a £20 note slammed it on the floor, scourged the assistant over her clean, but slightly worn shoes, and shortly after stormed out of the shop, scooping the scarf up from where the woman had finally dropped it.

"Janice, back shop!" The openly weeping girl vanished behind a curtain, into the Manager's inner sanctum. Karen collared another assistant,

"Take me through. To the Manager. Take me now." The assistant drew the curtain back,

"--are my best shoes, I haven't got any others."

"Mr. Seekitt, a customer wants to see you." With Janice evicted and the Manager in Customer Relations Mode, Karen assertively persuaded him that his staff had acted honourably, beyond the call of duty.

"-- She did brilliantly, Mr. Seekitt. Polite. Exonerating. She's obviously a caring and loyal member of staff. But she might need a break and a cup of tea after her ordeal. I know I would."

When she regaled the family with an account of the incident that night, she added her conclusion,

"Now we know why he is as he is."

Pealle came up with an alternative explanation.

"You're most likely correct, but don't forget the parable of the scorpion that was given a ride by a horse swimming across a river, on condition he didn't sting the horse. Half way across he stung the horse, thus ensuring they both drowned."

"When asked 'why?' By the dying horse. He answered, 'Because I'm a scorpion.' There's always that. I suppose. He knows he's superior. White collar is right. Blue is servant."

"I wonder how he viewed that notorious Protect and Survive document?" The blonde paused as she passed her daughter some wine. "You know the one that advised Joe Public, that in the even of nuclear attack, they should prop their internal doors against a wall and hide under them until it's safe to come out."

"He probably wrote it. Considered that it would provide for the survival of enough proles. Enough to serve his needs after."

"I didn't realise I'd brought you up to be quite as cynical as all that."

"My darling daughter's not cynical at all, she's a force field. The way in is to ease gently, ask permission, if you hack your way in, you might get there, but you'll live to regret it."

It was strange re-appraising her attitudes in bed that night. Did she feel more benign towards Bullethead now she possibly knew why he was as he was? Or was it just that 'come the revolution', she wouldn't be absolutely sure which of them to shoot first?

"Karen Robinson. Behave!" She admonished herself, but giggled nevertheless. "I only hope when it's my turn. There's a guardian angel standing by. Looking out for me."

* * *

A few times a month she went home with Snowy for a friendly frolic whilst sprawled over a chair, with the older man usually succeeding in getting her off. Once, when she offered to stay overnight, to let him have a longer session at her, he refused, but the following day booked her for that Saturday night. Karen enjoyed being pampered on the Saturday, and pampering him on the Sunday, but he never asked again and she didn't offer. She was aware of an undercurrent of unease the whole time. The hairs on the back of her neck were rarely completely down. Despite the ex-wife staying an ex, she was still the most likely reason for Snowy being unable to relax as he should and enjoy his guest, who was trying hard to be eagerly acquiescing, even compliant.

The Severed Head
Part Ten

The ferry in her brave new livery entered her home harbour on the falling tide, intentionally just as darkness was setting in. She would be unable to clear the harbour mouth again for four hours. Her captain was eager to have her away before dawn, well before it was light enough for some busybody to notice her Plimsoll Line and start asking stupid questions. Although the tides meant she had a comfortable ten hours to load and leave before the falling water trapped her again, scurrying to fulfil the other requirements ensured that they managed it in just six.

Dockside, the passengers, boarding by the weak light from a few sad bulbs, were checked desultorily by a bored official swatting flies and, when that became too energetic, scratching himself. The cargo meanwhile swarmed up netting lowered from the seaward side. Most of the passengers had paid for their short legal trip with a few dollars, many of the cargo for their longer, illegal one, a much higher price and occasionally not in currency.

Among the many human interest stories crammed together, a honeymoon couple finding themselves pressed in on one side by a group of brigands, who made no attempt to hide their occupation, and on the other by a scrum of drunken salesmen, consoled themselves that it was only for a few hours. Elsewhere in the crush, shrouded in a dark cloak, the fugitive from justice kept her head down, physically and metaphorically.

As the ferry slipped her moorings, a pretty but penniless young girl, followed four seamen up onto a tarpaulin-covered bale of deck cargo, to pay the next of many instalments on her ticket out. The passengers had expressed surprise when they were herded together into a single lounge. They would have been astonished to see the cargo lying on their shelves, shushing distressed youngsters, fearful of discovery.

Hot, weary and tightly packed together, they all stoically settled down to make the best of it.

The old, but freshly serviced engines, built the revs up steadily. Outside the harbour, the old lady turned and punched her way through a quartering sea, as the gale built behind her, hurrying her southwards.

Seasickness now began to add to the misery aboard.

Like a disdainful dowager cruising her manor, the ship brushed aside a large piece of flotsam. An oversize bolt head, of a design never intended to be used in a ships hull, and standing proud, caught the log and spun it around, the tiny sea creatures securing themselves to their new floating homes took no notice. Despite carrying high tensile steel markings the bolt snapped like a carrot under the force of the impact, revealing its true, base-metal identity.

The hull plates it had been anchoring together sprang apart.

After a moment's pause, the increased strain upon them caused the bolts either side to fail.

The next two failed instantly.

An L shaped tear opened up in the hull, like a zip in a hurry.

The still powerful engines drove their craft on, in a shallow dive, like a scoop thrust into flour.

With no bulkheads to prevent it, she flooded in seconds.

She was still doing a respectable forward speed as the waters closed over her, in an orgy of slaughter.

There were five survivors, the four seamen and the girl at the centre of their attentions. The unsecured deck cargo had turned out to be buoyant.

The official fatalities ran several hundred short of the true figure.

A British broadsheet gave the incident three inches on page five. Of the many details given about the loss, it managed to get the day the tragedy occurred correct.

The tabloids ignored it. It had happened in a hot part of the world after all; and no dogs or horses had been hurt.

Karen

The humorous Christmas card with Santa sweating over changing his sleigh runners to wheels, from 'John and Sunrise', was a nice surprise and arrived at work, complete with address, in good time to return the compliment. Instead of signing it, Karen drew a penguin, with huge crests over its eyes. She thought for a while before including her home address, but John had given her his in his card, so --

The other nice surprise was her Christmas bonus, which turned out to include an upgrading. A few months later she got another, only Paul now earned more than she did, among the warehouse staff.

* * *

The letter arrived a month before her birthday.

Dear Rockhopper,

-- So, once I'm over the jet lag, and able to do business again without being shafted in my sleep, I'll be flying up to Novochester on the Friday, for a meeting.

If you are feeling up for a cuddle, I would be more than happy to enjoy your company in the Wilkinson for another weekend --

Eagerly she wrote back,

Dear John,

-- I'll pack my School Uniform --

The warehouse had emptied promptly, as usual on Fridays, and Karen settled down to get on top of her paperwork. Presently she was able to tidy her little desk, as the printer worked through the last of the hard copies; she criss-crossed her papers, scooped them up, and headed for administration. As she passed it, the warehouse telephone rang. It was John and it was less than an hour before she was due to meet him at the Wilkinson.

“What’s the matter? Can’t you make it?” She kept her voice as calm as possible.

“Do I detect a slight feeling of disappointment?”

“Not slight and I hope I’m wrong.” Her weekend would be comprehensively ruined if he couldn’t get.

“There is no problem with us Rockhopper and if there had been, believe me, I would have sorted it. You have no idea how much I have been looking forward to this weekend. Can you get any more girls? I have a couple of colleagues who will be spending a lonely two days otherwise.”

“The works shuts promptly on Friday. There’s nobody here. I’m only here because I’m meeting you.”

“Okay I’ll not say anything to them, you don’t miss what you didn’t know you could have had, had you planned it better--Unless --”

“Say it John. We know each other better than that.”

“I was thinking of your friend Lisa, depends how friendly you are feeling--It would give you the chance to be in total control.”

“My decision?”

“Is final.”

“Colleagues is a bit vague.”

“They are extended family, younger cousins, very good friends, Sunrise likes them.”

That was probably the highest accolade he could bestow.

“Let me think about it. Don’t say anything. I’ll see you at six. Goodbye.”

“Bye Rockhopper.”

She collected up her work and walked through to administration, laid it neatly in the sections most useful to the office staff on Monday morning and then retired to the wash-room. She checked every cubicle before she doused her eyes, with cold water and spoke to the girl in the mirror.

“Well?”

You’ve already decided.

"I still want your opinion."

We went through all this at school. What if their plane crashes on the way home? I know. I know all the emotional responses. Unlikely. Desolate loss. Tragic for their families. But what if? You've been there. Do you want all that grief again?

"No!" said the girl in the wash-room and her reflection nodded to her, turned away, and left through the door in her own universe.

"Good evening Miss and welcome to The Wilkinson, do you have a reservation?"

"It's probably under Greengold Tree Ferns."

"Ah yes and you would be, Miss?"

"Rockhopper."

"Yes, Miss Rockhopper, we have the two suites adjoining option still available if you want it, are you able to confirm, or do you want to wait for Mr. Kurchach?"

It wasn't right, but it was a closer approximation to John's real name than Karen could have made herself.

"Two suites adjoining will be fine." The board was turned to her and Karen signed L. Rockhopper in the space indicated. "Would you have my bags taken up? I'll wait here for my boss."

"Certainly Miss Rockhopper." Karen first went through the dining room into the kitchen. The chef grabbed her from behind and swung his sister around.

"Are you being naughty again?"

"Could be. Happy certainly. I called in to see you. And ask for one of my special salads."

"That would be fat and gristle, only the yellow ends of scallions and finely chopped, no roots or fruit and smothered in oil."

"And Frisbee-ed straight back to you!"

"How's Dad?"

"Like a young swain on his honeymoon. The only problem is my presence. I need to move out. Can't afford it."

"I always thought you would--you know--have consoled him, did you ever? I wouldn't be mad at you for it."

"He turned me down. More than once."

Len nodded, unsurprised,

"And one Rockhopper special?"

"Yes, please. I'll try to catch you. Before I leave on Sunday."

"There's rod caught wild salmon on their way down from the Tweed overnight, I've been asked to do a sculpture. I'll serve you a Salmon Salad personally tomorrow, if you want?"

"There might be four of us."

"Okay."

"I'll order Rockhopper Salmon. How's Lisa?

"Blooming."

"Are you saying what I think you're saying?"

"I'm saying nothing yet, but we have suspicions, watch this space."

He was glowing in hope, anticipation. Karen kissed him and crossed her fingers, while pirouetting away from him.

The broad grin was still in place and lights dancing in her eyes, when she returned to the desk. She glanced quickly at the list. John's party had not yet arrived. She selected one of the hotel's brag sheets and sat down to peruse it in a seat commanding the entrance. They hadn't had time on her first visit to sample many of the delights on offer; she hoped that she could squeeze some in this time. She particularly wanted to try--

John was walking in through the front door.

Karen stood up.

Stepped towards him.

He saw her and dropped his hand luggage.

She was running.

He caught her and swung her around.

The kiss was total.

He set her down and turned her to his two companions, following him through the door, who were standing open mouthed at the display in front of them.

"Tom, Dick, this is-'

"Lisa," interrupted Karen, closed the gap between them and kissed each of the younger men a firm moist smooch on the mouth. Then she cuddled back into John's side. "The two suites adjoining option was still available. I confirmed it. Shall we go up?"

“Total control then?”

“It’s an option! Yes, of course.” The three businessmen signed in and together the quartet went up to their rooms.

Karen went straight over to the communicating door, opened her side and knocked on the other. After a moment it was opened and John followed her through to join his friends.

“Lisa and I are going to get ready for dinner; it’s informal, shirt and slacks, be ready to go down at six forty-five for seven. Between dinner and bed it’s party time.” He turned and drew Karen through into their own suite, securing the door behind him. He gathered her up and kissed her, a tender lover’s kiss.

“Now then Rockhopper, peel that kit off and get in the shower; I’ve got a load of surplus stock waiting to be unloaded into you and I want to hear you squeal and feel you fold up while I do it. So get nude, get in there, get your bum pouted and those fingers working, and get ready to come on me. Lisa can enjoy the boys later, I want my Rockhopper now!”

“Make me.” She whispered, as the discarded top revealed the bare breasts.

“Make me.” She was leaning forward, playing the simple girl, smiling a vacant smile. She stepped out of her shoes and her jeans followed.

“Make me.” She slipped her hands down her knickers to her clitty, caressing, feeling, preparing.

“Make me.” She was nearly there, just another few caresses. John, now naked, turned the shower on and bundled her, knickers, hold-ups and all, into it. He pulled the soaked briefs down, they formed a twisted rope hobble half way down her thighs. Karen began to squeal, she was bent over and snuggled up to. She felt him searching for entry and wriggled into place, lining herself up to receive him. She felt herself entered, filled, fucked and she collapsed squealing her joy.

She came to sitting on his lap on the floor of the shower having her fanny delicately, sensuously washed, with a large natural sponge. She pulled his head down to kiss, as the softly probing fibres sent little after-shock orgasms through her, with his tender ministrations.

After dinner, they all met up in John and Karen's suite.

"Would you like to play what if?"

"How do we play that?"

"Someone asks what if? Someone else answers. I make some decisions. Perhaps give some instructions. Then we ask what if again."

"Okay R-Lisa, ask me what if?"

Karen gathered her men close around her,

"If you could. Were allowed to. What is the very first thing you would like to do to me?"

"Unbutton your blouse."

"That sounds nice. Three buttons, one each."

Tom and Dick watched amazed as John undid the top button of Karen's blouse. She turned and offered her chest to Dick, beckoning him even closer. He edged forward, reached out nervously and clumsily slipped the second one. Tom followed, slightly more controlled.

"What if I wanted my blouse out of my skirt? I do. Tom would you do the honours?" Karen presented him with a hip and rotated slowly facilitating the withdrawal of the silk from her skirt. There were still two buttons fastened, but her bra and cleavage were now in clear view. "Dick what if?"

"I don't know."

"Okay how about--What if I touched your skin under your blouse?--Say it."

"What if I wanted to touch you under your blouse?" Karen raised her arms and turned sideways onto him.

"Feel my skin. The bare bit. Tickle my belly button." Dick reached out as if she were nettles. Karen had to take his hands and guide him into her, to feel and caress. "Tom?"

"What if I wanted to lick your skin?"

"Anywhere on the bare bit. Don't suck. Don't leave hickeys." She guided his face in to her belly button and giggled as he probed her rapidly with his tongue. "What if I wanted to feel bare tummy? I do. All boys take shirts off." As the shirts were removed Karen sensuously caressed tummies and belly buttons. She was careful not to go above a high waistline, that was being saved for later. Tom was doing okay now, but Dick still needed encouragement to match his actions to his level of arousal.

"What if I wanted a skirt off?" John, grinning at her.

"I would need all trousers off."

John had popped his waistband as she finished talking,

"You heard the lady, trousers off boys," he said, already stepping out of his.

"Would you do the honours please Dick?--please--it's what I want--I'm enjoying our game."

Encouraged by her comments Dick found the fastenings and the skirt loosened and slipped, she supported herself on his shoulders as he held it still for her to step out of it. The thin silk blouse came almost exactly to the knickers legs. There was a zone, several centimetres wide, of bare thigh above the tops of the stockings. What could be seen of the suspender belt suggested erotic titillation. All three men were sporting huge bulges in their boxers.

"Tom?"

"What if I wanted a hug?"

"Good hugs win kisses."

"What's a good hug?" Tom was anxious for his kisses.

"Firm. All enveloping. Not too tight, just nice. It's the contact that counts. All the way from scalp to toes." As each of her men snuggled up to hug her, Karen pointedly guided him in, looking down to check, matching her thighs and mound to his erection.

"Oh what if--what if I couldn't wait any longer?"

Karen smiled deeply into her 'boss for the weekend's' eyes.

"I'm shy. You would have to cuddle up close. Hide me from prying eyes. Blouse for your shorts. Bra for Tom's. Knickers for Dick's." She turned from him and cuddled the other two to her, kissing them alternately as John shed his briefs, released her blouse and cupped her semi-concealed breasts from behind. She gently eased the boxers in front of her downwards, first one pair a bit, then the other, then the first a bit more --

"Take something off her, gently, don't force it, she'll wriggle to help you, as soon as she realises what you're at." Slowly and gracefully the clothes came off. Karen cuddled her boys back into her as soon as she could. She eased John's access to her, to couple her doggy style, and consequently began gently bumping about.

"Tom, diddle my clitty. Make me spend--Oh Dick kiss my titties --Oh--Oh' Karen's arms unlocked from around her boy's necks as the climax stormed through her, they had to grab quickly, she was already falling.

"Hold her, keep feeling her, help me get her to the bed, don't stop frigging her and snuffling her. Gently--Carry, don't drag--Lay her down sideways, keep feeling her--While I--Uh--Uh!

John slowed, stopped and uncoupled from his girl. Karen flopped over onto her back convulsing in hard rhythmic jerks, squealing and whimpering.

"Right, now Tom, get up her, it's what she wants, this was all her idea--Give her a good time."

Tom settled gratefully to enjoy his treat.

"Ready Dick, he won't last long--The hole is further under than you might think, if you can't find it, try further under."

"She's squealing, is she okay?"

"She's fine. Trust me, she's fine--Gently at first. Once you're in just do what comes naturally. Right he's gone, he'll finish in a moment--climb on now--You're pleasuring her, it's what she wants, don't worry about hurting her, you won't. That's right--Lick her, all over her mouth as you're coming--That's right."

* * *

"You've been most polite Dick. Consumed with curiosity. Politely hiding it. I am John's mistress in the Wilkinson. We are very good friends who fuck. He asked me to get more girls to partner you. I couldn't get any. He has been very kind. Given me the option of sharing myself among you. If you would like a weekend playing pass the parcel. I don't mind being the parcel. Eager to be it."

"You are a nice girl, so why are you doing this?"

"Doing what?"

"Spending a weekend fucking strangers, doing what nice girls don't."

"Is Dick your real name?"

"No. It's a-'

"Lisa isn't mine. This weekend I have let the wild child out to play. I'm going to let her be really, disgustingly naughty. Do absolutely anything she wants. On Monday morning I'm going to lock her up again. You will go home to your family and pretend that nothing happened. I will do the same."

Dick went to speak.

"No. No comment. I do not want to know. I will do the same. But, I will relive the nice bits of being wildly naughty. For months and months inside my head. This is a time out Dick. You are having a good time with Lisa. Relax and enjoy it. Besides which, my first love conferred freedom upon me. The freedom to do this. And still be a nice girl."

"Did you really enjoy it, the three of us, taking turns with you? Again and again?"

"Did you enjoy it?"

"Well--"

"Did you?"

"Boys always enjoy it, we're hard wired to enjoy it!"

"I enjoyed it too. Times three. It was wonderful."

"Oh--It's just that you were--making noises."

Karen pulled a Styx face,

"Thrashing about? Yelling?"

"Yes."

"Sorry. Sometimes I lose it. Let go completely. When I'm having a lot of fun. Sorry."

"I thought we were hurting you."

Karen pulled his face in and kissed him tenderly.

"No man. You weren't hurting me one bit. You were wonderful."

"Tonight it's pretty formal. Black tie. And we are having fish 'n chips."

"Fish 'n chips? But out of The Times I assume?"

"Her fish 'n chips, Tom, bears as much resemblance to what's in your mind, as her meal last night bore to a hamburger with leaves."

"Not The Times then?"

"You never know."

Even in her shortest heels Karen would be over-topping her man, she surveyed the options regretfully in the mirror.

"Put the stilts on, I honestly don't mind, you'll feel better and look stunning."

She smiled at her about to be comprehensively over-topped lover,

"Thank you."

"You are one of the few girls who can make me feel small, it's strange, different and unusual and really no problem." In her heels Karen over-topped the others too.

Len strode out from the kitchen, resplendent in his full regalia. Behind him, forming a column several metres long, came assorted chefs, waiters and waitresses, pushing trolleys bearing large serving dishes, some with glass lids. The column came to a halt beside their table. Len glanced at his sister's unobtrusively pointing finger and addressed Tom directly, his voice carrying across the dining room,

"Your Fish 'n Chips, Sir."

The waitress behind Len stepped forward and placed a covered silver salver in front of Tom. With a flourish Len removed the cover. Dead centre of the platter was a huge chippy wrap. Tom had his Times after all. He put his head back and roared with laughter, instantly joined by his companions, the hotel staff and several nearby guests. He reached out to open his prize and nearly dropped it, it was heavy and cold. As he unwrapped it, the platter was removed and replaced by an ice bucket; he slid the pre-cooled bottle of Champagne into it, as the waitress relieved him of The Times.

"Compliments of the kitchen staff, Sir."

"Thank you. That's lovely." The largest trolley was rolled forward and opened, the lid slid away out of sight to reveal Len's sculpture, a fresh run salmon taking a truly enormous Silver Wilkinson in a furious head and tail lunge. The wild white water was ice and salad over a river bed of potatoes. John immediately applauded the creation; his reaction was taken up and spread through the crowded room with people craning to see. Len included his staff with a wave of his arm, then bowed briefly to the room,

"Thank you." He turned his attention back to the table. "I

know that Mademoiselle is having the salmon, anyone else?"

"Oh yes," replied John. "I think it's salmon for four."

"Very good, Sir." Their plates, pre-loaded with Rockhopper salad arrangements were placed in front of them and Len added a man-sized salmon steak to each plate.

Dick leaned forward and examined the salmon fly,

"Appropriate choice of lure," he murmured.

"Yes, Sir. And it adds a single flash of colour to an otherwise subtle, subdued scheme."

"Yes, a Silver Wilkinson is just about as gaudy as salmon flies get and that's saying a bunch," added Tom.

"It's almost a shame," said Dick as the sculpture was vandalised,

"Nothing is for ever," replied Len. "Food is just the same, only more so. Bon appétit."

"Thank you."

The column progressed to the next table and subsequently around the dining room. By the time it reached the kitchen doors again, there were few servings left to be had, despite backup from additional fish, secreted inside the trolley. Dick laid down his irons and surveyed the room,

"You know, I've just remembered, I heard of The Wilkinson last year at that conference in Sydney. No restaurant could possibly have lived up to **that** hype."

"And now?"

"No hype could possibly live up to thi-' The rest was lost as the table was enveloped in giggles.

* * *

Foreman Paul was sad; he drew Karen away to one side for the unpleasant task ahead.

"Your ideas are to be put to the lads, but I have been asked to warn you, on the quiet, that they are a non-starter. The general feeling upstairs is that they will be seen as cost cutting in preparation for job losses."

"No. Just--"

"That's how they will be seen. There is nothing fundamentally wrong with the ideas, they are just not right for today."

"Don't sweeten the pill Paul. I can take sour medicine when required."

"But --"

She turned away, blocking out the further consoling words her foreman was trying to say.

That night, when she had squashed the disappointment down to a bearable level, Karen set about writing a detailed report covering all work related matters that bugged her. As with the stinkhorn, however, she found that her ire took over and what had been intended to be a simple paragraphed essay, when she included examples and references and dealt with counter arguments, the essay rapidly grew to a small book divided into chapters. Rather than condense on the fly and possibly unintentionally discard Baby Bunting too, she continued her appraisal, intending to précis and resubmit later.

Pealle

"What's she doing?" asked Dennis. "Closeted away in her room all hours."

"Writing a report about increasing the efficiency of her workplace. She was asked for a combination where the pipe was too big, the hole too small and the glue suitable for neither again today."

"Again! That's the second time this month!"

"Yeah, but because it's on paper, every time she does a rewrite --" Pealle simply stopped talking. After a few moments her man picked up the telephone.

"Hi Reg, it's Dennis. How are you? --" The opening pleasantries didn't take long, then he settled to business. "With our conversation a while back, I know all about the trust fund while Karen was at school. What if she decided to go to university as a mature student?--What if she was studying at home, or doing work that would enhance her chances of getting a university place, later?--A computer--Really--You're kidding me--I'll call in to see you about it, thanks Reg, I need a long think about this." He put the telephone down and regarded his love steadily. "They've just had an in-depth trustee appraisal. Several other clients have raised the same points, that the trusts were set up at a time when you had to buy apprenticeships, computers were clerks in finance houses who did arithmetic, travel was on horseback and such. They've had a test case and it's been ruled that the wording, in essence the spirit of the trusts, clearly intend modern equivalents to be included. There's a letter coming out to all clients, as far as education is concerned the world is being offered. And it includes us as her parents."

"You're telling me that she can have a computer?"

"Yes and also her car, as the modern equivalent of a pony and trap. The trustees are interpreting that as a family hatch, but, and get ready for this, so can you, as her mum. The only stipulation is that the expenditure is not to exceed the income from the trust in any one year, with any adjustment for inflation. In our case that is a very easy stipulation to obey.--Well say something darling--

Okay I'll get you a drink, you look as if you need it."

Sometime later:

"I'd like to get her the computer as a surprise present, but I suppose I can't, it's one of those things where you need to choose it yourself."

"If it's any help, I know which one she wants, a real elegant class act, but it's not cheap. It is a PC but not an IBM compatible. In its day it trampled all over anything else in its price band, although you wouldn't think so to read the specification."

"Go on, you're talking Macintosh."

"I'm afraid so, yes. And I know where there are some, the particular model she loves, yesterday's cutting edge technology, mislaid stock, recently rediscovered. They have all the other necessary hardware too, printers and the like."

"And you too?"

"Yes, please. As the firm is a mail order Mac specialist they have all the software that she would need available. MS Office, it has a really tricky and temperamental word processor, but the World uses it, Apple's own stuff which is more friendly, but not as featured, Anti-Nasty protection, there's drawing packages as well, but they are robbery with extreme prejudice. One telephone call would do it."

"Make a list."

* * *

"We've dumped a load of stuff in your room, can you sort through it; decide what you want to keep and sling the rest? I don't want to come the heavy father, but can you do it tonight?"

"What stuff?"

"Some end of line bargains we managed to acquire as a deal, Darling Daughter. They might help you with work; I've got some too."

The end-of-workday-tired footsteps up the stairs. Silence. Odd steps, some scrapes, gentle thuds, then Richard J. Gatling himself, gunning down the stairs.

"In order: One, thank you. Two, there's nothing to sling. Three, how come? And four, if this isn't for real. Tough. They're not going back."

Karen

The downturn in the economy was really biting.

The first casualties had been the IT mushrooms with no substance. The latest however, was in her own field, industrial and domestic fluid processing, and in her own back yard. Located a mere half–mile down the road from D'Illion, Crossers was rumoured to be in big trouble. In retrospect Karen guessed there would be several contributory factors, but thought she knew at least one reason why. They had expanded too fast and the balloon was going to pop at the thin spot, cash flow. It was nearly always cash flow. Never mind. The local mopper-up of hopeless causes, with its impressive track record of save and bring back to prosperity, would do the necessary. If, but more likely when, it became necessary.

Then Crossers rejected the Monta deal. Some folks just have to commit suicide.

She was very happy that she didn't work for Crossers and Bullethead specifically.

Sometimes circumstances change with astonishing speed.

Part Three:
Crossers' Hardware
Chapter 1
Monta: January 2002
Karen

There was a flash of red to her left, Karen smiled inwardly. Stacey was on patrol, certain warehousemen would not be concentrating on the job in hand.

"Next please."

A middle-aged man in a Tweed jacket approached her,

"Can I talk to someone qualified in pipe work?"

"You're doing it."

"Can I talk to one of the lads?"

"Certainly." Karen turned to leave but was held still by Foreman Paul, signalling to his own customer, that he would be back in a second. The customer turned, leaning into the group, his eyes were flicking from Tweed jacket to Paul.

"Which do you want, a lad, or to talk about pipe work?" The foreman asked. The face above the jacket coloured slightly and there was a distinct air of 'Well if you must know!' about the reply.

"I want some highly specialist information about plastic pipe work and low cost, high output pumping."

"You'll want our top expert then?"

Tweed jacket lit up,

"That would be ideal."

"Talk to Karen, she's the best they've got," interjected Paul's customer nodding at her.

"She's not just the best we've got, she's the best in the district."

Tweed jacket haughtily turned his attention back to Karen. She felt her arm taken from the other side; Stacey pitched the volume at comfortable hearing for Tweed jacket,

"When you've proved what Paul has just said about you, would you come up to my office? The Big Boss wants to see you, probably needs some specialist advice about plastic pipe work and low cost, high output pumping."

Karen never took her eyes, off her customer, whose complexion was pulsing like a sex crazed cuttlefish.

"Yes, I'll come straight up."

What undiscovered crime isn't any more? Was the only thought in Karen's mind, as she trekked up to Stacey's office. The girl in red met her with a hug,

"I can see from your face that you're worried, don't be, it's nothing bad, not for you that is. Come straight through, he's waiting for you."

"Ah Karen, come and sit down please." Mike D'Illion was indicating easy chairs in the little conference corner, near the window. "It's black coffee, scalding hot, isn't it?"

Oh Telemarks! A manufactured alibi, to evade prosecution for assault causing actual bodily harm, to wit, tissue damage requiring removal of a testicle, two off, has come back to haunt.

"Don't look so worried, it is me that is worried, you're about to be head hunted."

Karen couldn't hold the shock.

"Me. Whatever for?"

"To do a specific job, but I won't get you back. This is just a little family firm Karen, with a not-ambitious boss. I can't afford to pay you what Shirley Monta will be paying you."

"Crossers?" *It had to be.* "But the directors rejected the deal. The news said."

"Yes, but keep it very quiet for now. Officially the deal is rejected. Unofficially it will go through as soon as they've sorted out the details."

"Like the firing squad list being finalised."

"A ruthless evil needs to be ruthlessly cauterised."

"So. If she's firing. How come she's also hiring?"

"I'll let her tell you that. But, I will tell you that it wasn't the directors who rejected the deal, it was the workers. Meanwhile I want you to interview your replacement. The rest of this week and all of next week. I've got twenty applicants. I want a good plumber, who is interested enough in the products we sell, to research them in their own time. I want you to find that special worker among those applicants."

The interview with the boss became a general chat about work, aspirations and her personal objectives. Presently Karen realised she was enjoying herself and it seemed so were the other two, because it was with obvious regret that Mike D'Illion terminated the meeting,

"After lunch go to the car park, there will be a taxi waiting, it will take you to Monta. The very best of luck Karen, we will be sorry to lose you. Your driver is called Joe. He will call you Miss Robinson. And Mrs. Monta specifically asked that you tell no one."

The warehouseman was quite sure that Miss Robinson being driven by Joe was a concept she disliked.

After lunch Karen walked out looking for a black cab, but it was a dark red, top of the range rep-mobile that awaited her. As soon as she appeared at the door looking around, the driver stood up straight and stepped towards her. Almost as if he knew about her reservations, his greeting was warm and friendly, neither smarmy nor subservient,

"Good afternoon Miss Robinson." Joe obviously had no problem about the situation; he opened the passenger door and guided her towards it. From correctly picking out his fare first time from several possibilities, through treating her with respect and courtesy, to delivering her safely to her destination, an expert in his field was taking pride in providing a peerless level of service. Karen promptly did a mental readjustment and proved that she was worthy of receiving it.

"Good afternoon Joe, are you well?"

"Very well thank you Miss." He settled her in and took his place behind the wheel. "And you?"

"Fine thank you. Which taxi company do you work for?"

"Monta Miss."

"Oh. I didn't see a logo."

"On the bonnet Miss, the flying M. Subtle, discreet and elegant, and I can hide it by pressing a button." The figurehead disappeared, plucked down from below. "It was concealed when I picked you up."

"Oh."

The taxi rolled straight in through Monta's car park and on into the shuttle terminus where the little red haired woman that Karen had last seen singing carols, was waiting. The driver was out and had the door open before the warehouseman could move.

"Miss Robinson, Mrs. Thompson."

"Thank you Joe," said the redhead, held out her hand to Karen and added, "Hello. I'm Janie."

"It's Karen. Thank you Joe."

"A pleasure Miss."

Karen was taken through reception where she was specifically introduced to a decorative and smart, middle-aged lady,

"Sonya, this is Miss Robinson, Sonya is Mr. Monta's PA."

"How do you do?"

"Hello. It's Karen."

As the girls shook hands Karen realised she was meeting the nut that holds the wheel on, Monta's equivalent to Stacey. Janie moved Karen on to a central office, quizzing her gently, the whole time. Over to one side a mature woman in Monta coveralls was struggling to negotiate the passage of a bumper through a door, Janie jumped across and held it for her.

"I'll get it Maisie."

"Thank you, Mrs. Thompson."

"How's Keir?"

"Improving thanks, doing really well. They're talking about him coming home at the weekend, might even be Friday."

"Give him our best."

A glowing smile welled up from deep inside and Maisie nodded as she began pounding the lino. Karen was interested to note that the reaction of porters, janitors and other comparatively lowly employees, was exactly the same as that of the cleaner bumpering the floor, she hadn't expected a large corporation to be able to have the family feel of D'Illion, but Monta had it by the tanker-full. It took several more pauses for corridor conversations to get to Janie's office, during which time she swapped smiles with several people, but apart from Sonya was introduced to no-one, which, in view of the friendly exchanges going on right next to her, she thought mildly odd.

Inside Janie's outer office however,

"Emily this is Karen Robinson, Karen, Emily Miller, my PA." The two girls exchanged greetings and Karen was taken through to the inner office where the gentle interrogation continued without a break. By the time another girl joined them, Karen had given Janie, and note taking Emily, a skeleton outline of her lifestyle and hobbies.

"You're a canoeist? Do you know Anna, the Boss's daughter?"

"I've heard of her. Anna Monta? She went to my school."

"She's Anna Teale now."

Karen couldn't speak, her all time canoeing heroine was the daughter of the girl about to head hunt her. There was a knock on the side door and a beautiful face surrounded by thick, dark hair appeared,

"Ah." It said and the whole girl entered. She was tall, nearly as tall as Karen, and busty, and wearing clothes cut to show it. She stepped towards the warehouseman extending her hand. "You must be Karen Robinson."

"Karen this is Mrs. Shirley Monta, our boss-'

Mrs. Shirley! Mike D'Illion saying 'Mrs. Monta' flashed Karen's brain. *There must be some mistake,* she thought. Anna Teale is thirty-ish, this girl's too young to be Anna's mother--and anyway, she was Margaret Stybes, wasn't she?

"-and Anna's stepmother."

Ah, so simple. Not Sister Len, step-mum.

"She's older than I am."

The hand was being held out invitingly, but the vibes were quite clear, Karen guessed Mrs. Monta already knew and was offering the opportunity.

"Mine to be is older than me. But only just. A few months." The answering nod, as the girls shook hands, confirmed it all.

The interrogation continued, Karen found herself warmly filling in the details about her home, her dad and Pealle, Lisa and her brother,

"My friends are providing both my sister-in-law and my step-mum!"

Her interviewers made her feel quite comfortable talking about her dreams and her, as yet, virtual own place complete with cat. Suddenly it all stopped. The other girls looked at each other,

"Board all green?" said Janie.

"Board all green."

"And me." Added the young secretary, looking down at her pad again.

"Karen we want to hire you, but I must be brutally honest, if we do, there will be times when you will put yourself in danger. We'll deal with that later, but you must know it from the start. We intend to head hunt you and we want you to go to work at Crossers."

The young warehouseman needed to conceal her shock at Mrs. Monta's words until she had it under control, so just kept her end up with a throw away remark.

"Crossers, as in empty lorries mysteriously become full ones?" To Karen's surprise the redhead pounced,

"Do they?"

"According to rumour. A friend twice drove an empty lorry to the lorry park. But the following morning. It left full."

"How did he know?"

"You can tell straight away. From the tyres. Then it was obvious when she got in to drive it."

"From the handling of course, there's a big difference between ten tonnes and twenty tonnes."

"She knew before. From the axles 'n that."

The secretary looked up from her notes, speaking directly to her red-headed boss.

"What's really strange is empty to full, so it's apparently not a theft scam. It could even be legitimate; we need to check that the load manifest says the lorry is full. It is when it leaves the next day. Mind, I wouldn't waste the time required to write out the bet."

"Me neither, but it does give clues as to the mechanics of a possible scam."

"We could do with knowing if the docs actually match the load. Or even just what they say."

The tall and busty, dark-haired girl turned back to Karen.

"Karen, how do you feel about taking the job at Crossers?"

"I don't want to leave D'Illion. To work at Crossers. If they're going under Mrs. Monta. And I'm sure they are. I'm out of a job. And no prospect of that changing."

"How about Monta?"

Karen didn't reply, that needed some thought.

"Your contract will be with Monta, not Crossers. It will have to look as if you're with Crossers, otherwise you'll stand out like a beacon, a Monta spy."

Under cover, no introductions totally explained.

"I'm hired five minutes after a failed takeover. Not subsequently fired. Isn't that a beacon?"

"Not when the company records show they've been after you for months."

"What?"

"Which they do, because they have. You've had upgrades in the past year, because Mike D'Illion's been desperately trying to hold onto you."

"Okay. I sign for Monta, What then?"

The redhead took over,

"Without going into details Karen, we want you to get up some noses, sideways! Find faults and publicise them, complain about injustices, drive some reforms through, including the one you failed to get through D'Illion. If something happens which you consider unjust, challenge it, up to and including reasonable force, if you feel threatened."

"Be a trouble-maker?"

"The opposition will see you that way, but we see it more as a trouble-shooter. Find the problems obstructing progress, those inside the works, relationships, morale, traditions that may have been of some use once, but are now merely a nuisance, and loudly proclaim they have to change. What we need to know is who opposes you and how they do it. The methods used. That's the primary target, you've just raised a second one, the lorries." She looked at her boss, who nodded. "Which we actually knew about, but it was useful to discuss it with you as if we didn't. Sorry about that. It will be a scam of some kind, you help get us the evidence and together we'll work it out."

And how much else have I told you that you didn't already know? Thought Karen. *Nothing I've said has fazed any of you. I bet it's not enough to taint your coffee.*

"And if I fail? In my reforms?"

The boss replied,

"Oh you will fail, at first. We're counting on it, so make sure you go for the jugular, the big stuff, things they cannot let a young upstart get away with, we'll give you a list, but if you spot a real biggie which isn't on the list, **go for it**."

"Why are you employing a failure Mrs. Monta?"

"I'm not. Janie was quite right in saying the one you failed to get through at D'Illion, but she spoke with respect to time. History will show that you didn't fail at all; your reforms are going through, six weeks after you leave. The two that left under mysterious circumstances were not replaced. Two more are coming up for retirement, your friend Snowy and little Jamie, with you that will make the warehouse five under strength. Only you will be replaced, your system will be required, the lads will be screaming for it."

"Is there anything that you think you need to tell us, before we discuss the nitty gritty of hiring you?" asked Janie, all three were looking at her with open, innocent, interested expressions.

"You already know don't you?"

Emily might have said little during the interview, but she wasn't there merely to take notes,

"Would you like to tell us?" she asked softly.

"I tried to castrate the two mysterious leavers. I used pipe wrenches."

Emily pressed again, gently.

"Would you tell us why?"

"They raped me. They failed to knock me out completely. So I knew who they were."

"We heard that your attempt succeeded."

"Half succeeded. They were on other people's most wanted lists. People with serious backup waited for the hospital discharge."

"That's the other thing," continued Mrs. Monta. "A minor, but important factor in our choice of you. You are strong, athletic and willing to take on unfavourable odds, but you are untrained. I'll not pretend that you will not be putting yourself in danger, quite the reverse Karen, you will be in danger."

"So castration as a reply to being raped. You would consider that reasonable force?"

"Restrained, I tried to kill mine! And he didn't even get to rape me. As I was being jumped on, I went straight into autonomic self preservation mode. He was a serial rapist, drunk on his own power, arrogantly expecting no resistance, so I got my retaliation in first, easily. So yes, Karen, very reasonable. Our Head of Security will give you some basic training on how to handle confrontation effectively." Karen glanced at Janie.

"Not me."

"Tub Symes, Director of Security. Janie's in charge inside this building and other specific tasks. Operation Crossers is one. You will report to Janie, copies to Tub. If you accept the job, Tub will give you a course in basic self survival. He will teach you when to soothe, or disengage, and on occasion when to aggravate, when to run, when to stand and fight and when you have to, how to fight. Can we talk serious hiring details?"

"Monta is a caring family business. Well run. I knew it before. Everything I've learned today fits that."

"Do I hear a 'But' in there?"

"So why did Crossers' workers reject the rescue package?"

"We have suspicions, but I'd like you to discover that for

yourself, not channel your investigation. You are completely free to ask anyone any question, the only thing we insist you keep to yourself is that you are a Monta employee and even that is only temporary and solely for your own safety."

"Do the Crossers' management know?"

"Not the management, Mr. Crossers and the administration generally, no."

"Just one or two specific people?"

"Yes, your Monta colleagues of course, but you can safely assume no-one else, those that do know will keep it to themselves. Can we talk details?"

"Yes."

The hiring details didn't take long, with the salary set at a level which brought Karen's own place from 'Some Day I'll have my' to 'Tomorrow I'll go looking for my,' Karen was so shocked she had to check.

"Is this my salary?"

"That's the gross, including your wages from Crossers, so you'll be paid in two instalments, one weekly, the balance monthly," explained Mrs. Monta.

"I don't earn this at D'Illion."

"At D'Illion you are a warehouseman, as one of Monta's Boys you're paid Miss Fixit rate. Don't worry Karen, you'll earn every penny and be worthy of it."

Janie handed her a box containing a state of the art mobile telephone.

"It's all charged up, and some useful numbers pre-programmed, play with it tonight, get a feel for it. It's registered to Monta, with a password, all enclosed in the box, you'll have to re-register it in your own name. Send us the details afterwards. Keep it on, and with you at all times, even when charging it up. It's got the new memory free batteries, so you don't have to completely discharge it before charging it up again. As it's a company telephone, Monta pay the bills, you will always be in credit. We just ask that you don't ring New Zealand too often."

Karen looked sharply at her new boss, who merely smiled and said,

"If you have to switch it off for any reason, hospital for

instance, report in first."

"We're not sending you into Crossers alone," said Emily. "Their new consultant works for Monta too, a heroine of yours I believe, Stevie Bollard?"

"Triple bob major heroine. Will I get to meet her?"

"Probably, also it's common knowledge in Crossers that they have hired a whiz kid to sort their finances, what isn't generally known is that he's our whiz kid. His name is Richard Keating, by the time you meet he'll know about you. Crossers is a deeply divided company, and getting worse, he's management, you're blue collar, in Crossers the two rarely meet amicably. You're both free to investigate everywhere, but most likely you'll do best in your own sector."

"Are those the one or two specific people?"

"No," said Emily, pointedly terminating that topic of conversation.

"Now," said the Boss. "This flat of yours, complete with cat. Our 20-year mortgage service offers 100% of what you need to borrow, repayments are £1 per thousand, per week, plus full interest, variable at 2% above inflation on the outstanding debt. That also covers insurance premiums on your life for the outstanding arrears, so if the unthinkable ever happens, your heirs are not saddled with your liability. In rough round figures a £50,000 mortgage over 20 years would cost you £100 per week decreasing to £50 at a constant rate of inflation of 3%. It's actually slightly less."

"You'll go broke."

"You've been doing your homework I see. I regard it as a deal, with honour on both sides. I give you the chance to buy a dream, without robbing you in the process. In return, not only do you refrain from taking me down into a cellar to shoot me, you stop anyone else who tries."

"Have you got my brain bugged Mrs. Monta? Or is it just you've done your homework too?"

The other three girls all smiled and Janie continued,

"The figures don't include the property insurance of course, fire, theft, storm damage and the like, apart from covering death liability, we don't do insurance, but we can recommend companies which do, which offer packages that we think are fair, reliable."

"Where there's a minimum of sneaky small print," interjected Emily. "Can't guarantee none, but we've weeded out quite a bit over the years."

"We also have properties for sale Karen. You do not have to buy one of our properties, you do not have to take up our mortgage, you do not have to insure with our recommended insurer. It's just you'll be very hard pushed to find better in the open market--But we don't do cats."

The meeting broke up in light-hearted banter and Emily took Karen through into the outer office and loaded her up with reading material and contract of employment and a loose-leaf file entitled 'Properties'.

"We bought one, ten years ago. They let us pay extra off the debt, it'll be ours next year."

"What's the catch?"

"The choice is quite narrow, older properties that came on the market cheap. Apart from that there really is no catch, no lock in, no hidden extras. The properties are good, and cheap because Monta make virtually no profit on them, visit a few, you'll be impressed. There's one other thing, you've agreed to take the job, don't sit on your contract. Monta pay from you submitting your signed contract to them, every day you sit at home thinking about it costs you money."

Karen left her contract, duly signed, with the young PA, before she went home.

* * *

"I'm thinking of changing my job. Well, I have changed my job. Next month. I'll have enough money to buy my own place. Would you mind?"

"Of course not, go for it. Where did you have in mind?"

Pealle closed up to her and hugged her,

"I'm not pushing you out, Darling Daughter, you're welcome to stay as long as you like."

"I know you're not. But it's right I should go. And now I've got the chance. I want my own place. I want to fly. This house will never be completely yours while I'm here."

"Where are you going?"

"One of these." Karen spread the Properties file in front of her dad. She handed some to Pealle. He leafed through the selection of older, larger, thirties and fifties houses and flats, priced at a level substantially below what he would have expected.

"They look very nice, but they're too cheap. There'll be a catch."

"Can we go and look? Particularly at those two," indicating the two in the other girl's hands. "On Saturday?"

"Yes, hang on, can you afford this?"

"Yes, Dad. I can afford them. I am well paid. I sleep with the boss and all his mates every Friday."

"Harrumph!"

Pealle waited until he'd left before she whispered,

"No, that was Lisa." They stifled giggles.

The very sceptical father, his very interested fiancée and his trying hard not to appear too eager daughter, viewed the first of the selected properties, a flat.

It was a ground floor flat, one reception room, two bedrooms, combined bath and W.C., fitted kitchen, gardens front and rear, {shared with the owners of the upper flat}.

The floors were carpeted with a new hard-wearing cord, in various shades of light brown, except in the kitchen, where the tile pattern of the vinyl was in shades of terracotta. The walls were absolutely matt and even, Karen suspected that they had been re-plastered and Pealle agreed with her. They were painted in different shades of mushroom, peach and apricot.

The electric split-level double-oven was huge, as was the gas hob, its five burners ranging in size from one glass of milk at bedtime, up in stages to an impressive three concentric burner ring complex with optional wok support.

"That cooker's the top of that range," said Pealle. "It's the one Mum wants for her new kitchen."

"But it's electric! Immoral!"

"Yes, I'm working on that. We got the gas in for the central heating a couple of years ago, so connecting in would be a breeze.

Mum's like you, you have to wheedle subtly, I'll show her your hob and then leave a few gas cooker brochures lying about, with the price lists prominent. The only down side is they are a bit smaller capacity, but it's only Mum and Dad usually, she won't really miss the extra few litres."

All the switches and electrical points were brand new and neatly labelled with peel off plastic stickers advertising which light they controlled, or that they were part of the ring main or, in the case of the bathroom, shaver only. Every light fitting was shaded to match the curtains in the theme for the room.

£60,000.

Dennis opened a kitchen cupboard only to find an automatic washer inside it. Pealle quickly revealed fridge, freezer and dishwasher. When they did discover a cupboard and pushed the door closed again, the hinges took over and shut the door flush, with a satisfying quality clunk. There was a full height pull out larder, which neatly wiped out the waste space in a corner, and an under bench slender version for condiments next to the hob. The breakfast bar was situated so that it overlooked the back garden.

"There has got to be a catch somewhere." Dennis was adamant. "There will be subsidence, or damp, or dry rot, or power cables, or the local riff-raff will have an easement of access. There's got to be something."

"Let's go and look at the other one. That back garden's East aspect. The other ones North. I really want South. But North's better than East."

The second viewing was a house, a post war semi at the head of a cul-de-sac, on a gentle south-facing slope, which was just steep enough to prevent a clear view from the road into the rooms through the picture windows. A wide drive led to a carport and the mature back garden could be seen beyond. Fresh pointing and new double-glazing drew the eye, as did the straight and horizontal ridge, unlike that next door which showed a suggestion of swags. Inside, the same luxuries greeted the viewers, set in the same bland empty canvas waiting for the new occupant to create upon it. Having more space available, the house was even better equipped than the flat, with the silly corners that creep into house designs, utilised creatively with cupboards and shelving.

"Gas oven!" Exclaimed Pealle pointing. "It's another top of the range one too."

Half way up the stairs was an about-turn, half landing and the second flight ended in a full wrap around landing encased in a balustrade. The thoughtful design ensured that none of the three generous sized bedrooms lost space to the stair-head. Nor would there be a problem about getting large furniture up the stairs, as a pair of French windows led from the rear bedroom out to a balcony overlooking the garden. The combined bath and WC was large enough to include a fountain bidet. Downstairs there were two reception rooms and they were all proportionately larger than the flat. In addition there was a small cloaks/W.C. in the entrance hall and, leading off the kitchen, there was a utility room housing the washer, dryer and an enormous chest freezer, as well as another sink and preparation area. Pealle opened the freezer.

"Oh look!" She exclaimed. "Hamster baskets!" Eagerly she slid the ones in the upper layer side to side. They moved like silk, sliding on the lower layer. "You'll not lose stuff in the bottom with these, they're one of those rare great theoretical ideas, which turn out to be even better in practice."

The generous back garden rose gently up to a high fence. Beyond the fence lay another cul-de-sac, its wide, modern road ran right up to the fence. Broad white bands, at intervals across the abrupt end of the metalling marked out parking places, some of which were occupied; large and expensive, open plan, recently built estate houses lined the sides of the street.

Karen had really liked the flat, but now she was smitten.

"Hello." The neighbour hanging out her washing was about the same age.

"Hello." The three girls closed up to the dividing fence, smiling at each other.

"Are you going to buy?"

"Looking yes."

"You'll not need to do anything to it, they gutted it, rewired; heating; roof; the lot, mind it needed it, but --"

"Have you been in long?" asked Dennis, joining them.

"About eighteen months."

"Any problems?"

"No, it's a quiet area, the biggest problem is getting out of the estate to work in the morning, avoid 8.15 to 8.45, if you're heading East, you have to queue."

"What about buses?"

"The terminus is under ten minutes walk away, but they're frequent, reliable." She nodded at the house. "Who's it with? There's been no board."

"It's a private sale. No agent."

"Ours cost one hundred and fifty, but we had to spend another ten on wiring, floors and things."

"So one hundred and sixty would be a fair price then?" Dennis was nodding encouragingly.

"Oh yes, about that. A good price with all that was done to it. We've still got to see to the roof."

Back in the car,

"Every electrical fitting and appliance is superior quality. We only put those in the really expensive houses."

"The plumbing's the same. The very top of the middle range. To get any better you have to double the price."

"Are you sure that you've got this right? You're sure it's not one hundred and sixty thousand?"

"Let's go to Monta and find out." *Ouch Karen, that was a mistake.*

"I thought you said you were going to work at Crossers?"

A big mistake!

"I am. But I'm buying the house from Monta. Don't ask Dad, it's private and confidential. Don't tell anyone. And I do mean that. I work at Crossers, end of story." She looked from one to the other, they nodded,

"Okay."

Dennis drove through Novochester in silence. Eventually,

"Sorry, it's just a bit hard for a Dad to let go and let his daughter fly by herself."

Pealle turned through between the front seats and reached out to touch her,

"If you ever need us darling, you know where we are. If you

are ever wondering if you should tell us, you should have already done it, don't delay."

There was plenty of space in Monta's car park.

"Stay here, I won't be long."

Monta was on skeleton staff, being Saturday, but Emily was in, reorganising Janie's suite of offices, and being assisted by an older, punk-rock groupie with wild eyes. Karen Robinson was introduced to Jessica Miller. The relationship was obvious from the start and confirmed every time they passed close enough, the pair would reach out and touch each other. Speaking to them was like talking to one person. The warehouseman wondered if they needed to talk at all at home, she felt comfortable and involved.

"I really like this house. But it's tens of thousands too cheap. I can't see the catch."

"There won't be one, it'll be an older property, bought a bit run down, cheap, refitted--"

"Offered for sale at cost plus administration, that's about 1%, barely what an agent would charge--"

"Plus VAT, of course."

"The only thing you'll have to agree to, is an undertaking not to sell it on quickly at a fat profit--"

"If you do, you'll never get another thing from Monta."

"What if I needed to sell quickly?"

"Monta would buy it back, at a fair price, depending on what you had paid--"

"Go for their mortgage too, it's unbeatable."

"And if there are any problems, they'll fix them. We had trouble with our drains--"

"As soon as it was discovered, it was fixed, no charge."

"How do I put an option in for it?"

"Keep the keys. If you have the keys nobody else can view it--"

"Let's see? Yes, three sets, you'll have them all--"

"While you've got them you've optioned it. Keeping the keys is tantamount to saying you want it, subject to contract."

The tall brunette, making her first tentative steps into under cover work, made her decision. Only a few weeks later the house at the head of the cul-de-sac was hers.

* * *

Moving the latest of Monta's 'boys' was to be a relatively straightforward event. The contents of her bedroom accounted for most of her own possessions at home, so the other rooms had to be furnished from new and she didn't have the money.

"Can I borrow the folding table and a couple of chairs? Until I get some money together for furnishings."

"No. We'll go to Billars' Saleroom, see what we can pick up there first."

"Dennis!"

"I'd rather not have second hand stuff. Unless I knew where it came from. And the good stuff they sell is antique."

"Get your hackles down you two, it was only a conditional 'no'. Billars have a factory clearance sale, every so often. It's not Mousey Thompson or G Plan, but it's new, it's serviceable stuff and it's cheap. They've got one next week, we'll go and look, see what we can pick up. Everything but your bed darling, we will buy you that as a house warming. Your choice of headboard on a double divan and pocketed spring mattress, when you lure the boss and all his mates back to your lair, you need a firm push in your back to hold you still."

"Dad!"

Dennis just gave his daughter the eyes and went to sort out the Billars' advert.

"Sadly it seems as if it's mostly bedding, but there is casual mention of club chairs and dining suites, we'll see."

* * *

The Auction House Saleroom was packed, mainly with furniture to sell. The Robinson trio noticed several people carrying numbers. Dennis murmured,

"Don't go far, I'll be back in a minute." And returned to the office. When he returned, he too was carrying a card with the number 2576 on it.

Dennis noted down the lot numbers of several items of interest. The nicest dining room suite was a very well constructed copy of a Mackintosh design. The girls were besotted; it was very nice but probably, even as a copy, out of financial reach.

"What do we do?"

"No idea. Lets watch for a while, see how it's done." Presently they noticed that most of the chairs facing the front of the room had become occupied, the auction was about to begin. As time went on punters were moved off lots in order to display them properly.

Several items went to bidders who called their money out clearly, others went to dealers who merely nodded at the auctioneer, then came the first bed.

"A dozen single beds, divan, mattress and headboard. They are perfect, but there is a dye number change between divan and mattress, the colours are still quite close however. Shall we say £10? Who'll start me at five?"

The bidding rapidly rose to £9.50 and stuck.

Who on Earth could possibly need a dozen beds? thought Karen: He must run a boarding house. The auctioneer had managed to boost the bid to £10.50 but there it stuck fast.

"All done? Sold 2528, How many do you want Sir?"

"One please."

"Eleven left. You Sir?" The under bidder was being addressed. "At £10.50?"

"I'll have two please." The beds were rapidly optioned at their give away price. When a man known to the auctioneer offered to take 'The rest', Karen wondered just how long it would be before they appeared in an out of town store priced as 'Special Purchase £49.99'

It took another hour for the Mackintosh suite to appear. During that time Karen worked out her strategy and her price. In a high street store, even poor copies would come in at five hundred plus and poor copy it wasn't. It was very well made and she did like it. Very much, stupidly much. She reached out and Dennis gave her their card.

£200! That's your limit Karen Robinson, not a penny more! Well-- Not A Penny More! You need easy chairs as well--Okay.

"Lot 204. Twenty dining suites in the style of Rennie Mackintosh. These are quality tables and chairs consisting of --"

Twenty! Right, Plan B: Get noticed. Bid firmly. Don't drop out until others have.

"Shall we say £200? Who'll start me--"

"Eighty," said Karen, stepping forward and raising their number.

"I have a bid of Eighty, Eighty-five? Ninety? Ninety-five?--!"

The bidding rose quickly in £5 jumps and she punched her round tens bids in firmly, with single flicks of the little card. At £100, £10 jumps cut in and by £120, Karen was fairly sure that there was now only one other bidder, an agitated young man who hadn't bid for anything else. She put in a £140 call just to make sure, but then at £150 she shook her head. The auctioneer tried vainly for other offers,

"I'm selling! Sold! How many do you want Sir?"

"One please." Karen had neither taken her eyes, off the auctioneer nor blinked.

"And you Miss, at £150?"

"Two," said Pealle, straight into her ear.

"Two please." The roaring was loud in her head, she'd just bought her very first dining suite, for the price of an everyday-dinner-service-less than what she would have been prepared to pay and mere shrapnel compared to its true value. The little group made their way forwards, and edged self-consciously across the front of the room to obtain the chitties to present to the cash desk later, while the auctioneer sold off the remaining suites.

"Lot 205. Five, three-piece lounge suites, four red and a green one, these are in leather, on ash and beech frames, built by a local firm who are justifiably proud of using traditional mortise and tenon joints. They are insurance salvage and there is a little cosmetic water damage. Shall we say--"

"Fifty." Karen's confident bid had come from right under his nose, she hadn't even reached the register desk.

"You won't get them for that Miss. Sixty." He'd never looked away. There was a reserve on the suites.

"Seventy."

"Eighty."

"Ninety."

"Ninety five, will you give me the hundred Miss?"

"Hundred."

"Selling now, at one hundred pounds," was greeted with total silence; the auctioneer wasted little time. "Sold! How many do you want Miss?"

"The green one please."

"Four red suites at a hundred pounds? Come on, a single chair's worth more than that."

"I'll take them," said a quiet voice from one side.

"Milliom," said the auctioneer. "Lot 206. Fifty club chairs --"

"Two Mackintosh style dining suites £150 and one green leather three piece lounge suite £100. Do you want them delivered?" asked the girl on the main desk.

"Yes, please," Karen gave her address.

"And one of the dining suites to my house," said Dennis.

"Yes, Sir, which would be where?" Dennis furnished her with his card.

"Can you take delivery tonight, between five and six?"

"Yes."

The VAT proved to be a larger item on the bill than the commission and delivery combined. When Karen had received her credit card back, Dennis hustled his women outside,

"Let's all get away from here before we are done for robbery with violence."

At ten past five that evening the sage green three-piece suite and the table were unloaded from a white delivery van. In addition to the four chairs expected, to Karen's surprise, two elegant carvers also appeared.

"Oh, I didn't know about them."

"There's nearly always six chairs in a dining suite, Darling."

Karen got out her leather care and tackled the water damage. Dennis screamed, gave up, and in mock disgust went home to help Pealle find room for the other Mackintosh suite.

As soon as he was safely out of the cul-de-sac, the grin surfaced and he screamed again, punching the air repeatedly.

The proud new homeowner carried her meal through from the

kitchen and settled down in one of the carvers, at the head of her dining table.

The mobile rang,

Trubshaw Symes
Answer?

Her first official Monta business call.

"Hello Mr. Symes it's Karen Robinson. What can I do for you?"

"First call me Tub, second dig out your appointments diary and fill in your Security Training sessions."

She couldn't keep the giggle in.

"Are you all right?"

"Yes. Sorry. I'm sitting here with an inane grin on my face. I've just spent tens of thousands on a house. And hundreds on furniture. But my appointments diary will have to be the back of the Cornflakes packet."

"Naughty. We'll have to teach you about nutrition too."

"Generic Cornflakes. It's whole wheat cereal really."

"That's better. Would you like to come before or after work, or at weekends?" The sessions were arranged and she finished her meal still grinning inanely at her house and its new contents.

During her training, Karen was forthright with Monta's Head of Security, whose job also covered all subsidiary companies. He turned out to be a Mr. Universe look-alike, with an incongruously old face, contrasting with the toned up and still young-looking body.

"So who will I be setting the dogs on?"

"We are hoping you'll come up with names, meanwhile steer clear of anybody connected with the union. Says they're connected with the union, just do what is reasonable, but keep out of any dark corners when they're around."

"Particularly who?"

"Frank Stooppley and his tame gorillas. We think there's the odd executive who hangs about on the fringes picking up scraps, in particular a blonde pretty boy salesman called Brian Bevans. The manager most instrumental in divisively dividing the work force is P. E. Jeckobs; he requires that he be called Mr. Jeckobs by the workers. They dubbed him Pej of course."

During other sessions she pumped him gently about 'The Boys', as cover for her true inquiry.

"What is the problem, will you mind being referred to as one of The Boys?"

"No. It'll just take a bit of getting used to."

"That's what they all say, I think it goes with the territory, the type of people that would mind don't want to work for Monta."

"Or Monta doesn't want them."

Tub's eyebrows went up, but he made no comment on that.

"The first time I saw any of the boys it was Flint, Stone and Jack. So I was told. And of course I was looking for the third male."

"Naturally, have you any preference as to your security name?"

"Rockhopper please. If it's available?"

"It is."

By the end of her training she had found out what she wanted to know. Her target was twice her age, available and heterosexual.

* * *

The National Chain Store's delivery van was an early caller. Karen couldn't understand, she hadn't been expecting anything.

"Miss K. Robinson?"

"Yes."

"Sign here please."

"I haven't ordered anything."

The delivery man consulted his sheet and then indicated the parcel,

"It's gift wrapped Miss. Our gift delivery service," he consulted the label. "Sourced out of our Glasgow branch, relayed from--"

"Benguthrie?"

"Yes."

"Oh, from Grandma. Thank you."

The enclosed card read:-

Happy House warming Karen,
It needs one AA Battery, enclosed.
It listens to the radio time signal
from Rugby.
You still get the one you want
when we no longer need it.
We are looking forward to
visiting you soon,
Love,
Grandma and Granddad

Inside the box was a little revolving pendulum mantle clock, in a transparent domed case. Not the classy antique she would inherit, but if it listened to Rugby,[3] it would have the distinct merit of being always right.

* * *

"Big Kay." Paul's voice from the counter; Karen pushed herself away from the computer leaning back into the passageway to see him,

"Yes?"

"Personal call, from New Zealand."

She rose and made her way to the counter, the telephone was on its hook.

"Over here. Called in person," said the familiar NZ accent.

"John." She dived halfway across the counter to kiss him. "This is a lovely surprise. What can I get you? Curved radiators to keep your tree ferns warm?"

"You have just put a silly idea into my head, thank you Rockhopper, it's just daft enough to be a winner. I'll name it after you, we'll negotiate a royalty later."

3 The signal was relocated to a transmitter in Anthorn in Cumbria in April 2007. *P.C.*

"You-'

"Sh! Not another word until we slap the patent in. Listen, what I really called in for is I'm on my way up the West Coast, all the way up and out to the Isles. Can you come with me, until next Wednesday?"

"I can't John. Sorry. I'd love to. But I can't."

"Just the weekend then?"

"I'm leaving. On Friday. I'm going to Crossers, I start on Monday. A weekend away would be lovely. But I can't. Come on, I'll walk you to your car."

"Well-'

"Come on. Remember our conversation about money? Settling for the best you can achieve?" Karen drew him away.

"Yes."

"You were right. I've moved up a couple of leagues. And it's still compromise. Prioritise. Just at a different level. You're absolutely right." Once out of range of all possible eavesdropping she moved smoothly on to the classified details. "We're in the middle of an investigation. My change of job is part of it. I couldn't even take time off in The Wilkinson. I'll be working all weekend. Thinking. Planning. Working out where the bodies are buried."

"Crimes I presume, not actual bodies."

"Someone has disappeared. Is unaccounted for."

"Rockhopper, that's not funny."

"No it's not. I stopped laughing a while back."

"Are you in danger?"

"I could walk under a truck tomorrow."

"Rockhopper."

"Nobody knows I'm onto the plot. I'm perfectly safe. While my secret's secure. No. Get in. Belt up safely and keep in touch." She flipped a card out of a breast pocket. "New address. Keep in touch."

"But--"

"Go. I'm safe. Nobody knows how close I've got. Go." She kissed him tenderly.

"Make sure you tell somebody."

"I've told you. Now go."

John got back into his car.

"I'm fine. Honestly. Don't leave me worried. Leave me smiling."

He obeyed her.

"I'll send you a copy of the patent. Royalties 50-50 split?"

"High Telemarks No! 25's too much!"

"25 UK tax paid, that'll be easiest for you, unless you've got a magic accountant."

"25 of nowt, tax paid, is more than fair. Go."

"It won't be nowt. Bye Rockhopper."

"Bye John. Love to Sunrise. Hi to Tom and Dick."

Karen brought in a tray of cakes and a bottle of wine for her colleagues to share on her last day and was pleasantly surprised when Mike D'Illion called the entire Warehouse Staff into the Management Suite, to mark her departure with more food and speeches. Speeches from which the word Monta were significantly absent.

* * *

Bushy Hair met Karen at the front door of Crossers and introduced himself as Mr. Crossers, handed her over to her foreman, Winston, and promptly left them to it. The abrupt departure was odd, but the warm handshake from the greying Nelson Mandela clone was reassuringly friendly. Karen took to him immediately, even though she was instantly aware of an undercurrent, the welcome was too respectful, not obsequious, but there was something genuinely unexpected in Winston's manner. She shelved the vibes for examination later, as they walked through to the warehouse, there were important formalities to be observed.

Chapter 2

Home-making: February 2002

Karen

"Do the lads have their own chairs?"

"Very largely yes. Most were provided by Crossers--"

"But used by a particular lad?"

"Yes."

"I've got my own outside. I'll bring it in."

"You have your own locker, these three are all vacant."

"Why are they all open? Is it company policy?"

"I keep mine locked. There was a certain amount of pressure to leave it open, not from the company, from the union, but I don't do what a thug tells me, just because he tells me." Karen smiled reassuringly into her new boss's eyes,

"I've got a lock."

"And a wedding ring, married girls have less hassle than single ones. I'll do what I can if it gets too much, but a ring will go a long way."

Winston picked up a large spoon and banged on the tea urn,

"Okay everyone, this is Karen. Mr. Crossers has been trying to capture her for months and finally succeeded." The reaction was not what Karen had been expecting, not joy nor hate, neither expectation, nor even indifference. What she could feel was a contradictory, watchful-apathy.

You're going to screw us all, there's no escape, but I'm making sure I'm last.

Karen gave a small smile and,

"Hello everyone." She got two or three half-hearted grunts for replies. It would seem that she was going to earn every penny Shirley Monta was paying her, but, apparently, not for humping plumbing supplies.

She dropped her chair down against a spare piece of wall under a poster advertising Crossers Spring Ball, now less than a month away, dumped her bag on it and unpacked into her locker. The usual assortment of boots, coverall and food and drink facilities were joined by a seriously high tech pair of gloves, hung inside the door. The top shelf fronted jars of barrier cream and hand cream, a large box of quality condoms and an even larger box of high tech tampons. Winston surveyed the line of ultra personal supplies.

"You making a statement girl?" he asked quietly.

"Who, me? Would I do a thing like that?"

He paused for a moment, then,

"You are gonnabe trouble!" He rolled his eyes, skywards and turned away. "Ask and ye shall be given. Praise be!"

It was another strange reaction and, as Karen wasn't entirely sure he'd meant her to hear, she left it at that.

* * *

The Cat and Dog Shelter was quiet, Reception deserted, it took the girls a few minutes to find someone. Eventually Pealle called generally into the empty yard,

"Hello."

"Hello, can I help you?" The call had come from around a corner, they followed the sound and found a girl binning some newspaper bedding.

"I'm hoping to buy a kitten. Vaccination certificates and everything."

"We have some in. Come and see if you fancy anyone." Karen slipped her reading glasses on, as they followed.

Six kittens were nestled in a basket. Two ginger and white kits were wrestling with three black and white ones, while a tortoise shell, who was significantly smaller than the other five, looked on,

"May I?"

The girl waved at the basket, Karen suspected that she was being assessed as a potential owner, as much as she was assessing the kits as pets. She reached out and picked up the tortoise shell, as her hand approached the kitten stood up as if to assist her.

"She's a queen cat."

Karen put the kitten to her chest and stroked it,

"No," she replied. "She's an Empress." The two girls, feline and human, looked steadily into each other's eyes. "She's chosen me. I'll take her please."

"How much?" asked Pealle producing her purse.

"Free to a good home, but if you would like to make a donation, it all helps. If you haven't already got one, I can sell you a cat box to take her home in--and there's some official forms to sign."

Back at the car, Pealle kissed her friend,

"She's our present from your mothers, mine and Jane's present to you, your house-warming present."

Karen glanced skywards,

"Thanks Mum," then at her friend. "Thank you Mamma."

"Cheeky baggage, get in."

Her Imperial Majesty, Catherine II, Empress of all the Russias, or Imp for short, settled into her new home and took charge of her bed, litter tray and feed station immediately. Only once did she test her new servant's resolve, and have to have her nose rubbed in it, after that she continued to queen it over everything and everyone, but obeyed the house rules.

Less than a week into her employment Karen had sent off an e-mail list of prime suspects involved in unsavoury activities to Janie with a copy to Tub, along with a footnote that she was sorry, but which precise activities were as yet mysteries. She meticulously catalogued the evidence on Mac every night, because it was so utterly ephemeral. Arrogance, rudeness, indifference to the suffering you cause, as 'evidence' would all be laughed out of court as merely undesirable human character traits, but the subtle vibes associated with them had Monta's new truffle hound keeping records that quickly picked out a group of employees. A number of people had left suddenly in recent months. Could Janie trace them and find out if any were willing to say why. The e-reply had come back by return,

Big K,

Stevie Bollard: Will meet you for high tea in The Brasserie after work on Monday.

Recent leavers: Not yet, but I'm working on it. As far as the two girls that left suddenly are concerned. It was Philippa who was never seen again and Janice always wears a glove on her left hand, even inside her house. She will not go out on her own. It was something really bad, be careful.

It was a few days later, during a busy morning, full of big, complicated orders that Karen first saw the bouncy little blonde, all bust and bum, visually the personification of bimbo. The urge to feel the gentle caresses of a girl enveloped her, whilst simultaneously she lost a hand.

She had a piece of pipe in the pipe bender, bending it for a customer and caught sight of the passing girl.

She risked a quick glance.

The unaccustomed wedding ring caught in the mechanism.

Her hand was whipped towards the jaws.

Sirens screamed as the Kill All button lit up, flashing bright red.

The whole warehouse came crashing to a halt, electrically.

Within moments she was surrounded.

Winston fought his way to the front.

"I'm okay. I think. It stopped in time. I just can't get my hand free. But I'm sure I'm okay. There's no pain." There was no hand either, whatever the damage, or lack of it, Karen's arm disappeared from view at the wrist.

Winston slid the handle onto the shaft and gingerly reversed it one ratchet click, looking hard at his worker. Karen's hand began to re-appear from deep in the mechanism.

"It's okay. It's coming free. Keep going."

Another click.

The hand appeared palm out.

Where there should have been fingers, was jammed firmly against the smooth face of a cutting wheel.

But neither blood nor gore.

Winston glanced quickly under the machine.

Then reversed it another click, the watchers couldn't see any reason for Karen not being able to withdraw the stump of her hand, but she could obviously feel one,

"One more should do it."

Another click.

The hand slid out revealing the fingers, intact, but bent back at an impossible angle to the rest of the hand. Karen slowly clenched her fist and opened it again.

"Thank you. My ring caught. That could have been serious, but thankfully not."

The debriefing over the incident, and thorough rollicking by Winston about her momentary lapse, took place in the presence of the big boss. Karen took the tongue lashing without a murmur, it had been entirely her own fault and she understood that Winston was scourging himself as much as her.

"I'm sorry. I'll wear it on my coverall in future."

"You do. I don't ever want to be that scared again."

Later as they returned to the warehouse,

"The first I knew about it was when someone switched the works off, who was it that hit the button?"

"Me."

"Show me." The brunette and her boss surveyed the impossible gap between bender and Kill All button.

"You can't have, it's out of reach."

"I think I used my foot. Yes, my foot." She put her left hand on the bender and reached her right leg out. Even straining, she was still a full hand-span short. Man and girl looked at each other wide eyed,

"There was nobody else around."

"Do you pray girl? Offer thanks."

"Regularly. Tonight it will be special--Again."

"When your hand first appeared I looked for your fingers on the floor. Have you ever had them bent back like that before?"

"Do it all the time," she showed him. "I'm told I do anyway."

After work she went on a belated fact finding mission, touring the works to find her way about, and of course on the lookout for the girl, but, as it was after hours, more likely any information about her. The blonde had been formally dressed in white shirt, Crossers rich red tie; navy suit skirt, flesh coloured stockings and navy court shoes, so the Administration block was probably the most profitable place to try.

That first night, when she arrived at Administration, she walked in confidently, stopped, spun around and hurried back out, closing the door softly behind her. A similar outfit was there, but not being worn by the luscious body she was researching, quite the reverse.

She spent the rest of the evening avoiding the office suite, it could wait. The following night she peered through the door first, then closed it without entering,

"You're new aren't you? I was just going to say don't go in pet, he's a horrible man." The young cleaner obviously knew the large balding man, who was swearing at the computer he was working at in the reception office, and apparently shared Karen's opinion of him.

"Yes, I'm new. Exploring. Trying to learn where everything is. While not getting lost."

"Don't disturb him, come back some other night, it's not worth the aggro. He holds me up a couple of nights every week. I wish he'd do his overtime work in his own office, on his own computer, then I could get done, come back and do his office later. I've got babies to see to."

The following Monday, Administration was deserted; the station she was looking for was easy to find. Propped up on one of the desks was a photograph. The neatly typed rubric read 'Lara and the boys'. It had apparently been taken at a party with everyone enjoying themselves, glasses were half full, silly string and party popper streamers were everywhere, with some caught in flight.

The bouncy blonde, smiling deeply into the camera lens, was surrounded by several happy men, some of whom were holding her in a proprietary manner.

"She's a lovely girl." The cleaner had joined her so quietly that Karen hadn't heard her enter. "Everybody likes her. You wouldn't believe it, but that was taken on her honeymoon and her husband's not even in the same room, she's quite a girl, but lovely too."

Karen re-examined the picture, she wouldn't have minded being held like that, especially by the tallest of the boys, but would have kept the photograph in her secret album, not displayed it openly on her desk at work. She was sure that only strategically placed hands were hiding the fact that the young bride was popped out of her top. And her husband not even in the room?

The desk, dominated by the state of the art telephone exchange wasn't tidy, but Karen could see a kind of mad system at work. She sympathised, keeping her tiny corner at D'Illion's uncluttered had always been difficult. Centrally placed was a laminated notice,

'Crossers Hardware, Lara speaking, how can I help you?' The small clutch of mail was addressed to Lara Jeevers and a swivel chair allowed its occupant to turn sideways to work on a computer.

The girl that did lovely things to Karen, inside her head most nights, was Crossers' telephonist.

The Easter Ball's not that far off,

"Okay," she murmured to her dim reflection in the monitor, killing the volume just in time. "Easter Ball, we go for it."

What do I wear? She knew full well what she wanted to wear,

"You can't," she murmured again. "Not since you spread your thighs on Llew's bed."

At home Karen regretfully spread out the family heirloom, bead, dancing-bodice that, to those who could read the code, proudly proclaimed its wearer was virgin.

A sudden thought, a catch of breath, what if?

She dug out her treasure chest and sifted through the strings of beads. Smiling, she held up one for a negative, another one signifying many and the symbol for apology.

That will do lunch nicely!

Karen went shopping for a ball gown for the Spring Ball. She saw several which were attractive, but just lacking in the something special that she wanted. It was on the third or fourth trip out that she saw it and knew immediately it was what she was after. Importantly, they had the colour she liked in her size.

It was a simple dress, with a short full skirt and very sheer top. Karen slid her hand in under the bodice to check. She could have read a newspaper through the dusky green material. Her sexiest black bra would set it off nicely and it would form a perfect backdrop for her beads.

Having found the dress, she tackled the beads. With some careful shortening of strings, and judicious rearranging, she built a neat bib that hung down over her impressive breasts, hopefully camouflaging and drawing attention away from them. She tried the entire outfit on and examined herself critically.

If you didn't know, you might almost think that this lot was a single outfit, She thought with satisfaction. She gave a twirl, whereas the skirt flared quite provocatively, lewdly flashing undergarments, the heavy beads largely stayed in place.

Yes, you'll do girl.

Chapter 3

Lara: March 2002

Karen

Crossers latest recruit dried her hands carefully, in front of the mirrored wall in the female blue-collar wash-room. That was the only problem with being the only female warehouseman she knew, that and the official money of course, hand care was at a premium. She examined them closely. Karen believed they were her best feature and, so far, they seemed to be standing up to the severe demands of her job reasonably well.

I wonder if she'll be there tonight? I can't go for it if she isn't, she thought, staring at her reflection. The scene behind her changed in her mind's eye to a disco, the bouncy blonde was gyrating sexily, looking at her standing embarrassed in her blue coverall.

"Don't be embarrassed." Her reflection spoke out loud. "You won't be wearing this tonight." The outer door squeaked as someone entered and the disco dissolved back to the wash-room. Karen turned to leave and met the incomer face-to-face, coming through the inner door,

"I'm so sorry, it's urgent."

"Be my guest," replied Karen indicating a vacant cubicle. The girl vanished inside and Karen left in a hurry, unwilling to let the girl of her dreams see her in her coverall again, totally unaware that ‘Karen in her coverall’, shared orgasms nightly, all over the city. The high spot of many a young plumber’s day was a glimpse of Karen in her coverall, which, like her canoeing waistcoat, had had to be specially heavily tailored to accommodate her spectacular bust.

The girl in the cubicle was muttering with feeling, uncaring if she was overheard, cursing her luck,

“Of all the blue collars who could have been here to witness my ‘crime’ it had to be her. Her face said it all. Okay! Tonight you seek her out specially to apologise, it won’t work, but it’s a start. She’ll cut you off as soon as she can do so politely and you will have to start again, but it’s your own fault! The worst that would have happened if you’d waited until you could reach the management wash-room, is you would have wet your knickers. Wouldn’t have been the first time you’ve gone home with none on!--Yes, but the first time because you’d wet them!” The accompanying giggle, revealed equanimity restored.

“Winston, is there a reason why the warehouse is set out like it is?”

“Yes, girl, there is.” The warehouse foreman surveyed the counter and frontage, there hadn’t been any customers for some time. With the day winding down to closing there probably wouldn’t be any more until tomorrow. He turned and leaned against the counter, looking at her, “You wanna know it?” He barely paused long enough for her nod. “I drew out the plan when I got the job and we’ve modified it since, as and when we realised it was wrong. What do you want to change?”

“The arrangement by item. The entire layout. From pipes here, joints there, bends somewhere else. To one manufacturer in one place.”

“That is not a change, it’s a transformation, anything else? Pay scales, time clock, leisure and wash-room facilities, executive perks?”

“I can’t change the pay scales. Fact of life. And anyway, they’re fair. Not generous, but fair.”

It was several seconds before Winston realised he had his answer and that she was serious.

"What are you, a one girl wrecking crew?"

Karen smiled and raised her eyebrows.

"Building crew. Don't necessarily need to wreck first."

"Draw up your plan, in detail, if it's worth looking at, I'll look at it, but no other promises."

"Would you tell me something else? Why the workers rejected the Monta deal."

"I would if I knew."

"Oh. I can't find anybody who does. Or even wants to talk about it."

"I'll talk about it, ask the right question girl and you'll get the right answer."

She pulled a Styx face as he went on, turning the volume up.

"It was decided at a meeting, that nobody I know knew about, held in a secret location, don't ask, because I don't know, on a date and at a time, which are tighter secrets than next Saturday's lottery numbers." Winston hadn't lowered his voice; he obviously didn't give a randy ape's who was listening, if anything, wishing to be overheard, making a public protest. "But --" The volume went right up. "-- But the entire workforce rejected the Monta deal, unanimously. Well that was a lie, because this one didn't. I can only speak for myself, but one against means it was not unanimous." He was projecting his words towards the corridor to Administration, but it remained silent and empty.

"A virtual meeting?"

He turned back to her,

"We came in one morning to find notices on all the notice boards, all over the works, congratulating us all for resisting the takeover and voting to save our jobs. Within hours anyone who had challenged the validity of the announcement had suddenly found excuses to agree with it, except me, they ignored me." Once again he addressed the corridor fortissimo. "Nobody consulted me."

Lara

Utterly unaware that they both regretted their afternoon encounter, and for virtually the same reason, Karen and Lara got ready that evening, decking themselves out in their most royal finery, specifically to please the other one, each utterly ignorant of her opposite number's intentions. Lara had gone for the black, allowing her to wear her rubies without them fighting another red. The black was low cut too, revealing that the little blonde's peaches and cream complexion extended, not only down her arms, but probably everywhere else as well. George Jeevers watched his wife putting her face on,

"If you're late back, don't wake me, I've got an early start tomorrow." Lara regarded him steadily in the mirror,

"Does that mean if I want to be laid tonight I have to pull a desperate youngster from Stores and have a knee trembler behind the car park wall?"

"Well you won't be getting one from me," grunted George. "And he will be desperate, all the decent ones will already be up to their nuts in the top P.A.s, giving them their annual bit of rough." He looked back down at the evening paper and pulled it straight. The footy would be on soon.

Lara knew, late or not, he would be asleep before she got back.

She knew he hadn't meant to be crushing, just that he didn't know any better. A wife was an accoutrement to be there for shagging on the odd infrequent occasion when the desire arose, but between those rare occasions, anyone else could borrow her for shagging too if they so desired. The realisation of this had come as a big shock to the nubile little blonde, when George had topped her up to the playful level with vodka and then handed her out to three brothers for their pleasure, on honeymoon, while he retired to watch his beloved footy. The boys had taken full advantage of the situation and returned Lara, so well fucked she could hardly stand unaided, to her hotel bed and slid her gently in beside her snoring husband, without even waking him.

At least, she assumed it was the brothers.

Karen

Karen compared her watch with her little mantle clock; twenty minutes, then she'd leave, then sat down to compose herself and make sure in her mind that she'd done everything. Checking yet again that the unaccustomed wedding ring was in place had her reviewing the reasons for its existence. She had worn it at Crossers from the day after she arrived and like a brooch on the lapel of her coverall, since her adventure with the pipe bender. There had to be a husband. He was an essential additional barrier to the unwanted sexual overtures in the darker corners of the warehouse and she kept his most prominent evidence of existence on view whenever possible.

Mrs. Monta had been correct, Crossers was not D'Illion. Although she had no concrete evidence of it, according to rumour, unmarried blue collars were expected to put out, and several times a day, to any unsavoury predator who happened to wander by, feeling randy on a whim. Not just girls either, the vicious bullying extended to weaker boys and men. The quietest whispers had it that it had been known for pretty boys to be forced to acquiesce to buggery, no matter how foreign their inclination to do so. She couldn't find anyone who would confirm it, but there was confirmation in abundance that victims were subjected to sadism.

Five minutes were left when Karen came out of her musing and she began her finishing tour. The cheap, sparkling champagne-substitute, that she much preferred to the real thing, was cooling nicely in the fridge, not that there was any chance she'd be sharing it later, but what's a life without dreams? She twisted and turned in front of the full-length mirrors. Yes, she'd do, young Mrs. Lara Jeevers, of the immaculate wardrobe, almost certainly wouldn't find anything wrong with the full, most formal gown of a Zulu princess, even though the beads now humbly apologised that the wearer was no longer maiden--several times no longer. She looked hard at the black gauzy bra. It was almost hidden beneath the beads and sheer bodice and then shook her head; it would have to stay, to start with anyway. Without it, one good shoulder shimmy and no-one would be looking at the beads. She checked the house, kissed Imp goodbye, and left for the Annual Works Spring Dinner Dance. One of only three nights of the year that everyone was on an equal footing.

The Warehouse Gang were standing together, with a sprinkling of wives and girlfriends among them, supping their first drinks. Karen, {'Pepsi, no ice, twist of lemon please, I'm driving,'} was fending off gentle enquiries as to the whereabouts of her husband and trying very hard, so far with success, to do so without actually lying. When a question she couldn't duck came up, she resorted to replying with a question of her own, especially one that raised other issues, for example,

"Karen, how old is your husband?"

"Is someone running a book on this? Who is it? I want to get my bet on!" or similar, had got her out of many a tight corner.

From time to time, the group got smaller as couples left for the dance floor; during one such depletion,

"I love the dress."

The voice had come from directly behind her. Karen whirled around, the face she had been searching the disco hall for, ever since she arrived, was looking up at her.

"Oh, thank you." She nodded at the blonde's outfit. "That's lovely too."

"Thanks and -- I want to apologise -- for using your toilet," added Lara as she read the confusion in the tall girl's eyes.

"I offered it to you. No problem. It's the company policy that's wrong. There should only be one for everyone." Karen could see the astonishment at such a radical view and mirrored back forgiveness, friendship and delight. Go for it, ask now! Ask!

"Are you dancing or sitting out?"

"I'd like to dance."

The brunette took the little blonde's hand and led her onto the floor. Then she encouraged her to dance as though her partner was a boy, it wasn't long before Lara was bouncing to the music, putting on a display, specifically for her partner's pleasure, and smiling into Karen's eyes, as she did so. Karen transmitted positive answers to the smile and all its messages back to her on full power.

After a couple of numbers, a pushy young executive slid between them neatly cutting the taller girl out. Karen, was an old hand at this game, two boys were usually accepted for a dance, and nice boys for a couple, but she and Jet had learned early on how to handle pushy singles and, using his residual momentum, assertively eased him on his way. Lara too, had learned a few tricks in her youth, she flicked her foot out and back, at just the right moment to prevent sideways movement of his, so he tripped over and nearly fell and had to shoot off sideways to save himself.

The neatly synchronised teamwork designed specifically to ensure their continued partnership was not lost on either girl and very much not lost on the executive, who, having regained his composure had to come to terms with the fact that neither girl was worried that they had precipitously ejected him from their locality, they weren't even looking his way. They had at least left him the option that he could now pretend that it was merely the drink and not have to live down a public humiliation by mere girls and one of them a blue collar!

"Who was that?"

"Brian the Greatest, Brian Bevans, the great lover. The great love in the life of Brian Bevans that is. I've known him since school, let him into my knickers once, never again. It might be less boring than listening to grass grow, but it'll be close."

When the music changed to a smoochy number Karen reached for her partner's hips and pulled, intending to get her close. It became apparent that merely close was not what Lara had in mind, she moved right in, sprayed herself up Karen's front, slid her arms up around the brunette's neck and luxuriated against her.

"Look behind me, blue suit, that's the other main poser, Harold Wreegues. The girl he's trying to impress is the Boss's daughter, Claire, she's only twenty, but it looks to me as if she's sussed him." Although the other poser seemed to be reading Claire's responses as acquiescence, Karen agreed with Lara, she was merely being polite.

"Does he play tennis?"

"Yes. He's not as good as he thinks he is, says he is, but he's better than me."

"Bit of a ladies man? Is he?"

"Fancies himself that way, I've seen girls who ought to know better getting into his car. But who am I to talk, not that I've been there, no thank you very much, but I've been where I shouldn't, on occasion."

During the pause between records, filled with the deafening and unintelligible yawnage of a D.J. who doesn't understand how microphones work, an older man excused himself into the couple. There was something vaguely familiar about him, but Karen couldn't place it. Claire continued her polite frontage but now it was failing to mask interest in her new man, not boredom, and she was dancing much closer to him. Karen gently eased her partner around so that she could share the new development,

"Who's the newcomer?"

"The new accountant, Richard Keating, he's lovely, tough with the books, trying to stop us going bust, but a lovely man."

"She's tuned in now."

"Who isn't? He can check my figures anytime."

The buffet opened and in perfect harmony the warehouseman and telephonist joined the queue for the food. Karen watched Claire being steered into the queue with silky smoothness by her partner.

Well done Richard, she thought and gathered that the boss's daughter, who was talking animatedly to him, with almost constant eye contact, touching her ears, open palms, was sharing her thoughts. With just a smidgen of luck both Monta's undercover operatives had pulled. She picked up two plates and two sets of irons rolled in napkins,

"You load, I'll carry," she said, neatly prolonging the encounter.

"What do you want?"

"Whatever you're having will do fine." When she had loaded the plates, Lara asked where Karen wanted to sit, which the tall girl read as acquiescing to having been picked up.

"Anywhere, I don't mind." So the blonde led the way to a small corner table tucked away out of the main flow.

Presently,

"How do you keep your hands so nice?"

Karen looked down at her hands, which she had been self-consciously half hiding all night.

"You work in the most punishing environment."

Two slim and gentle hands took one of hers in their grasp, holding, feeling. If Lara was doing to Karen's cunny, what she was doing to her hand, Karen would consider that she was being fucked; she surrendered totally to the blonde's caresses.

"Yet you manage to keep your hands clean and soft. I've seen you humping pipes and joints, I know you often wear gloves, but still."

"I only very rarely don't wear gloves. Lots of barrier cream before. And hand cream after, like sex."

The blonde pulled her new friend's hand down into her lap and continued to caress it sensuously out of sight as she giggled at the incongruous visions the taller girl's statement was conjuring up. Karen inched around the curved corner bench towards Lara, who closed the remaining gap, smoothly snuggling up thigh to thigh.

"You're very good at what you do, aren't you?"

Karen made no reply, her hand was having a gentle orgasm in Lara's lap, she didn't want to break the spell, and anyway she didn't know what to say to that.

"When people ring in to speak to the warehouse we get asked for only two names, you and Solomon. Oh and Winston of course but that would be expected."

"Yes, well. Solomon knows the difference between gunk and gonk."

"So do you, apparently."

The caresses, hidden by the table, were now blatantly sexual. Karen reached her other hand over, intending to reciprocate the lovemaking to one of Lara's hands, she couldn't reach and had to settle for a stockinged thigh. Lara gently tweaked the hem of her dress out from under the wriggling mass in her lap. Karen was now snuggling stockinged thigh with both hands. The naked hands, making love to hers, slid up under the dress, now naked thighs above the stocking tops were being snuggled. The conversation continued without a pause. A plump knickered mound had now joined the game.

"Several times I've heard people say to ask you, you would know if a product could do the job they had in mind for it."

"Some things stick with no effort to remember. I'm interested, that's all."

Their small table filled up and the girls smoothly replaced everything in full view. The conversation reverted to hand care.

They finished their food and danced some more and Karen broached the subject that she had been working up to, for several records.

"How are you getting home?"

"I'll have to get a taxi'

"I'll give you a lift if you like. As long as it's not too late. My car turns into a pumpkin soon after midnight. I don't normally join nightclub crawls. But I could manage one or two. If you want to."

"No need, I'm not a night club person."

Natural blonde hair, pneumatic curves, pretty face and dancing which is sex on legs, but you're not a nightclub person. Okay dear, if you say so.

"You could take me for a drive if you like, out into the country and look at the stars; I like country driving at night, it's so peaceful. We could find a quiet place to park for a while. Talk and things. Hold each other in the dark again, somewhere we won't be interrupted."

Karen's heart cart-wheeled about,

"Okay," she said.

Lara opened her bag and gave Karen her cloakroom check,

"If you get my jacket, I'll get a doggy bag."

The buffet staff were issuing bags to fill with the remaining food.

"Toilet first," replied Karen and smiled when her friend replied,

"Yes, we want to be nicely relaxed for our drive." And held

her gaze afterwards, to confirm that the undercurrents were intentional.

Twelve minutes away from the bustling centre of town, the B road ahead was suddenly empty. Lara turned in her seat, looking at her hostess; Karen kept her eyes, on the road but smiled as she spoke to her companion,

"This is nice. Nearly as nice as dancing with you. If I could hold you. And drive as well, it would be perfect."

Lara reached out and felt Karen's thigh,

"May I hold you then?"

"Yes." The smile softened, tenderly enveloping the blonde even though Karen still wasn't looking at her.

"Is there anywhere off limits?"

Now she got a quick glance,

"Don't loosen any clothing. Not while I'm driving. Once we stop, only missing bits out is off limits."

The giggle was happy and engaging, the subsequent caresses sensuous and slow. The hand moved smoothly up the dress, caressing the thighs above the stockings and the knickers covered tummy beyond.

"That's perfect now." Karen kept going, concentrating on the driving, not facilitating access to herself, but not preventing either, whatever Lara could get at, she could have. Thighs, tummy, neck, ears, the proud swell either side of the bead bodice. Lara's hands fluttered over her, avoiding any attempt to invade her cunny, or now bra-less breasts and, if anything, being more erotically exciting as a result.

Karen also usually enjoyed peaceful night drives. There was that one memorable one that she hadn't enjoyed, but this one had now become merely a preliminary to better things. The few reflective painted signs they passed glared at them from the scene, but most of the time everything was picked out in the same half dozen shades of grey, soothing and calming. Occasionally the higher branches met overhead, the impression now was like driving through an empty tunnel, or of driving into a picture to become part of it. Karen knew of some scenery nearby that she would like to make the background to the next stage of their progressing relationship.

Turn left here, then right after a hundred metres, up the farm track for half a mile, careful on the bumps and check the cattle grid is still safe, then a sharp left through an obscure entry.

She navigated her way to the picnic area off the main tourist track. It would be a little chilly, but thankfully not freezing, if Lara could stand it, so could she. The inclination of the area to peel off to go clubbing, rather than get dressed, was now so well known, it had become a national joke. There wasn't much more to peel off Lara, before she could get at everything, their jackets were on the rear seat. She turned into the tiny car park and froze at the tableau before them, the Astra skidding gently to a halt on the loose metalling. A panda car was parked side on, right in her headlights.

A young female Police Officer was leaning against the back of the car, her tights and knickers around her ankles, her skirt rucked up around her waist. Her blouse and bra were up around her neck allowing free access to her breasts. Standing behind her, thrusting steadily into her, was a burly Police Sergeant. As the astonished girls watched, he spent into the younger officer, to their obvious mutual pleasure. Karen grabbed Lara's hand, a moment later the blonde had thrust it hard against her cunny and was squeezing it tightly between her thighs. Having finished the business of the moment, the Police Officers quickly, but without haste, rearranged their clothing, climbed back into their car and smoothly drove off.

"Oh Shit!" said Lara. "I've never seen anything so horny." She caressed the hand that had grabbed her when the car had squealed to a halt. "I nearly shoved this right up my cunny. I still want to!"

Before Karen could reply Lara had released her, jumped out of the car, shut the door behind her and was leaning against it. Karen extinguished the lights, plunging everything into inky blackness, switched off the engine and secured the car. She walked around to join the embarrassed little blonde and had to reach out to grab the pale shape to stop her from walking away. Now she leaned against the car and cuddled the other girl in, pressing her to her own body.

"It's okay. It's nice. It's what I want." Obediently Lara snuggled in tightly to her. Karen kissed her forehead and as the smaller girl's face came up, her eyes and finally her mouth. Lara's arms slid up around Karen's neck, pulling her in, encouraging the kisses. Karen caressed Lara's back, fondling her bum through the thin dress, she slid her hands further down so that she could slide them up under the dress. Her heart spun with excitement, her impression, in the car, that the back of her hand was fondling cunny, not knickers, had been correct, the thighs that had been firmly encased in stockings still were, but the silky bottom they led to was bare. Absolutely bare, she checked, there was not even a thong or G-string between those luscious cheeks. Lara too, had shed some undies during her trip to the toilet.

"Come on," said Karen, drawing her girl over to one of the picnic benches, finding it mostly by memory and feel and sat down upon it with her back to the table. "Sit on my lap, facing me, with your legs under the table. I'll shove it right up your cunny for you. I've wanted to do it for ages."

Lara slid one leg through the gap and, steadying herself with her hands on Karen's shoulders, swung the other leg over and into place. Fingers thrust gently into her, even as she was settling. She took the brunette's face in her hands and tenderly kissed her, thrusting her tongue into her mouth. She sat up smiling at her friend in the darkness and gently slipped the thin straps of her evening dress off her shoulders and down around her waist. This was followed by the strapless bra and she presented each of her nipples in turn to Karen for suckling. Then she was cuddling her friend's head to her breasts, jerking passionately,

"Oh Karen, I'm coming, I'm coming--Oh!--Oh Karen--I've come--I've come--Oh!--Come--Darling--I've--Come!" and she was a dead weight in Karen's arms.

"This is lovely, but it's chilly. Can I take you home for a couple of hours? It's nice and warm."

"Where's Mr. Karen?"

"He's camouflage netting. Doesn't exist."

"Oh--Yes, then, that sounds lovely."

The pair climbed back into Karen's car and she drove home. Lara leaned over, into Karen's lap, to let her friend fondle the breasts she hadn't bothered to cover up. It was a careful, sedate and highly illegal, one handed drive back to the tall girl's house.

"How many girl friends have you had?"

"One. One and a half. One and a bit. Oh and a one night stand at a party."

"Tell me about the bit."

"My friend at school. On a sleep over when I was fourteen. And quite a few times since. She felt me up and got me off. But she didn't want me to touch her. She's living with our General Studies teacher now."

"Naughty."

"And me. The one was another teacher. Junior-school teacher. Not one of mine, I didn't meet Siew Mui until I was in the sixth form. I used to help her at her swimming club. Go home with her. And make love all night. Walk around school like a zombie all Friday. Then go down and fuck the General Studies teacher on my way home."

"Didn't your friend mind?"

"No. It was before they got together. They disliked each other then. They don't now."

"So you've had boys as well?"

"More boys than girls. I like it every-which-way."

"So do I, I think my best dream is one of each, with me in the middle and, before you ask, not yet."

"Erm--Every-which-way but one. I don't like being raped."

"I was tied up and fucked once, but it wasn't rape, it wasn't done against my will. I just didn't know everything about what was happening, when I found out, I was okay about it--nearly."

"I wasn't. I put them in hospital."

"Oh my darling, I'm sorry, are you okay about it now?"

"Now? Yes, I am now."

At home, Karen ran her car in under the carport and paused, looking at the gates, in her driving mirror.

"How long have we got? I would love to fall asleep in your arms. But I suppose I should take you home soon?"

"No hurry, as long as you get me home in time for work. If you're prepared to give me a lift in, I can stay. At least half my office will turn up in their party frock and last night's face. I won't be alone, far from it, but you might not get much sleep, I'm feeling languorous, but incredibly horny."

Karen was consumed with curiosity, but decided to leave it for the moment, incredibly horny described both of them and priorities, priorities! She walked over, shut the gates and escorted her guest inside.

"What do you want to do?"

"I want to --" The blonde thought for a moment. "If you were a bloke I'd be being a fellatrix."

"You want to eat me?"

"Yes!"

"Cunnilingus. What would you like me to do?"

"Lie there and squeal a lot."

"No, I mean do to you."

"Squeal a lot, when you can't stand it any more, grab me, upend me, spread me, mount me and fuck me cunny to cunny until you faint."

Smiling broadly Karen set about stripping Lara bare. The nubile little blonde facilitated the process and reciprocated. As soon as Karen's breasts were revealed she closed in to suckle and didn't stop, eventually Karen had to take over the undressing totally.

By the time Imp crept into bed to snuggle, the bottle of relatively cheap sparkling plonk that had been left to cool as a defiant gesture was largely empty and a new pair bond was well on the way to being established.

The following morning,

"How can we manage this? I start at seven-thirty. But you don't start 'til nine."

"It's okay, I'll work some flexi, we've got to get you in to clock on."

"Which is the very first thing I'm going to change. Then the warehouse storage system. Next up the blue collar, white collar divide. And after breakfast I'll --"

Lara laughed,

"For a minute there I thought you were serious."

"I am. Not about the time scale. It'll take me at least 'til lunch."

Lara laughed happily and continued putting her face on.

The following Monday, the tall girl began to earn her Monta salary.

Chapter 4
Contact: April 2002
Karen

There was nobody at the warehouse counter.

A moment before there had been several of the lads knocking about.

In the utility area leading to the rest-room, the shop steward was leaning against the drinks machine and a young obese subordinate was opposite him, lounging with his back to the domestic end of the workbench. Behind him, one of the spiral rings on the electric hob was glowing bright red-hot.

Some people look like their pets.

Frank Stooppley owned a red setter that lived in his car every Monday, Tuesday and Wednesday; the union official's lank curls however, were black.

The subordinate would keep a hippopotamus.

Karen moved between the men to the metalworking end of the bench, smiling minutely at the newcomers.

Just like that morning among the pipe racks at D'Illion, as she passed, all the hairs on the back of her neck went up.

And her pipe wrench was locked away in her locker!

Just look, murmured Tub, inside her head: *There's usually something.*

She turned up the valve on the acetylene torch.

"We run a strong union here Karen, I can call you Karen, can't I?"

She just turned and looked at him steadily, the flame hissed beside her. Huge blobby clouds of carbon looped up from it into the exhaust extractor.

"We don't need to lock our lockers, but we do need strong subscriptions. So you can take the lock off that door." He nodded through towards the staff room. "And give it to Mr. Blote and I collect £20 from you in cash every Monday."

"It's okay Mr. Stooppley. I pay my union subs through my bank, direct to head office."

"This is in addition, to keep the work force strong and resist takeovers that threaten our jobs. Monday, have it ready in an envelope with your name on."

"No way. That's a substantial percentage of my gross."

The tub of lard at her side grabbed Karen's hand with surprising speed and forced it firmly onto the cold cooker plate. She watched him impersonally, passively, as if the assault was allowed and happening to someone else.

"You have lovely soft hands," Karen turned her attention back to the boss. "You take real good care of them, it would be a shame if they got pressed to the hot plate, by mistake. The lock now, £20 in the envelope Monday. Your name on it." It was a confident smirk; Frank knew he was in charge. Karen looked away from him again, into the burly labourer's eyes,

"Let me go," she said calmly, while with her free hand she grabbed his testicles and gave them a sustained squeezing twist with the canoeing-exercise-honed muscles that hefted heavy pipes for eight hours a day. "Please."

She was released as he dropped to the floor in a tight ball, silent, clutching himself.

Stooppley laughed, a sudden guttural snort.

She plucked up the torch,

"If it ever happens. I will personally castrate you Mr. Stooppley." She switched the oxygen on, the flame's hissing developed a shriller, angry tone, and the intense blue flame was now hurtful to look at directly.

He wasn't fazed, she could see it clearly in his eyes, all it would take would be reinforcements, empty threats had obviously been shouted before.

"Have your little tantrum, you'll squeal as loud as the rest when your skin begins to sizzle."

Karen finished her ultimatum, speaking in the same matter of fact voice, as if he hadn't interrupted.

"You! Not your minion. You! With this hot spanner."

She lunged her weapon,
like an expert swordsman,
hard into his groin,
and held it there.
Frank leaped up and away,
beating at the flames enveloping him,
screaming.

He plunged himself into a fire bucket, the water rose up in a Crown Paint advert and splattered onto the floor all around him.

Karen stepped over to him,
grabbed him by the hair and,
despite his best efforts to prevent it,
snapped his head back with a flick of her wrist.

The flame, giving out intense blue light, but remarkably little radiant heat, squilled next to their faces, competing with his screams; she had to speak loudly over the noise,

"Just a taster. To show you that I really mean it. Next time, it'll be flame up. Don't ever come anywhere near me again. You or your thugs."

She slashed across the base of the hair she was holding, scything the flame through a broad strip of it down to just short of the scalp and slung the handful of greasy curls into his lap.

Frank was quiet now, his eyes, rolling white in real fear.

The young warehouseman snapped the oxygen off; the contrasting silence was tangible, like jelly permeating the building,

"And No! You may not have my lock. You may not call me Karen. You may not speak to me ever again."

She turned to the big boy, unsuccessfully attempting to struggle to his knees, still clutching himself.

"This torch accidentally fell in his lap. Take him to Medical." Then she replaced the torch in its rest and ostentatiously ignored both the union delegates as she checked her makeup in the mirror, but on her toes watching for any hint of a counter attack.

The younger man helped the union official to his feet and they limped slowly away, bent over, with small steps. With the emergency over, she began to shake so badly that it interfered with turning the acetylene down and she couldn't even take deep breaths, because the stench of burning keratin was urging her to cough.

It was a while before anyone reappeared at the counter and, when they did, Karen found herself the centre of an exclusion zone, being spoken to nicely, but from a distance.

The customers arrived on a tour bus, as they always did and for a few minutes the warehouse was rushed off its feet, a jovial heating engineer deliberately held back to get served by Karen.

"Have you any of that imperial three-quarter pipe left? Just a couple of metres would do, make the job simple."

"And some converters?"

"Half a dozen," he was proffering a job sheet.

She took it and glanced at it, parts for a major upgrade, he would need radiators too, she waved the sheet,

"I'll get these first."

He nodded his agreement, hunting in other pockets. When she returned, she arranged the different items in a series of neat rows for inspection.

Snarled shouts as yet unintelligible, but audible and getting louder, floated from the corridor to Administration. Bullethead was still several seconds out of sight, but he could be heard, then the words became more distinct,

"You're fired blue collar, where are you? Shag anything 'case it dies before she gets to it. You're fired."

The voice was coming closer, but Karen had had enough warning to organise her thoughts. She slid the wrench into easy reach. The puce face topping the egg shaped body roared around the corner, striding along the front of the warehouse counter, pushing customers aside impervious to their complaints.

"You're fired, Savage Shagger! Get off the premises! Don't bother with your cards!" Karen's customer, a tough little cube of a man, politely gave space before he was involved in a collision. Bullethead's fists crashed down on the counter disarraying her neatly itemised order.

"You're fired! Instant dismissal! No payment, no references! Fired! Get out! I knew it was a mistake. Schoolgirl plumbers? Ha! Promiscuous slags! What y'waiting for? Get out!"

Karen, on attack alert, shocked and angry, but determined not to show it, not to react to his abuse would annoy even more, reached out and straightened off the order,

"Anything else?" she asked her customer politely.

He looked from her up to Bullethead's face and back again.

"It's okay. I don't work for him. He can't fire me. He's not my boss. Just a jumped up clerk. A loud noise and a bad smell. Ignore him, he'll go away."

"Four radiators pet." He handed her another paper. "These are the specs."

Bullethead, rage blind to the reality, would have swept the order onto the floor, except that just as his arm hit the nearest items it stopped, firmly grasped by the chunky little heating engineer's hand. Karen fenced in the rolling fittings with her arm and neatly caught an escapee radiator-valve as it skidded off the counter. The restraining arm bulged as force was applied,

"That's my order Jack, don't touch it again. Be a good boy and do as she says, go away, before you get hurt. Before either she parts your head with that wrench, or I break this arm." He pushed the arm and Bullethead out sideways with no apparent effort, leant on the counter, and looked straight into Karen's eyes. "Four radiators pet." Other customers that had been forced to give way on his arrival now closed up, easing and assisting Bullethead away along the counter, as he staggered about squealing through clenched teeth, whilst cradling the lifeless arm.

By the time Karen returned with the radiators on her trolley, Bullethead was nowhere to be seen. Her chunky little customer thanked her for her service and towed the trolley off to accounts to pay the bill, having made no mention of the altercation.

Shortly afterwards, the reappearance of Winston from the management briefing dissolved the force field around her and allowed colleagues to brush past her and talk to her normally.

Karen slipped away to the toilets, and checked that she was alone, Janie answered at the second ring,

"Karen?"

"I think Bullethead's running a protection racket. He's just fired me. Verbally abused me. And fired me."

"What for?"

"Torching his bagman's balls I should think. I also think I know why Janice wears a glove. The bagman got a gofer to hold my hand to a cold electric plate. Threatened to transfer it to the red hot one. I got my retaliation in first."

"Just let me jot things down--What was the outcome of Bullethead's firing of you."

"I ignored him. A customer restrained him. Bullethead made a mistake. Tampered with the customer's order."

"I'd like you to put in a formal complaint, about the firing."

Janie had obviously not appreciated the scene,

"Janie. I used the acetylene torch. On the bagman. It was the only thing handy."

"I guessed which torch, make sure the complaint's backed up in writing."

The seriousness of the assault was not getting across, Karen tried again,

"With the oxygen on."

"Specify the abuse in detail, exact words if you can, send me a copy in your report."

One last attempt,

"His clothes caught fire."

"I should Red Zones hope so, naff quality acetylene if they didn't. Don't go down any dark hallways off guard."

"No--Janie --" It was very difficult to say, if she was correct, it involved betrayal. "There's something else. I'll tell you now. Just in case." Janie listened in silence. "--Hello?"

"Still here Karen, I've written it all down. Damage limitation, search your memory, assume all cover is blown. Make a list of all sensitive information that may have leaked."

"Stevie might be suspected. Pure bad luck. I used to sing her praises for years before I got the job here. And you told me who she really was."

"Stevie's had threats for months, but we are getting concerned for her, very worried. I'm thinking that it might be best if we pulled you out."

"Sorry Janie, no deal. Not after this morning. That level of insult comes expensive. It's a big bill. Payment in full at the end of the month. And no discount."

"Karen."

"Sorry. No. Bye."

She went straight from finishing her call to lodge a formal complaint with Winston. As soon as business permitted, he took the complaint, now in writing, up to Mr. Jeckobs personally.

Half way through the afternoon her foreman pulled her,

"Pej wants to see you. You ready for this girl?"

"Ready as I'll ever be."

"I'll come with you if you want, or the union," he held his hand up. "There is a decent official, at local HQ."

"Thanks for the offer. But no thanks, I can manage. Time I met my line manager. Raised some points with him."

Winston looked steadily into his young warehouseman's eyes, for a couple of seconds,

"Look out Pej, you got trouble, man. Don't judge him purely on what you've heard, he's always treated me right, your face might fit too. The appointment's for three, but go now, be in good time."

"See you later."

When she arrived several minutes early at Mr. Jeckobs' outer office the receptionist jumped nervously; they could both hear the row going on inside the inner sanctum.

"It's Karen Robinson to see Mr. Jeckobs.

"You're a few minutes early, he's not ready for you."

"Business was slack. Obvious time to come."

"Please take a seat then."

Pej finally gained the ascendancy next door, the two girls sat listening, stolidly looking straight at each other, while he summarised,

"You attempted to sack a member of my staff because you claim that out of hours she is promiscuous."

The receptionist's steady gaze never flickered.

"On every count that action was unacceptable. Her sexual inclination, off the premises, is her own affair. You have no jurisdiction over my staff. You have no authority to sack anyone. Are we now agreed?"

Total silence.

"Fine. You have a choice. Apologise unconditionally to Miss Robinson, and never molest her again, or your resignation on Mr. Crossers' desk by close of business today. Which is it to be?"

Another awesome explosion blasted its way through the wall, the gist being that there were no grounds for dismissal, without warning.

"You had your written warning for poor timekeeping two weeks ago, yet you still leave the premises early every night. Apology or resignation for poor timekeeping, choose."

Bullethead chose. The intercom buzzed, the other girl lit up from inside,

"Miss Smithers, please send Miss Robinson in as soon as she arrives."

"She's here now Mr. Jeckobs. I'll send her in." She pointed at the door; Karen drew herself up straight, tapped on the door, which gave under the tiny pressure and walked in. Bullethead stood over to one side, black with rage. Mr. Jeckobs met her in the middle of his office and politely shook her hand,

"Miss Robinson, I'm afraid you were the recipient of the outcome of a misunderstanding this morning, we are sorry for any distress caused to you." He looked at Bullethead. "Mr. Johnson also apologises to you." Everybody was waiting.

"Sorry."

"Okay."

Mr. Jeckobs nodded and Bullethead turned and left, leaving the door open behind him. Her line manager walked over, pushed it closed and offered her a seat. The conversation was gentle and supportive, asking about her welfare and progress, and Karen quickly felt at ease. Presently,

"Are you okay now, about this morning?"

"Yes, thank you."

"May I ask a very personal question? You are under no obligation to answer."

"Okay."

"Certain allegations--concerning your private business..."

He was not at ease asking. Karen couldn't help wondering why he was putting himself through so much torture, especially when he'd given her a get out free pass.

"-- I can't help being curious--Would you tell me, are you a--modern, liberated girl?"

"Am I promiscuous Mr. Jeckobs? Yes. And not ashamed of the fact. I don't steal other girls' men. That apart. I consider that I can take anyone to bed that I like. If they want to, that is. I'm not promised to anyone."

Mr. Jeckobs smiled gently, a suddenly, surprisingly, attractive smile.

"I've never met anyone quite like you, Miss Robinson. In the highly unlikely event that you ever find yourself alone, but eager for male company." He gave her his card. "You could give me a ring, I'd consider it an honour to assist you in assuaging any loneliness."

Karen gently returned the smile,

"Are you lonely sometimes?"

"Yes, there are few emotions less pleasant."

"Are you married?"

"Divorced, entirely my own fault, as I now admit, I didn't then, but I do now."

"What about Miss Smithers?"

It was her line manager's turn to light up from inside,

"My secretary is a lovely girl, Miss Robinson. Very proper. I like her very much. I couldn't, you know, ask. I could only ask you because of what you told me, otherwise I wouldn't have dared." He stood up and offered his hand again as Karen too arose. "And I'm really sorry about this morning."

"Must our talk end? Or can I raise something else?"

"What?"

"You might not like it."

He pointedly sat her down again and also himself.

"In that case, I think it's very important that I listen."

Karen quickly summarised the divisions in the company, Pej watched her, his face blank of all expression,

"-- And I intend to change all that." She paused.

"What is it that I'm not going to like?"

"Most of it is down to you."

"Me?" He was wide-eyed and gold fishing.

"The general feeling outside. Outside this office. This company."

But he was also brave,

"What do you think?"

"Until this meeting." She shrugged. "Now, I don't think so."

"What did I do to earn this stigma?"

"Demanded that you be called Mr. Jeckobs. Everyone promptly called you Pej."

"Pedge?"

"Your initials. Pee Ee Jay. And they stopped listening to what you had to say. Which is unfortunate. You talk sense."

"I never demanded to be called Mr. Jeckobs--Oh yes, I did, but only by Stooppley. I caught him terrorising an apprentice, there was an ugly scene. So, I've been Pej to the workforce ever since, have I?"

"You can bet he broadcast only his view of the ugly scene. And suitably edited."

"Karen I too disapprove of the blue/white collar divide." He breathed deeply, considering, then took the plunge. "The company is in trouble, I thought we would go under months ago, but R----the new accountant is--"

"Called Richard. You just discarded the blue/white collar divide. Don't put it back."

He slowly relaxed into his chair,

"Richard is turning us around, we might get out of here alive yet. If we do, I'll assist you in dismantling the divide. Will you do something in return, I'm not keen on Stooppley's nickname for me, purely because it's his, he stands for everything I abhor, will you call me something else, including to my face?"

When he suggested what, Karen laughed and so did he,

"But I prefer it to Pej."

"Okay, it'll earn a few giggles. But respect may follow."

"Is there anything that we could do now, to begin the anti-divide process?"

"A full staff briefing, like the management one. In company time. To let everybody know new developments."

"The logistics of that's horrendous, hundreds of people, many of them transient, like the drivers and cleaners, a huge room needed."

"Nobody said it would be easy."

Her line manager closed his eyes and sighed deeply through his nose,

"Next Wednesday, nine o'clock, representatives first, to sniff out its development?"

"Lowly representatives. The ones that normally don't get heard."

"Can we leave it there Karen, you've given me lots to think about?"

"Sure." As she stood up with him and shook his hand again, she noticed that his door had failed to latch, again. "There's one other thing." She had been debating exactly what to say and, fully aware that the lovesick and probably by now heartbroken girl outside, had been an unseen participant in the conversation, decided to go for the jugular. "Miss Smithers. What is her given name?"

"Santoria, but I've heard her friends call her Sandy."

"You like her a lot more than you said. It's obvious. And she fancies the pants off you. She'd love to show you her improper side. My guess is she's just waiting for the invite. She also probably thinks of herself as your PA. Not your secretary. And I'm sure she'd prefer Sandy, to Miss Anything." She laid the card down carefully. "Give her first refusal. You can send me that if I'm wrong. Internal mail. But I'm right."

Outside she walked straight past Santoria Smithers with just a wave of her hand in her direction.

Back in the warehouse, Winston collared her at once,

"Was Pej okay?" Every antenna within 100 metres was straining to tune in. She turned the volume up,

"Okay enough to earn the title of Mr. Jeckobs from me. From now on."

"That okay. Wow!"

"But he doesn't want it, never did. All Stooppley's lies, I think I'll call him PeeJay. It fits, soft, cuddly, protective."

"You sleep with them."

"I could think of worse things. Than sleeping with PeeJay. A lot worse. He's very nice. Very tough, but very nice too. I wouldn't say no."

The silence that greeted that, rivalled the one in Llew's General Studies lesson. Karen waited. The silence stretched out and out, a message had definitely got across, only time would show if it was the right one.

The clock ticked past 4.30 and the warehouse closed up.

In the high-on-her-hit-list, blue-collar wash-room, the warehouseman checked her clothes and repaired her face. A man walked past behind her checking the cubicles, Karen watched him in disbelief, of all the warehousemen at Crossers, Solomon was the one she had identified as the person to have washing your back when taking a shower in Bates' Motel.

"Sorry to barge in unannounced, Miss Robinson. I don't often walk into ladies toilets, but I need to talk to you and Janice insisted that I do it in secret, she doesn't want her right hand crisped up too."

Karen leaned back against the basins, watching him.

"The workers rejected the Monta offer by not accepting it, not objecting when we were told it had been rejected. I would have done, but I was afraid, they took my previous objection out on Janice."

"Ah."

"Crossers employ quite a few hard men. They toe a line they hate because most of them are family men and you can't guard your loved ones all the time. It's just that after this morning, I have a feeling that this Joan of Arc will be doing the crisping, rather than being crisped--So--It was the union that held the meeting at which we rejected the Monta deal."

"Were you there?"

"No, I would guess there were less than a dozen there. Stooppley, Blote, possibly Bevans, Johnson for sure, but who else I don't know. My guess is that their crooked little protection racket wouldn't last two seconds under Monta so they rejected it on our behalf."

"How do you know Bullethead was there?"

"Philippa saw him pinning up the notices."

"And the notices were just accepted?"

"It would never occur to management to ask the troops, we're living too close to the edge, a strike or other similar damage could send us over."

"How come Philippa saw him? And nobody else did."

"She was in early, she was doing the breakfast shift in the canteen, it was her day to open up. Philippa disappeared that night, nobody has seen her since. They probably think she didn't tell anyone what she'd seen, but she telephoned Janice, and told her, and Janice told me."

"Janice is your girl?"

"Yes, she's my soft underbelly. Don't make any mistakes, Miss Robinson, the cost will be too high. And, take care, after this morning you'll have a price on your head."

"What do you think happened to Philippa?"

"Something nasty and I suspect permanent. If I'm right, and I hope I'm not, it's an impressively excessive over reaction, unless she knew something else, something she didn't tell us."

Karen had to agree.

"Your hide might be riding on this, you take care now." He sketched a wave before checking the exit and sliding silently away, like a wraith.

"I will," she said to the empty wash-room, took a deep breath and headed for her get-together. The hard lump in the long pocket of her coverall was firmly reassuring, bumping against her right thigh.

Meeting your heroine face to face was not something to be approached without care and Karen was excited. UV goggles might be needed, or clay feet revealed, but either way, life would probably never be the same again. She saw her from right across the restaurant, spotting the famous comedienne's blonde bob hairstyle first, then the pretty face and voluptuous figure confirmed it. Stevie wasn't alone, she was talking to a smartly-dressed slightly older girl. As Karen approached the pair, she recognised with a shock the girl who shared the female lead in Stevie's sex videos. The hair was different in both colour and style and the makeup was conservative and understated. Queen Cleopatra had been packed away, but it was the same girl. Stevie saw Karen and, correctly assessing the body-language, stood up.

"Like you must be Miss Robinson, I'm Stevie."

"Karen." Stevie closed with her and kissed her gently on both cheeks.

"And this is--"

Karen needed to show her hand,

"I know you as Chicago Lynes I'm afraid."

The other girl kissed her gently too.

"It is my real name, that is, it is one of my real names." The elder girls sat Karen down, poured tea and offered cakes.

"I want to say thank you. For teaching me my pipe-work skills. Both kinds."

The other two laughed and Chicago added,

"You are welcome. Thank you for purchasing the videos, I needed the money." The conversation covered several topics over the next few minutes. Chicago was smart, well spoken and came from a comfortably off background,

"That was, like, before she needed to star in the videos."

"How did you start? I mean, I'm seriously grateful for them. But it must have taken real balls to do it."

"No. Nothing in the larder, children with big round eyes, waiting patiently, uncomplaining, for Mummy to feed them."

"And she does mean nothing Karen, like, absolutely nothing."

"Oh, I've never known that. To have nothing. I can't imagine--I'd like to think I never will be able to."

Chicago assessed Karen's reaction correctly.

"I did once, so refrain from doing what I did, I married for love but chose wrongly, we ended up seriously destitute, on the wrong end of several Somebody-Gets-Screwed business deals. Eventually the bailiffs arrived, they said they were bailiffs, but now I no longer think so. They took everything. When they ripped the jacket from my back, I grabbed it back, took the children and blasted out."

"But by then, everything had gone, like, they even took her watch."

"I had the children, but my total assets were me, indoor clothes, the jacket which I had snatched back and three hours of daylight."

"Then, like, along comes the ultimate temptress, have some naughty fun and get paid for doing it."

"Karen, my employer knows that it was that, or on the streets, my school curriculum taught me to be a good seat on a horse during the day and to be a good ride during the night. I have no other talent, there was no temptation involved. It was a straight choice of doing the same activity, in safety, in a nice warm bed, with nice warm people who were already signed up, or down a cold, wet, back alleyway with possibly unpleasant strangers who I had to go and find myself. Add employment stamps, pension rights, not to mention an equity card and the fact that being a Porn Queen is legal, whereas soliciting is not, and the choice was easy." Karen was impressed, there couldn't be that many actresses down the years that had had pension rights, as part of their job. "I talked it over with my children. My son had difficulty accepting it."

"It's a favourite source of school bullying. What the bully did to your mother last night."

"Sadly yes, but my daughter was most supportive, she suggested using my middle and maiden name for work. The Mary Snowdon of the school run, would not obviously be the Chicago Lynes on the television. She also thought up the Queen Cleopatra makeup disguise to help James cope. Her exact words were, 'If you are to be a Porn Queen, Mummy, why not be a real Queen?' It was her pragmatic approach that got us through." Chicago checked the bracelet that Queen Cleopatra had been known to wear in front of the camera, several millennia after her adventure with the asp, against the clock on the wall. Almost hidden in the design was an unobtrusive, tiny, watch face.

"It has been lovely meeting a genuine fan Karen, thank you,"

She stood up. “I must go now, but I look forward to seeing you again soon. Goodbye.”

The other two girls talked about Karen’s life and times for a while when suddenly Stevie asked,

“Would you mind if I wrote a story, loosely based on your life? Like, the trouble with writing porn scripts is that they’re never as interesting as what real people do.”

“That’s why candids have their unique appeal. They may lack cinema quality, but not interest. It’s the enthusiasm of amateurs. Doing it for the buzz.”

“Just like you, even though you haven’t said as much. I can see it in your eyes, your brother and your Dad, being a Conference Hostess, the canoeing coach. I could weave something, like, really erotic from the basics you’ve told me.”

“I’ve never actually committed incest. I would have done, had I been asked. Got telemarking close sometimes. But just never did.”

“You would do in my story, not interesting not to, not what the punters want, but it would be just a story, like, fictitious.”

“Do me a synopsis. If I like it I’ll add some authentic details. I’m strongly tempted to offer to star in it, if I could play opposite your boys. I’ve never seen anyone so well endowed as that thinner lad.”

“Well endowed and good with it. Not as a stunt stud, like pointless sexual gymnastics, a complete natural, gives a girl a good time because he likes giving girls a good time. Turns him on, it’s how he gets his, like, buzz.”

“It shows in the videos. But can I suggest a good hairdresser? Both your boy stars need one.”

“No they don’t, it’s all make-up--yes, like, good isn’t it. I nicked the idea from the drawings of the bearded Wild Man of the Woods in “The Joy of Sex’.”

“Most people thought they were just cartoon characters. When the book came out. Hardly anyone guessed that they were real people. Closely associated with the project.”

“Or that the chaste housewife model that the Wild Man was

playing opposite, his wife in real life, having decided to do it, was the driving force behind getting the pictures done on time and like, I would guess, on budget."

"I really admire her. Over that."

"And me, my boys perform mildly disguised, but they are listed in the credits under their own names, look on the video sleeve, but be prepared for a shock, because you know one of them, both of them for all I know. Just so you, like, know the score, when you realise who they are, it's not a state secret, just don't put a bulletin on the palace gates."

The video sleeve screamed 'Starring Stevie Bollard and Chicago Lynes' on the front, with effusive, although Karen now accepted, justified, claims as to the contents, but no further reference to the cast. She turned it over and had to hold it steady in good light to read the tiny print listing the rest of the Production Team. Stevie Bollard, Richard Keating, Chicago Lynes, Jim Teale. Produced by Stevie Bollard and Jill Keener. Directed by Jim Teale.

Monta's whiz kid accountant and Miss Anna's brother-in-law were Porn Studs and perfectly willing to put their name on their work, if not their unadorned face. Mentally she unlocked her Heroes' Hall of Fame and rolled in two more names.

After such a varied, jam-packed and eventful day, Karen knelt by her bed for longer than usual that night,

"I answered violence with violence. Again. I know it's wrong. But if the same thing happened tomorrow, I'd do it again. Please show me a better way. I'm sorry for sinning. But I will do it again. Please show me a better way."

She felt much calmer afterwards, but the better way remained tantalisingly elusive.

On the Wednesday, Karen intercepted her friend on her way home.

Chapter 5

Re-Evaluation: May 2002

Karen

"Work late tomorrow Lara."

"I've got to stay anyway, with Mr. Crossers being away."

"I would like a conducted tour."

"Yes, please."

"Of your office."

"I had hoped you meant me."

"I'll take you home and tour you later. Whole Bank Holiday weekend if you like."

"I like!"

"There's a huge football fest on the satellite channels. It starts tomorrow. So we could too, if you want. Make it a long weekend."

"I want."

"Mr. Lara won't even notice you're not there."

On the morrow Lara went to meet Karen, clutching a holdall,

"Weekend gear."

"What did you tell him?" They stowed the holdall in Karen's car and returned towards the offices.

"I'm going away for the weekend with Karen for a shagathon. I expect to be undressed tonight, and not need any clothes until

I go to work on Tuesday morning, I'll see you on Tuesday night."

"How did he react?"

The smile, although still present, had become professional and slipped out of her eyes.

"He didn't even ask about tomorrow, he probably thinks I'm to spend it tied to your bed. He said 'Don't bring anything home with you that will infect me.' I didn't think I'd heard right, but I had. If I'm to catch anything it has to be Venereal Instant Death, nothing slow acting that I might pass on to him at Christmas when he next condescends to screw me."

Karen held the little blonde and softly kissed her,

"Oh my baby. Sorry. What about Karen?"

"My guess is he doesn't know. If he has realised who my lover is, he doesn't care. He loaned me out to be gang banged once, probably thinks you're going to do the same and most probably for financial gain. I think I earned him a fat fee one night on my honeymoon." The taller girl cuddled the smaller one into her,

"Oh Lara. I'm so sorry. I didn't know." Lara returned the hug, but then disengaged just enough to continue the walk tightly cuddled together along to Administration.

"It's okay. I didn't marry for love, so I didn't feel betrayed, once I realised what was happening, I let go, surrendered and enjoyed it. But yes! It was a bastard's trick and I've never forgiven him for it."

"You can tell Mamma tonight if you like. I'll love you through it."

"I'd like that."

Claire Crossers appeared briefly from her Dad's office before vanishing down the far stairs.

"That smarmy git Harold was sniffing around Miss Crossers again today."

"Got no chance. Not if Richard wants her. He'd just have to crook his finger."

"People would be killed in the rush, me among 'em. I hope he does want her, for always, the poor kid's got it bad and every great man needs a good woman behind him."

"If he did go for her. He could be the MD in ten years time. Maybe even less."

"I can think of many worse outcomes, we could go bust, or be taken over by Monta--"

"What's so bad about that?"

"Well--would you be happy?"

"It would upset Stooppley. Bullethead. Fat Sid. Bevans. Wreegues. Do you want the other ten percent? Reasons to make it a unanimous vote in favour?"

"But we wouldn't be independent, we'd be a small unit in a massive complex, being dictated to by people who never come here, know nothing about us."

"Instead of Stooppley?"

"What?"

"Mein Führer Stooppley. The one who dictates to the workforce now."

"Does he?"

"He ordered me to remove my lock from my locker."

"Really? I mean he meant it, he wasn't just joking?"

"He really meant it. I said no. I had to say it loudly. We had a little spat. He really meant it. I guess he doesn't dictate to Administration."

Lara just shook her head slowly.

"Being dictated to. Not an option for blue collars. Just a reality. Why do you think they'd never come?"

"Well--Brian--said. It's the same isn't it, I've been fed lies, by known liars and I believed them."

"Have you ever been in a Monta company?"

Lara shook her head again.

"Visit one if you get a chance. Monta wouldn't be any worse, believe me."

"I'd never stopped to think about it, about who was against it and what they were actually saying, about it costing jobs, being dictated to by a big firm, just general fears, nothing concrete."

"It would cost jobs. Those five for starters. How much worse off would we be then? Which of them gives more to the company than he takes? Is missed if he's ill?"

"Harold was off the week before you came, it was Thursday before anyone in reception noticed, I even had him logged in. When you start thinking about it, the case for is very strong."

They had reached reception, the little blonde reached out and opened the door. "My office," she said with an exaggerated flourish of her arms. "Well that corner is."

Karen looked around the packed room, taking in the detail for the first time, on her previous visits she'd concentrated on Lara's corner and escaping Bullethead. The desks, nestling against each other, were tucked in whichever way they would fit. The room had once been the spacious home to three, one of which was Lara's. The original desks were easy to spot, larger and stylish, but six computer stations now jostled for space, besides the telephone exchange. Each hinted at the personalities of their owners. Beanie Babies cascaded over two monitors, while healthy shade tolerant plants clambered over two more. Lara's desk, with its scatty, mad, system-clutter, contrasted starkly with the one next to it, which displayed almost obsessive tidiness. No paper, notelets or correspondence interrupted the half-acre of polished wood, just three pens side-by-side, parallel to the edge of the blotter. There was even another station without a desk.

"And who's this poor soul? Has to work on a trolley."

"That's the office spare, in case any of us goes down, it never gets used. No matter how battered or beat up your gear is, it's your gear, you don't want to use any other."

As she walked past the trolley the sun glinted powerfully off the tab key, leaving a slight afterglow on Karen's retina.

"Tidy that desk up ready to go. I'll browse about. Look for evidence of buried bodies. Neb into where I shouldn't and cause utter chaos."

"Just set fire to the place, much quicker, we'd all be out of a job by Tuesday." Lara wasn't the least bit concerned about Karen nebbing into where she shouldn't. Apparently she wasn't worried about the possibility of her finding bodies, but then, apart from John's worry about her personal safety, nor had any other potential suspects been either.

Lara set about her desk and last minute chores while Karen hunted down 'Dispatch' and anything that she could find to link Bullethead to--to--well anything at all. What had been a long, but comparatively narrow, barn of a room was now divided into Reception, where Lara worked and several smaller alcove-like offices down one side, linked by a corridor down the other. The otherwise open offices were marked off by half glazed partitions. Karen found what she was looking for, much to her surprise, as a paper record, in an alcove two along from Lara's section; like her section, it was almost paper free, almost. She had to call her questions along the corridor.

"Why are some Dispatch accounts still on paper?"

"Firms, countries some of them, still pre 'computer age'. Those are mostly Third World countries, we do a lot of trade with them."

"Where would, say, last week's be?"

"Red file. Red for hot. Current business."

The file had five spacers for the four weeks of the month, odd extra days being before the first or after the last. Karen's randomly chosen 'Last Week' showed many lorries, all fully loaded to the Third World. One of them had a T against it.

"What's this T?"

"Tranship. Goods we send straight from the manufacturer."

"Goods never on the premises?"

"Oh yes. They come into your warehouse, well the lorry dock anyway, but are off loaded straight onto the outgoing lorry. They're just never unpacked. They always go by the case or sometimes the complete load. Not like the stuff you handle at your counter, by the dozen, or the each."

"Even a complete load would come into the warehouse?"

"Oh yes. Where else would it go? This is the only branch of Crossers."

There had been no entire tranship loads leave last week, not that she could remember, there had been several empty lorries. Several lorries had had clearance for abroad. Karen thought hard; she was sure that one of the empty ones had been cleared. Then she noticed the signature, who had authorised the tranship load, in effect, bought it and sold it on, untouched. She slid out the adjacent box file, dated for the current year. As expected, it turned out to be the previous months' records, back to and including January, she flipped back through the sheets. There were several sheets a month that carried a T. Three of them sprinkled throughout the file also carried the signature that had caught her attention. Further random checks, through the previous three years' box files, showed a similar pattern stretching way back. In addition she noticed that there were no sheets carrying the signature that did not also carry a T.

She watched Lara through the glazed top of the partitions, bustling about, ending her day. She was totally indifferent to Karen looking for bodies and specifically in a transhipped load, that left last week. It didn't make sense, unless anything she found would be innocuous, or she wouldn't live to pass it on. Strangely, despite that chilling thought, Karen did not feel under threat. When Lara glanced up to grin at her through the glass, she felt loved and cherished, not in danger. Nevertheless, just because you're wearing a belt, doesn't preclude using braces too, she rang Janie and reported in the latest development.

"Does Lara know you've rung me?"

"She knows I'm ringing somebody. It was just in case."

"I understand. Try not to break cover Karen, if you think you need to, say you've reported to the Police, you have in fact done that. We always work within the law. You'd best call in on your way home, Mrs. Monta's here, she'll want to talk to you. It won't take long."

"Okay. Bye Janie. She's coming."

"Bye."

"I'm finished. Are you ready?"

"Yes. Just reporting my findings to my boss."

"I bet he loved that, deep in that jam on the Sea-road."

"What?"

"But I suppose he could answer a mobile, standing still. I saw him, Winston? I saw him not ten minutes since, turn into the loop, I bet he hasn't got as far as Barkers Crossing yet."

"Oh no. He won't have. You're not bothered are you?"

"Darling, I'm living the start of the most torrid weekend of my life. If my world ended now, I wouldn't be bothered, because I'm so happy. It would be lovely to be this happy again and again, but anything beyond this is a bonus. Kiss me, love me, Tuesday is another country. Meanwhile, I'm living here in your knickers with you and loving every second of it."

Karen gave her trust to her lover, relying on the prostrate

hairs on the back of her neck.

"I've just been ordered to drop some stuff off at Monta. You can wait for me in reception. Get a feel of the place."

* * *

The visitor's car park at Monta had a space available, she didn't think she would be castigated for grabbing it. Inside she settled Lara in one of the easy chairs commanding reception.

"Be as quick as you can, please darling, I'm panting."

"I'll be back soon. Promise. Watch the cleaners and porters. See how proud they are of belonging to Monta."

Sonya waved her straight on down the corridor towards Janie's office,

"They're waiting for you," she said. Emily welcomed her with a smile and took her straight through to her boss. Shirley Monta was holding court,

"So don't book me anywhere on Tuesday night, I'm not available."

"Not even for me?"

"Not even for you, Suzi-Q, or the Dagenham Girl Pipers, that's assuming any of them would want to. If the universe is to implode next Tuesday night, it has to be later on, or it does it without me."

Janie put her tongue out; Mrs. Monta tossed her head, grinned at the others and bounced into an easy chair. Emily whispered the explanation.

"It's parents' evening at school, Mr. Monta's away, so she has four to shepherd around the building alone, she'll love it, but she'll be trashed by the time she gets home."

"Four?" the warehouseman whispered back.

"Two sets of twin girls, thirteen and nine."

Karen winced at the thought.

"Mum or Step-mum?"

"Oh, mum. She's been married to Mr. Monta forever. Miss Anna was her best friend at school."

"Okay Karen, open up."

"We buy a load of parts. Split it between customers. Dispatch the orders out. We also sell from the warehouse. A small percentage of the total. Less leaves the lorry dock than comes into it."

"That makes sense."

"We deliver locally. White van delivery. And a lot is collected. So lorries leave the dock empty. On a regular basis. Unremarkable."

"I feel another but coming."

"Joy was right. Some of them leave the warehouse empty. Rest overnight in the lorry park. But leave the lorry park full. I'm sure one went last week. Cleared for the continent. I'm certain it left the lorry dock empty. The docs said it was full."

"So orders are being filled in the lorry park?" Emily had paused in her notes, awaiting confirmation.

"It would seem so. A company jockey takes an alleged load to the park. On a trailer. Leaves it there."

"And usually never sees it again, the load manifest goes into the night safe and a long distance driver takes a real load the next day, from there to the destination."

"There are several ways to make the switch. Joy said. But she didn't say how. I didn't want to appear too keen."

"The easiest would be on paper, just change the load number on the load manifest."

"Or on the trailer," Emily looked up from her notes. "Even easier than on paper, Mrs. Monta, just swap the load numbers over from one trailer to the ne--" Janie interrupted, excited,

"That's it. I had been concerned about how many mouths needed sealing with bung, but it needn't be any. The driver is told to pick up load so and so, if it matches his manifest, and load number, he won't know it wasn't the empty trailer that left the works, he won't even need to be fixed. If nobody squeals, who's to know?"

Mrs. Monta began the analysis,

"Joy drives in with the empty trailer, unhooks, drops the docs, genuine docs stating that the trailer is full, into security, goes. Ungodly follows her in, with mystery load, and parks next to the empty trailer. When watchers are looking the other way, he swaps the load plates."

"People could still be watching and notice nothing, he would be expected to retrieve his number plate, nobody would notice a driver working at the back of his vehicle, more suspicious if he didn't. It would look normal." Mrs. Monta ticked her truffle hound's comment with a finger in the air and continued,

"Having done the swap, he too drops off utterly genuine paperwork, relating to an empty trailer and the load is on its way from Crossers, never actually having been on the premises and never having been in danger of any check or scrutiny. It could be anything."

Emily finished off,

"Ungodly comes back later, for 'his empty trailer that he needed a home for temporarily' and the last bit of evidence of anything unusual disappears."

"Crossers are not showing shortages, but they are running a big fleet of lorries for the business they do."

"So it's not theft of goods, most likely theft of money or transport. I don't see how anyone could steal the transport, without Crossers spotting it in the books."

"So money most probably?"

"But not from Crossers."

"Stolen before it reaches Crossers?"

"They'd miss it surely?"

"But nobody is squealing foul!" There was a silence, pennies were teetering on the brink, Janie collected them all together and gave a firm shove.

"The only time nobody squeals, is if everybody thinks they are getting what they paid for."

The four girls all looked up,

"Forgery!" They all said together.

"We'll grab a shipment and shove it under a microscope."

Karen was half amazed, half horrified,

"How can we do that?"

"I'll buy it in transit."

Of course you will, thought the warehouseman. *Get a grip Karen, you're playing in with the* ***big*** *girls now. Playing by different rules. Not 'How do we do this?' but, 'This needs doing. Do it! Fix whoever needs fixing.'* A further, less comfortable thought followed. *When awkward people won't be fixed, how many* *mechanics do you employ, Shirley Monta, to fix permanently?*

"I want the very next tranship load that's filled in the lorry park. Can you get the load number for me, owner, destination?"

"Yes. I know where to look. I'll look every night."

"Okay. Janie get Jill released and her truck camouflaged please, that will do for now ladies. Karen, who's that luscious peach that came in with you?"

"Suspect number two. But a long way behind the leader. No worrying vibes."

"Your telephone call to Janie?"

"Yes. We're having a dirty weekend at my place. She's staying with me until Tuesday. Despite all the damning evidence, I think she's okay."

"Are you sure you know what you're doing?"

"I'm following my emotions. They've never let me down. My brain sometimes does. Which Jill?"

"Your friend, the lorry driver, she's been on the payroll longer than you have. It was Joy and Jill that recommended we interview you for the inside job."

"So I could have subjected Joy to the thumbscrews safely."

"But you were right to be cautious."

Their first eager, frantic wrestle of the night was a tingling recent memory when Karen stretched languorously across her new bed,

"Do you want to tell me. About your honeymoon. You don't have to. I'm not pressurising you, darling. Just trying to be comforting. Trying to help. Letting you unload, trying to understand." She cuddled the blonde into a little ball on her lap and stroked her like a kitten.

"I was loaned out to some brothers, to get me out of the way while George watched his football. I was lucky, the brothers were nice boys, with big dicks, and they took the trouble to give me as good a time as I gave them."

Lara was unaware that she was being loaned out; she thought that she was being subjected to a gentle bondage sex game and was sufficiently merry to be up for it. George kissed her and loved her and buckled a belt around her waist and shackled her hands to the belt. She could move her hands and arms around moderately on the short velvet covered chains holding the cuffs to the belt, but not enough to get free, he then gently blindfolded her.

"Was it the tied up and fucked incident? When you weren't raped?"

"Yes. I was fucked, I was fucked stupid, but it wasn't rape. I was carried along into the bedroom, laid on the bed, frigged right off and fucked."

Lara expected to be released as she came back down to earth and was pleasantly surprised to be frigged right up again and wonderfully fucked for a second time. The suspicions that she might be entertaining more than merely her husband were confirmed when she was fucked for a third time and a fourth; and when she was picked up and moved to another bed--

"Did you lose count?"

"Somewhere between four and six."

"And by then it didn't matter. You'd surrendered."

"I just let them get on with keeping me in orbit." Occasionally, between bouts of fucking, she was picked up and carried about. The orgasms subsided down to blissful sleep, as soon as her blindfolded head touched what later proved to be her own pillow.

George woke, showered and left to watch a local game before she woke up. It was the young chambermaid who removed the blindfold and released her from her shackles. She managed to show neither surprise at the lack of cane, or other discipline marks across Lara's buttocks, nor shock at the torn and spunk stained dress, rucked around her waist.

Lara showered and checked herself carefully, but appeared none the worse for her mind-blowing session the night before.

"When I was just about ready to go down there was a knock on my door, I answered it to three brothers who presented me with a bouquet of flowers and thanked me for the wonderful party last night."

"You'd been shared out amongst three?"

"No, they were just for starters. I was enjoyed by loads of men, but it was the three brothers who took care of me and looked after me, as everybody took their pleasure of me."

"You were lucky."

"I know. That sort of good luck can't be relied upon forever. Since then I've been careful about the vodka intake. If I'm going to be handed out--"

"You want some say in to whom. Who gets to handle the goodies."

"When I thought George was carrying me to bed, he was actually carrying me to a bed in a room across the hall, he hadn't even been there. And I was definitely carried about, at least twice more. Shuck knows how many beds I'd been in and how many men had been in me."

"Lara and the boys?"

"Yes. That was taken a couple of nights later and that wasn't all of them, they kept looking for others, but that was all that were in the bar at the time."

"Are you popped out of your top?"

"Yes, but so was everybody else, it was a lock in."

"That tall Negro with his hand up your bum is a dish."

"And a fantastic fuck. He's the eldest of the brothers."

"You did him again didn't you?"

"In revenge for being loaned out, yes."

The following evening, Shirley Monta answered her mobile at the third ring,

"Hello Karen."

"I'm walking in the park. There's a tranship booked out for today. Gone to the lorry park empty."

"Understood. Have you got the details?"

"They're sitting in your fax tray. Should be."

"Thanks. Where's Lara?"

"Feeding the ducks. She can't hear me. But she knows I'm reporting in. But, not what about. She assumed I'm reporting to Winston. But, she never checked. I just didn't tell her different. She's absolutely not bothered Mrs. Monta. We're going to pick up a takeaway. Go home. Lock up and get smashed."

"Leave your mobile on, on charge but on."

"Can you hear me? Even if I haven't dialled out?"

"If you were to scream, yes, we're not listening in on your

love life, you haven't joined Stevie's club, you're not an audio porn star yet, unless you know something I don't."

"I'm almost disappointed."

"It's purely a safety feature."

"Yes. I gathered that."

"Bye Karen and thank you."

* * *

On the May Bank Holiday Monday, a lorry driver, bound for the continent, was annoyed to learn that he had to divert to a Manchester Warehouse to drop his trailer, collect another from Salford the following day and take it to Glasgow. He was already on the A1079 when the call came through. Having specifically chosen the A19 and A1079 to avoid the M62, he was now faced with the trashingly busy motorway, on a Bank Holiday Monday, being the only simple route. He was doubly annoyed as his plans had included a little junior school teacher in Hull; a dozen or so hours of her cuddly company had been the main reason for working on the holiday. He replaced her with thoughts of the barmaid in the Merman's Arms just out of Salford. She had at least listened to the patter before rejecting him last time. Perhaps tonight?

Several hours later, he dropped the trailer, cleared his documents and left for Salford to strut his stuff. As he pulled out, a filthy rig with the lurid paint scheme of some tropical fiefdom was reversing in to hitch up the trailer, he paused just long enough to let it reverse past and then departed, already rehearsing his new spiel in his mind.

The filthy truck was almost eager to get into the lorry wash, Jill was apologising profusely to the vehicle. The tropical fiefdom followed the mud down the drains and the truck, now sporting its subtle, elegant, D'Illion livery beneath the gleam, made the hundred and change miles dash back to Novochester, overnight.

Karen regretfully returned Lara home a day early and joined Richard Keating and Paul Crossers, freshly returned from holiday, to comb through the records in the office two along from Lara's.

"This entire load was bought from one transit company and has been sold to another transit company, by Lara Jeevers, it was never on site, just an entry in the books."

Paul Crossers was bemused.

"Mrs. Jeevers bought it? Is that usual? I thought she dealt with personnel and enquiries, not stock. I don't understand, the load was never here, and we neither made nor lost money, why do it? Nothing's changed."

"That's it!" and "Got it!" said Richard and Karen together.

"You're quite wrong Mr. Crossers."

"A vital thing has changed."

"Crossers are now listed as source," finished Karen. "It is forgery."

"Or possibly smuggling, but that's not where my money is. We'll see what the boys find. I'll photocopy these docs, then Karen could you take them back to Monta, Jill won't be long; you should be able to start checking in a couple of hours. And Paul, not a word to anyone."

"Okay I'll just get Mrs. Jeevers' job title changed-"

"No Mr. Crossers. That's having a word. Not a word to anyone. Not anyone. About anything."

"Oh."

When Jill arrived, in the early hours, the security squad from Monta got her to reverse the trailer into an isolated and deep sand-pit and then escorted everyone well away before sending in a robot to cut through the hasps and open the doors.

Chapter 6

Richard: Tuesday May 7th 2002, 0500hrs

Karen

Nothing went bang and the CCTV camera couldn't find any nastiness waiting inside; nevertheless it was some time before the rest of the Boys permitted Karen, Jill and Janie to investigate the trailer contents and then only after suiting up.

They began their research unpacking some cases and unloading others onto the dock. The crates were distinctly frail. One containing a hundred scaffolding clamps had had one forced half out through the gap between strakes, splintering one of them. Karen examined the clamp closely and then gave it a firm whack with her pipe wrench. The protruding piece broke off and fell to the floor, closely followed by the rest of it and pieces from two more damaged by the blow. In the silence that followed she looked around the ring of shocked faces, no one spoke, just turned away and continued the unloading.

Janie and Karen left Jill and the boys to continue their investigation and came up to Shirley's office to report.

"It is forgery, so far it's all spares and parts exactly as per manifest and I wouldn't even show one to my bike."

"That bad?"

"Shocking. There's a box of hoist brake mechs. They can't work. Some of them."

"Karen's going to test them anyway, but I agree, they can't work, we're telling you now."

"Nuts and bolts marked as high tensile steel. But made of pumice. Pumps with baling wire electrics. Cracked pipes with leaky flanges. At least they will be. As soon as someone tightens them up."

"They are claiming to be from lots of different companies, worldwide, but all the packing cases are made from the same grotty wood and the tying wire is off the same roll."

It was mid morning by the time that Karen made her way back to Crossers and gave her report to Richard and her bushy haired boss. She walked in on the new accountant apologising for being wasteful,

"Sorry, I cost you a fortune, I always forget when I borrow somebody else's computer and have to print it twice."

"I'll forgive you a few sheets of memo paper. Ah, Miss Robinson, you have some good news for me I hope?"

"Not quite Mr. Crossers. Quite bad I'm afraid."

The boss' face paled out as Karen confirmed to him that his company was plunged head first to its tootsies in a nasty illegality.

"What do we do now? We-'

She could see he was panicking.

"You do nothing. Absolutely nothing Mr. Crossers. You'd give the game away at once. You leave it to Richard and me. Go home. Go away for a few more days. But, do nothing."

Paul Crossers gathered up his coat and obediently left. A few moments later he could be seen wandering across the drive to his car. Richard shook his head sadly,

"He's a beaten man, that's why Bullethead could build his protection empire, nobody tried to stop him until it was too late, too late for Paul I mean. We'll get there. Do you think he's involved?"

"No. Not in the tranships. Crossers make no money on them. And that load was processed late on Thursday night. After Lara and I left. He was on safari. On the actual safari. Camped overnight on the far side of the moon. Lara had loads of trouble getting a message to him. The Rangers knew where he was. But he was out of contact. He's not involved."

"So who are we looking at?"

"I don't know. Until today we didn't even know there was a crime. Not for certain. I haven't even got a long list. Never mind a short one."

"Yes, you have. Working on the police theory that criminals usually are into anything going, duplicate your protection suspects, all of them, not just the proven few, onto a tranship suspects list."

"How much would the protection racket be worth?"

"I reckon less than £2000 a week gross, based on 100 victims. The White Collar staff seem clear of infection, I haven't heard any whispers. There's bound to be others who told them to choose between 'no' and 'drop dead', like Winston did over his lock, so possibly nearer a thousand, to split between principals."

"Not enough to buy an upwards of half million pound house. And, furnish it in the style it was used to?"

"Shit no! The mortgage interest alone would be close to a hundred pounds a week for each percentage point, with repayments it'll be nearly a thousand, possibly closer to £1500 a week depending on the interest rate percentage and the term and that's not counting the devious tricks the lender might be pulling, creative interpretation of APR for instance, insurance 'n that. Besides there's expenses out of that, Stooppley and Co."

"No, it's not enough. That would need regular payments of many thousands. And there's something else. Been bugging me. Solomon said something about Philippa. That she might have known something else. Which she didn't tell her friend. But, it could be something different. What if --"

Richard waited in silence, apparently unwilling to break her thoughts.

"How do we know Bullethead's involved? In the protection?"

"His immediate response to your attack, we don't know, we have inferred it."

"And hence started looking at him. Fitting him up for everything from Jack the Ripper to Jimmy Hoffa. That would be a mere minor irritant. For an innocent man. But, if you really had something to hide --"

"Realising you had drawn attention to yourself, might well make the observer become an expendable nuisance. You take heed young Robinson, if you disappear, Shirley Monta will raze this place to the ground and cook Bullethead over a slow fire, but that won't do you any good if you're already in a hidey hole, growing cold. I'll chase the cash, the inability to conceal the dodgy money effectively has proved the downfall of many a crook. Not only have we got our list, we've got important evidence to back it, add Lara until we prove her not and Harold as well."

"That would be convenient. Clear the ground nicely around Claire Crossers for you."

"She either accepts me or not, if she's really smitten with Harold, my being instrumental in gaoling him will seal my fate, not clear the way."

"I know. I was just testing to see if you did."

"You go back to the warehouse, cheeky baggage, I'll poke around in records."

"And it doesn't worry you? That she's only twenty?"

"Yes, it does, a lot. I've been around the park a few times. Lived a bit, as they say, so I've been up close and personal, with many very nice girls, who were very nice to me, several of them on a number of occasions."

"I know."

"Claire Crossers is a bit special. Merely walking her around the park is not what I have in mind and not just because she's the Boss' daughter either."

"You won't lose sight of the facts, will you?"

"Specifically which facts?"

"That they also like to walk in the park. The Claire Crossers of this world. With the right guy. Mebees **only** with the right guy. But all the same. I'm sure she'd appreciate an invite. Even if she says no. Which she won't."

Richard Keating, whiz kid accountant, and all round bookishly attractive hunk in everyone's eyes but his own, regarded her steadily.

"Those facts had completely escaped me, which is crazy, because I've known them for more than half my life. My first lover made a point of talking us through it. Thank you Karen."

"Us?"

"Yes, us. As I said, I've lived a bit, I won't tell you who it was because she's famous now, in three fields, academics, Media and hobbies. You will certainly have heard of her, you might even know her."

"I've had a gang bang too. Enjoyed it as much as your eyes, are saying you did."

"I'm still not telling you."

"I've got a full set of the videos. I presume we're not talking about Stevie or Chicago. Not when you were in your teens."

"Sixteen, no and I'm still not telling you."

"Good boy. Bye." She turned, took a step and paused. "Does Claire know about the videos?"

"The first time she spoke to me she said, 'Hello, I've got some of your videos,' that broke the ice nicely."

Karen grinned at him, nodded, walked away and waved without looking back.

Winston, was furious,

"Where've you been?"

"Sorry. Had a late night. I've seen Mr. Crossers. Sorry, I should have notified you. I'm here now."

"This why you want rid of the time clock?"

"No." The look to go with the reply warned her foreman not to push it, despite his anger.

"There's a pipe lorry in, go and unload it."

Karen grabbed her gloves and set off to the hated task without demur. She carefully worked at her punishment right through lunch and on into the afternoon until the lorry was empty. Late in the afternoon, with only a few bundles of pipes left, Richard called by.

"You wouldn't happen to know why Mrs. Monta wants to meet me at the new hotel site tonight would you?"

"I didn't know she did. What did she say?"

"Dunno, secretary gave me a message, it's for five so it might be to look around when everybody's gone home."

"I really have no idea."

"Okay. See you tomorrow."

"Bye Richard."

She finished the lorry.

As she made her way through the warehouse, to report back to Winston, the first twinge of worry splashed her thoughts and was gone, before she could grasp at it. Making up with Winston was her first priority. She grabbed him and reported on the completion of her task and the quality of the shipment, but went straight on,

"-- And I am sorry that I was late. And it's not why I want rid of the time clock."

"Don't be late again and don't work through your lunch break again, you've made your point."

Karen returned to her station satisfied. Winston was okay, not around when he was needed to protect his vulnerable workers, but it could be that the ungodly chose the times when he had to be somewhere else. It would help to know if he knew about the extra subs, or paid them, or collected them. That muttering worry at the back of her mind still wouldn't let, to allow itself to be examined. What was it that she hadn't done?

"--meeting with PeeJay. Am I in trouble?"

The voice of one of the more reticent apprentices had reached her through the racks.

"Dunno, don't think so, I'm going too. Karen might know," replied Curly, another of the warehousemen, and poked his bald head around the aisle. "Big Kay, what's this meeting, nine o'clock tomorrow?"

"The bosses telling us what's really going down. Instead of Stooppley's gorillas feeding us lies. Sounds like a good idea. I'm going too."

"Why us?"

"It would be everybody. But there isn't a big enough room. My guess."

"Oh right." The head disappeared. Karen returned to her task and smiled to herself. PeeJay, and not only had it not been challenged, it had been acknowledged. It was a start.

The end of the day slid past and Karen tidied through for a while before packing away.

There was a small envelope in the internal mail for her; inside it was a business card. Karen was surprised, she had been so sure about the Smithers girl. She turned the card over, scribbled across it was,

Thank You! Thanks a Million!
Love and kisses!
Not that these days
I've got that many going spare!
Thanks again!

It wasn't from Mr. Jeckobs after all, it was from Sandy Smithers.

Karen grinned, the day might have had its down side, but it was ending well.

Winston came through,

"Go home girl!"

Girl? Forgiven then. Okay time to strike.

"I will. Honest. Winston, do you pay extra union subscriptions?"

"No! Has somebody been pestering you for money?"

"It's okay. I said no."

"Who was it?"

"It's okay Winston, I said no."

"That Frank Stooppley?"

"It's okay Winston, I said no."

"Karen, there's something going on and I want to know what it is."

"Then what will you do?"

"Complain to Mr. Crossers."

"I already complained. It's being looked into. If I have any more trouble. I'll tell you. I promise."

"Make sure you do girl, they can't hurt me, I retire in a few weeks. I could go tomorrow, they can't touch me but I can torch them."

"It's okay Winston. I already did."

"I heard a rumour, is it true?"

"Probably--And I know you're retiring. I've applied for your job," she added as she turned to walk away.

"I know. That's why I was so mad about you being late this morning. The Foreman must set impeccable standards, especially when the time clock goes."

She stopped and turned back, surprised,

"I thought you were against that reform?"

"As it happens, I'm not, in principle, but my feelings are irrelevant. You'll have it in place within a week of taking over, if that long."

"I've got to pass the selection board yet. Be the best candidate interviewed. **And** good enough on top."

"What makes you think there will be an interview--a selection board--or even any other candidates?"

"Well--there'll have to--"

"The first time I saw your boss," Winston was speaking as softly now as he had been projecting forcibly at the start of their conversation. "She was eleven years old. I was past it, unqualified, fat and 40, unemployable by most firm's standards. A lowly immigrant black clerk on the lorry dock, spending all my time sorting the trouble that the mess in the warehouse passed to us. A month later, out of a clear sky, I was offered this job, to sort the mess. Paul Crossers offered the job, but it was Shirley Jayne Swyfte, as she was then, who told him whom to offer it to. Shirley Monta does not see you ending your career merely as Foreman in Crossers' Warehouse."

Karen stood still and quiet. Presently, Winston turned and walked away to his desk, selected a sheet of typescript from his personal file, signed it and dated it. Whilst sealing it into an envelope, he walked through to Administration and slid the letter into the top of Paul Crossers' mail. The Boss' PA would open it first thing in the morning. Karen was still standing where he had left her, when he returned.

"Go home girl."

"Oh--yes." Karen systematically forced the whirling thoughts out of her mind. She'd need her wits sharp for the difficult drive home, through Novochester's evening rush hour traffic. She and Imp would review the situation in bed with a cup of cocoa, when she had time to give it the attention it deserved.

From Winston knowing whom she really worked for, up to-- down to, she forced her mind clear again.

The Sea-road was very busy again that night and, with visibility diminishing rapidly under a glowering sky, Karen decided to cut her losses and turn left, taking the long way around the loop, but actually moving, rather than standing still, waiting for a chance to dive across the main flow. This also avoided annoying the brain-dead young bucks behind, who saw only the girl driving and not the fact that if they went, when they were cursing her for not going, they too would have an accident.

Half way around the loop, Monta's imposing pile rose up into her view and, with it, that niggling worry.

She couldn't quite nail it down.

Something to do with Richard?

Never mind, Richard could tell her tomorrow, after the Wednesday briefing. She smiled to herself,

'Wednesday Briefing' already and the first one not even having taken pla-- ***Wednesday****!*

Karen had already signalled left and assertively created space to allow herself to cross over to the inside lane and subsequently into Monta's slip road. Nobody actually blasted her, but she feared that they had felt like it.

"Sorry." She mouthed through the window, several times. There were no visitors' spaces available, she drove straight into the one labelled J. Monta.

She scurried, head down, half bent forward, shielding herself from the first heavy drops of the impending cloudburst, across to the main door, dreadfully fearful. She could be anything between too late and overreacting and she had no idea which.

She found Janie taking her end of day leave of Sonya.

"Sorry to interrupt. Does either of you know exactly where Mrs. Monta is?"

"At home, Goldrill." Sonya had neither checked nor chaffed. "Getting the kids ready for Parents' Evening, I spoke to her not five minutes gone."

"Richard got a message to meet her. He's gone to meet her. At the new hotel site. At five. I've just remembered what she said last week. About Tuesday." Sonya was already dialling.

"Tell me what he said," said Janie.

"He got--no, secretary gave him a message. Meet Mrs. Monta at new hotel site at five o'clock."

"Hello Shirley--Karen's just arrived with a disturbing report. Richard thinks he's meeting you at the new hotel site at five o'clock, secretary gave him a message --" Janie was already dialling, she paused awaiting the confirmation. Sonya held.

"Scramble the boys Janie." Janie punched her last digit. "Find him. Quietly, but find him! You are to stay right here and co-ordinate the campaign." She paused, turning her receiver slightly out over, while Janie spoke,

"Hello--There's a flap on. Richard Keating thinks he's meeting Mrs. Monta at the hotel site, but he isn't. We think he's been set up, get in quietly, top priority, find him and lift him and get back out undiscovered if possible--check--check--I'll tell her." She hung up. "Stone and five to the site, with the dogs, Flint on general patrol, the rest of the boys are minding the store, Jack is instructed respectfully, but assertively, to stay put and supervise."

There was a squawk from Sonya's telephone, She reached forward and pressed the loudspeaker.

"Okay! Okay! I'll stay put." Janie sat down.

"Janie," squawked the speaker, Mrs. Monta's voice clearly identifiable despite the tinny reproduction. "If Richard's in danger, it's because he's a danger to the ungodly. Can you start a list of possibilities?"

Janie had already produced a dictation recorder, as she laid it down, Karen could see the wheels turning.

"He knows something, he's been somewhere, something he's written or read. Seen, heard, smelled, touched, tasted something. He said little to Karen, so he might not realise himself that he's carrying burrs."

"Yes, Boss, I'm onto it."

Sonya re-established individual communication,

"Did you get all that Shirley?--Fine--Okay bye. Shirley will call when she gets to the school and as soon as she comes back out, for updates. Until then you are in command Janie, with the instructions to stay on site confirmed. Colonels should not go charging into battle with their troops, they are paid to think, not fight-"

"I'm staying."

"What do I do?" asked Karen.

"Have you got your mobile 'phone?"

"Yes."

"Keep it switched on, I'm sure Mrs. Monta will want to speak to you later. It would help if you prepared a little report, so that you know in advance what you are going to say. Meanwhile, just do what you had planned for the evening and thank you for the information."

"Thanks Karen."

"Okay."

In her car the warehouseman put her head back and heaved the deep breaths she'd been craving for some time.

Thank you, Guardian Angel, thank you. Now it could be something as innocent as a misunderstanding, or the absolute opposite, it didn't matter. In the eyes of Monta's Head of Internal Security and the Big Boss' PA, she had done the right thing. That was good enough. She put her lights on for the swishy drive home.

It was only when she went to select a supper for Imp, she remembered that there was only enough cat food for that night and the morrow. Go tonight, or --

Always catch the bus before the last, she chanted in her mind, and wriggled back into her coat.

On the return journey, her mobile rang as the United Reformed Church came into view through the thinning rain, just as she'd decided to turn left there, rather than right and on for home. She pulled into the side and rummaged it out of her bag.

SJM

Answer

"Hello, Mrs. Monta?"

"Karen, where are you?"

"Up the Lonnen. By the Church. I'd just decided to pick up a takeaway. I've been to the Supermarket."

"Are you alone in your car?"

"Yes."

"Are you sure you're alone?" Karen checked behind her.

"Yes."

"Lock the car doors now."

"Locked."

"Rain check the take-away for the minute, dear, drive straight to your home. Now! Flint will be with you in five minutes. We'll be right behind him."

"Check. Bye."

"Bye."

What had gone wrong was anyone's guess, but if Mrs. Monta wanted her to cuddle up to her own pet gorilla, there would be a good reason for it. She drew back into the traffic and completed her journey. Presently the wipers began stuttering on the drying windscreen and she was able to turn them and the headlights off.

The drive was uneventful.

It was the arrival that was traumatic.

Chapter 7

Flint: Tuesday May 7th 2002 19.00hrs

Karen

A couple of neighbours were gossiping across the gardens. Some children were grouped at an unruly hedge. They were touching the tips of their tongues on the raindrops stubbornly clinging to the privet leaves, giggling at the sooty taste, so utterly normal.

Karen warily got out of her car, but then went on to her toes as anger swamped her. Through her living room window, she could see that her computer was on and a darkly hooded figure was sitting at it.

She grabbed her constant companion and dashed forward, fishing for her house keys.

She clearly saw the Alert Dialogue Box come up on the screen and the figure okay it.

She thrust her key in the lock.

The figure whirled around, looked and whipped back to the computer.

He pulled a menu down, highlighted an instruction, jumped up and ran.

Second key in second lock.

As usual, just when you needed it most, it wouldn't go in.

Wriggle and twist.

Calm it a bit.

Yes, in.

Turn and push.

Dive through searching for intruders.

Progress arrested by furniture blocking the way,
not where she had left it.

He was already scrambling over the back fence.

She fought her way through.

Into the garden.

An engine roared from beyond the fence and raced away,
she dashed up to the boundary and looked over,
the cul-de-sac was empty.

He'd got away.

From her front door to the road behind was a tortuous drive. Pursuit was five minutes one way and eight the other and she didn't know which way. He'd got clean away.

"Miss Robinson, are you okay?" Flint was calling to her from inside her house.

"Out the back,"

He joined her and she explained.

"--He must have had an accomplice. The car didn't start up. It just roared away."

"Most likely."

"What do we do?"

"I stay with you, up to and including inside the toilet Miss, until Mrs. Monta says different. You may be in danger."

Karen said the first thing that came into her head, to cover up her shock, not to mention the lightning bolt of thrilling excitement that shot through her, at the possibilities.

"Are you ordered to sleep with me Flint?"

The ugly and scarred gorilla face softened and lit up, as it always did when its owner smiled,

"I'm looking forward to it Miss. Let's go and have a careful look from the doorway." They returned inside, Karen waved at the broken back door.

"Matchwood. I'm going to have to get decent modern

composite construction ones. I'd have come around the back first. If I'd thought it through."

Flint's eyes and the significantly skewed tip of his head, needed no words to endorse.

"I know. Mebees just as well."

"Especially with that in your hand, I've heard what you can do with it."

Now it was Karen's turn to speak with her eyes and tip of her head. In the hallway Flint gently restrained her,

"Don't go into the room Miss, not until the others arrive. He left in a hurry, he may have dropped a calling card. If he has, Janie will find it."

"How did you know I was being burgled?"

"I didn't. The call out is specifically to guard your person, your property is included, but only if doing so doesn't put you at risk."

Karen reported to her boss, whilst standing in her hallway pointing at her computer,

"It's all gone Mrs. Monta. Sorry. Disc wiped. Backup discs. Everything."

"That's a pig's bum. Janie get Jessica over here, ask her to wave her wand, you never know."

"Wait boss! Don't anyone move." Janie rang Jessica's number. "Stay absolutely still everyone, Karen have you got a-- Jessica it's Janie, grab a Power Mac tool-kit please and you and Emily get over to Bentham Grange yesterday, I need a hard disc unwiped --" Janie leaned forward and read the number on the front of the tower. "6400/200, looks like a Performa--Yes,-- Thanks. Bye. Have you got a dog?"

Karen only knew that Janie was talking to her, because the question was aimed straight at her eyes.

"No, a cat."

"I can smell wet dog too," said Mrs. Monta. Janie stepped over to Karen's leather tilt and swivel computing chair and plucked a hair off the towelling cover. She examined it with a hand-lens,

"Wet red dog!" She turned to Stone, but he was already there.

He was turning to leave.

"I'm on it."

"If he's clean, check bins and waste ground between there and here please."

"Check," called Stone over his departing shoulder.

"How long was he in before you got to him Karen?"

"Three minutes, five. I don't know. Long enough to wipe completely. I saw the empty trash dialogue box through the window. I burst in. He shut down and legged it. My hard disc's gone."

"Were you going to clobber him?" Janie nudged the wrench.

"Just a bit."

"We might be in luck. I don't know much about Wintel machines, but that's a Mac. Macs only ask you once if you're sure about irrevocable reforms, but keep their own little ways back occasionally, just in case. You're sure it was the empty trash box?"

"Pretty sure. Yes."

"Well if you did see that dialogue box, he can't have wiped the disc. That takes a while and Macs are very picky, they demand a high standard, and that takes even more time. Where are your tool-kit discs."

"All gone. Backups. Blanks. And they're special ones. The Que drive's even more picky than Mac. And my little audio collection."

"Okay, we'll wait for Jessica. Flint get a security squad over here please. Organise this house sealed and alarmed, tonight?" Mrs. Monta was regarding Karen, waiting for her agreement.

"Yes, please."

The big man nodded and dialled out on his own mobile.

While they waited, under Janie's guidance, they combed the room for more clues. Several more red hairs joined the first one in an evidence bag.

Karen took the opportunity of the pause to ask again what had triggered the alarms. Her boss drew her away into a corner and spoke softly,

"Richard did. Officially, he's missing; if anyone asks, he has disappeared under mysterious circumstances. Actually, he's stashed away under armed guard, several layers deep in Monta's private clinic, rambling and delirious, and with a very sore head, and it's all thanks to you."

Karen was horrified, but Mrs. Monta's tone had been one of gratitude, not censure. She went on,

"But for you, he would be part of the concrete supports of the twenty fifth floor of the new hotel by now." She nodded her head, smiling. "So thank you, he's a from-childhood-friend as well as a valued colleague."

The alarm squad arrived almost dead heating with Jessica, who had Emily in tow,

"6400/200, lovely machines these," she laid her tool case down and gently caressed the tower. "On paper, everything against them; 603e processor, one bay, two slots, so hardly expandable at all, a mere one-two-eight-plus-eight on board Megs memory maximum. Apple manufacturing the worst crap in their history and consequently going down the tubes, then, in the middle of it all, they produce this lovely machine to work on, work with." She selected a nondescript grey disc from a CD storage box. "Jonathan Ive's iMac might have saved the company, and got design awards from everywhere, but this is the baby for me." She held the CD by a finger through the central hole and restarted the computer from the keyboard. "As soon as I get this in, hold the C key down." A second later, she pressed the CD eject button, the draw obediently slid out and she swapped the CD inside for the grey one and closed the drawer. Karen held the C key down and a moment later the Mac started up. The CD drive was silent,

"Not quick enough, it's trying to start up from its own disc--hello--it's succeeding." The girls all stared at the 'Happy Mac' icon, heralding a successful start-up. "It's found a system folder--Mac OS 9 but look what we have here," Jessica showed the disc she had retrieved from the CD drive to the others.

"Mac OS 8 System disc. Don't despair yet Karen, I think that you interrupted him well before he had done the necessary. You said your hard disc had gone, what's that?" She pointed at the squat grey box in the top right hand corner of the screen.

"Not mine. Mine's gone. Pocahontas icon. I've got two

partitions, they come up as two discs." Janie began to grin.

"How are they set up?"

"System and Applications on that one, but all my files are on the other one." Janie highlighted the little grey box and hit Curlycue-I; the information dialogue box came up on the screen,

"Format Mac OS Extended." Jessica fanned the OS 8 disc in triumph. "So not from this boyo. I didn't think he'd go to the trouble of reinstalling."

Janie too was now grinning broadly.

"Pocahontas may be gone, but not forgotten and not actually gone either, just the directions to find it have been scrubbed. The disc, and everything on it, is still there. Emily will have that back on your desktop by supper-time."

"She sure will, he didn't have time to reformat your disc, so it's all still there, you just can't see it. And anyway, even if he did reformat the disc, we'd possibly get most of it back for you. As long as the heads can read the platters, Emily can raise the dead."

The younger girl grinned as she settled in front of the monitor, her hands reaching out to the keyboard and mouse.

Karen was disappointed; Flint's car had gone with the alarm squad and now the girls were preparing to leave,

"I thought Flint was staying. I felt better that he was staying."

"He is; several of the boys are ostentatiously on patrol outside, but Flint is hidden away somewhere inside, he'll reappear when you have drawn your curtains securely. The people who tried to kill Richard are still out there; I don't think you're in immediate danger, because they most likely don't know you're onto them yet. I'm guessing the activity will be being viewed as stable door locking and that's why I'm generating some very obvious 'Where's Dobbin' activities. But you're definitely a nuisance they want to go away, so in addition, I'm covering other possibilities too. Flint's the ace up your sleeve."

Silence enveloped her as she closed and locked the front door. When she turned back into the house Flint was standing in the hall.

"Oh. I'm going to have some soup before bed. Fancy some?"

"Yes, please Miss."

"It's home-made. Robinson recipe. More like stew than soup."

"Well in that case, very yes please."

She selected two mugs of soup from the freezer and popped them in the microwave. "They will be a few minutes. Two goes. One to thaw and one to heat."

He nodded.

"I need the toilet. Are you really coming with me?"

"Yes, Miss. But it's quid pro quo, I'll relieve myself too."

Karen nodded and led the way into the bathroom. She turned to face her bodyguard, pulled her jeans down, followed by her knickers, performed her ablutions, dried herself and replaced her clothes with neither flinch nor stutter. When she stood aside and raised the seat for him, Flint followed her example, also making neither real nor symbolic attempts to hide the mechanics of the process. The girl then washed her hands, as the man replaced the seat and flushed and handed him a towel after he'd washed his.

"Thank you for making that such an easy and natural event."

"Thank you for your aplomb. You made it easy too. But that wasn't the first time I'd done that. With a man in close attendance. A friend, not family. Or medical. And he was several orders of magnitude nearer."

"We're talking millimetres?" Judging by his astonished expression, Flint had thought through the logistics and appreciated their consequences.

"No. Much less. I might tell you about it some time. Depends how things work out."

Whilst still looking at her, astonished, Flint took a sip of his soup,

"Wow, this is more like meat and two veg in a cup, than soup and the bread's amazing."

"Can't claim credit for the bread. Other than having the sense to buy it. Those crunchy bits are sunflower seeds. But the soup is Grandma Robinson's recipe. And it's more like two meat and six veg. But in a cup."

"If this is supper, how do you stay that shape, not swell up like a Santa suit?"

"I work out." She waited while the look of disbelief achieved totality, then added, "But today has been unusual. I haven't eaten since breakfast. I wouldn't normally be scoffing a couple of thousand calories at midnight."

"What's that doing there?" she asked. One of the dining carvers, festooned with cushions and blankets, was secreted behind the bedroom door.

"It's easier to stay awake sitting on a hard chair Miss."

"You are not spending all night on that."

"I have to Miss, sorry, Mrs. Monta's orders. We've done the embarrassing bit, the toilet, twice, I have to be in your bedroom here with you too."

"I'm not trying to throw you out of my bedroom. I meant not on that all night." Karen wriggled out of her top and jeans in one continuous slinky sway. "If we must spend the night together, Flint. I insist on at least one fuck. Fair's fair."

"Miss Robinson."

"You can decamp to that when you've ridden me to sleep."

"But Miss."

"But nothing. I know you like me. That way I mean. I can see it in your eyes. There isn't a Mrs. Flint. Or partner to be hurt. I checked. There isn't a Mister Karen. And I know you won't hold my promiscuity against me. I've seen you talking to working girls. With much mutual respect. D'y'want a fuck?"

"Miss?"

"Do you want a fuck?"

"Yes, I do. But if you're serious--and I can see by your face that you are, we need an extra layer of security." Karen watched as her guest slipped a neat little jamming device under the door.

"Are you all mine now?"

"Yes, Miss."

"At last! Feel me up my boobies." The huge black hands were astonishingly gentle, the contrast incredibly erotic. "Tell me to take my bra off."

"Turn around, I'll do it."

"No! Tell me. Make me. Make me do it."

He took her hands and gently but assertively put them to her back,

"Take your bra off for me--Yes,--Slide it right down your arms, I want you naked."

"Now my--Oh--Oh! Tell me --Oh --"

He hooked her thumbs into the waist-elastic and leaned in to suckle her. He had to speak out of the side of his mouth,

"Take your panties off for me."

"Make--Oh--" The floppy hands just slid out and away from their designated job. Flint managed to carry her to the bed and lay them upon it, without a pause in his suckling.

"Lift your bottom, slide them down over your hips, wriggle them down."

She wriggled, as if attempting to obey, but the panties only peeled off because he provided the pull.

"Now--Oh--Mount, do--Do me--Now--Oh!" Despite her desire just to be taken and her commands to that effect. "You like--don't stop--come--Protected." Karen was losing it, her instructions degenerating to incoherent squeals. "Don't worry--Oh!--Have--Do it--Oh!" As the big man took over; pleasuring her. "Do me--Oh!--Ooh!" She had been mentally geared up for the nice feeling of giving pleasure, the reward of being in control, so she was totally unprepared to have multiple orgasms flooding through her jerking, surrendered body.

She lay in his arms being gently caressed. Growing together.

"There's a story behind that chair. I didn't know I'd bought it. I bought a dining suite at auction--I didn't know you could bid on a dozen things. But only opt to buy one of them--When the dining suites came up. Lot two hundred and something. There were twenty of them--I was so busy working out my strategy. I missed the detailed description. Four chairs and two carvers--I got the three piece for its reserve. Because they were water damaged--I was the only bidder. While we were walking down to pay for the dining suite--Then the water damage wiped off--With the first application of leather care. Dad went off in a big huff--Pretended to, he was pleased really--Is it Flint Somebody, or Somebody Flint?"

"Neither; I'll tell you the somebody sometime. Flint is my

security code name at Monta. We all have one, all the security and under cover staff, you, Richard, not Jill, she's a Monta driver, officially on loan to D'Illion, Janie's is Jack."

"Yes, I remember now. She called herself that tonight. It was only tonight. Just hours ago. What a day. Shock after shock. One of the more inexplicable. Winston, my foreman at Crossers. Knows who I'm really working for."

"Of course he does, who do you think screamed for help? Who do you think he screamed at?"

"Life can sure take abrupt turns. I left work tonight, knowing exactly what I would be doing now. Sitting in bed. Alone, except for stroking the Empress. Examining the detail of my future plans. Supping cocoa. Asking myself what I really want. Building dreams."

"Oh dear, I've wrecked a lovely evening. Do you want to tell me about those dreams you're building?"

"Perhaps later man, they'll keep. I'm living other ones. That was a really nice fuck. Would you like to do something else for me now?"

"Like what?"

"Make love to me. If you're up to it."

"Oh yes, I'd like that."

"Did you ever see the film King Kong? The Fay Wray one?"

"I played the title roll, with no makeup."

She kissed him tenderly.

"Silly boy. I'd like to play out a scene from it. But improvised. Unscripted. Going where the wind blows."

"Which scene?"

"Where he picks at her bather. Fay Wray's character didn't do what I will."

"Go and get wrapped up pet, I'll get my picking finger crooked."

After breakfast, the warehouseman tackled the job she'd been not looking forward to all night,

"Winston, it's Karen."

"You're going to be late again!"

"Yes. And I'm sorry about that. Honestly. Today especially I meant to be in on time. But I was burgled last night."

"Oh, sorry, I didn't know, much gone?"

"We've recovered most of it. I surprised them in the middle of it. So we've got most of it back. They didn't have time to dispose of the loot properly. It's the damage. They smashed their way in. Through the back door. And mess. I didn't get much sleep last night. I need the day off. I'll tell the office."

"Okay, sorry for barking at you, when will you be back?"

"That's okay." *Especially since I'm misleading you something rotten, Winston,* she thought. "Tomorrow I hope. I'll let you know. Let PeeJay know please."

Karen had barely wound up the conversation and replaced the receiver when it rang, Flint nodded.

"Hello."

"Karen, are you all right?" Lara's voice, full of concern.

"Yes, darling." Flint's eyebrows went right up. "I'm fine. Angry. Pissed off. But I'll be fine. I'm taking the day off to supervise the clean-up. Can you log me out?"

"I already have and me, I'm coming over."

"There's no need."

"I told Mr. Crossers, he's okayed it, and I'm on my way. Get the vacuum out, rubber gloves, paint, whatever's needed, I'll see you in half an hour. Bye."

"How did you know?"

"Mr. Crossers told me of course, when he called through to tell me to log you out. I'm on my way. Bye"

"Okay darling. Bye." Karen replaced the receiver.

"One of my other lovers. Also a suspect. Is coming over to help clean up. Mr. Crossers knew I'd been burgled."

"Mrs. Monta will have told him and that you need the day off to sort things out. Also she'll want to see you later, the boys will have been busy last night, there will be developments to tell you about, she'll have cleared the way."

Karen could see that Flint was struggling with his curiosity; she waited until he won, before she slaked it.

"It's the telephonist at Crossers. Lara Jeevers. She'll want to take me to bed. There are questions I have to ask her. In bed."

"Okay. Keep the mobile switched on Miss, help is literally seconds away, I'll go back to Monta, see you later."

Lara arrived as the replacement door company's fitter was taking his final measurements and shocked him speechless.

Chapter 8

Orders: May 8th 2002

Karen

"Where's the vacuum? Make us a brew while I finish here, then I'm taking you to bed to fuck you silly while you tell me what happened."

The door-fitter dropped his rule and groped around and couldn't find it because he couldn't take his eyes off Lara, Karen giggled.

After the fitter left,

"Well, I arrived home last night --
saw him through the window --
blocked my passage with furniture --
so he got away."

Lara had caressed her love all through the description of the night's events, from which Karen had carefully omitted every reference to the Monta contingent.

"Oh darling, all those wonderful ideas for reform, are they completely lost?"

"Possibly not. We'll have to see. He didn't have time to reformat my disc. A decent technician will be able to do something. Can I quiz you, darling? About procedures in Crossers?"

"Sure."

"About what you actually do?"

"Of course." Her eyes, lit up. "I know I bitch on, but it's all cover, I like my job, I love talking about it." Karen leaned forward and suckled a nipple, between sucks,

"--Tell me--what you do."

"I handle all enquiries about stock; I patch them through to the people who know. Those about technical details through to you and--Oh do that again,--through to you and Solomon. I'm the nearest thing we have to a Personnel Department. I handle the creature comforts, but I'm hoping when your reforms start--Oh--Oh--start coming in we'll start a proper Personnel Department, not just someone papering and patching. Can I tell you the details?--Oh--Do that again while I tell you."

"What about orders? You never mentioned orders."

"I call the service company and they fill everything up again."

Karen stopped her pleasuring, and stared at her girl, totally confused.

"You didn't think I get the stuff myself, did you? Anyway, I'm not allowed, it's in the contract, all machines to be filled by C-North Machine Vendors Ltd."

"Not the vending. The company products."

"Not me, I don't do any, that's all Michaela's department. That's where your friend and everyone's darling, Bullethead is. It's Purchasing and Dispatch but we just call it Dispatch the rest is too big a mouthful. It's what we wish most of them would do, Dispatch themselves."

"You never buy goods? Dispatch orders? Tranship orders?"

"No, I handle enquiries about them, I-"

"Not even when you're short staffed?"

"No. Never in the five years I've been there. You watch, it'll happen next week."

Karen decided to risk it,

"Lara, your signature is on some dispatch orders."

"No it isn't. Well yes, it is, in my personal file from the staff training when I started, but not on real orders."

"On orders that left the works as late as last week."

Lara lay shocked and silent, shaking her head.

"A steady trickle of orders. For as far back as you care to

check."

"No."

"They're all transhipped orders. Going back three years."

Lara would know even better than Karen that that was the current records, those held in the office; earlier ones would be in storage.

"No." She was still shaking her head. "I filled three order sheets in Staff training, four or five years ago, to learn how to do it. I've never filled one since." She was getting puzzled and upset. "Karen, I'm not an orders clerk, I'm a bimbo with bouncy tits and natural blonde hair that can answer a telephone correctly and do some typing, without making too many mistakes. What you see is what you get, all my brains are in my cunny. The best thing that can be said about my business acumen is that I'm a bloody good fuck. I said yes, to the first man who asked me to marry him, before he fucked me and it was a huge mistake. I've never filled a real order."

"Tell me what you were trained to do. Five years ago. About orders."

"Call the order up, assign it, tab it in, sign it, print it off."

"Let me jot that down. With a layman's crib. Call the order up. What's that?"

"Call the blank sheet up on the computer."

"Then?"

"Assign it, fill in the destination company and address, just type in the destination code, the computer does the rest."

"Then?"

"Tab it in, Product Code, tab, Quantity, tab. The computer works out what it is, puts in the price each and works out the part cost. When you finish, you check it then hit three fast tabs and it finishes with Delivery, VAT and Grand Total, with any conditions, or discounts for prompt payment and such."

"Then you print it, take it out and sign it?"

"No sign it and print it. You never see any paper you send out, letter, order, delivery note, invoice. Well you will in the warehouse, but we don't, it's packaged and processed by the computer, it's never even in our room."

"Well how do you sign it?"

"Hit F5. That's how we sign everything."

"Darling Lara. I think you've just explained a bunch. I'm going to fuck you silly. Then feed you. Then send you home for a while."

"Do I have to?"

"Yes. I have to go out this afternoon. But, you can come for the weekend. If you want."

"Yes, please."

"Starting this evening."

"Oh, yes, please."

"I may be buzzing about a bit. I'll give you a key. And the alarm number."

"Oh. I'm not good with those, ring me when you get in, I'll come running, panting. Better still, pick me up on your way."

After lunch,

"No you'll smudge our lipstick." Karen opened the door as she prevented Lara from smooching her goodbye and propelled her through it with her hand up the back of the blonde's dress, squishing her bottom. "Be gone, baggage. I'll see you tonight." Flint was standing on the step, half-hidden behind a huge bunch of flowers, about to ring the bell.

"And who's this?"

"A friend. On your way. I'll call you. Pack some sexy undies."

Lara examined Flint and then turned back to Karen.

"Lend me out sometime," she said and put on an exaggerated strut, as she walked off to her car.

"These are for you," said the big man, as he passed her the flowers. "Happy Wednesday."

"Thank you, they're lovely."

"I've come to escort you to the meeting at Monta."

"That's nice. I'll get my coat."

Shirley Monta was waiting for them in Janie's office; Karen briefly outlined her progress,

"I'm fairly sure Lara's in the clear. She chose not to have the run of my house. Despite telling her that I might get my work back. She sees herself as a blonde bimbo. She's not all that dim. But she thinks she is."

"That was still a big risk, offering her the opportunity to wreck everything."

"I was just testing. Ready to back out again if necessary. It wasn't necessary. And anyway, it wasn't that big a risk." Karen waved a jewel case and then laid it on Janie's desk. "All my work. And there's another backup at Dad's. And Flint kindly activated the password protection on Mac. They can break her. Burn her. Bust her. But they can't hack her. Not any more. Not without me."

"Okay. Let's go and see what your burglar has to say for himself. Jessica should have some forensic for us by now."

Mrs. Monta's office had the partition drawn; Janie was sitting at a centrally placed table, facing Frank Stooppley who sat opposite. He looked up and scowled when Karen followed the others into the room. She joined the group scattered around the walls, watching. Mrs. Monta sat beside Janie, on the only other chair. Several minutes passed in silence during which time the central character checked his watch. After the second check Janie spoke,

"You seem quite obsessed with the time, Frank. Is there any reason why?"

"I am imprisoned here against my will. It's only a question of time before the police find me and release me. Then I'm going to sue you to your knickers. I know who you are."

"And after me being kind enough to give you a cup of coffee and let you use the toilet; I don't think that's all that bad."

"I'm still going to sue."

"You came here quite voluntarily, because you needed two things. The first to know what we know and the second was time." Jessica appeared briefly at the door,

"Everything, every item on your list," she said to Janie who nodded and turned back to the Union official.

"Why do you think I gave you the coffee, Frank, then let you use the toilet, in that order?"

"I'm here against my will that is going to cost you."

"Perhaps, perhaps not. An independent witness to all that's happened would be nice, have you got one?"

"I don't need one."

"That'll be a no then. But we have, a high ranking police officer who is itching to arrest you for burglary."

Frank insolently surveyed the room,

"I can see Monta gorillas, and the young dykes you keep for your pleasure, but The Filth is significantly absent."

The two women looked at each other, then back at Frank. Presently, Mrs. Monta looked at her watch and nodded at Janie who broke the silence again,

"Last night you broke into Miss Robinson's house and wiped her hard disc on her Mac. You stole all her backups and incidentally her audio collection. Why did you do all that, Frank?"

"I didn't, I was never there. You can't prove I did any of it."

"Depends what you call proof. Means: You left a Mac OS 8 CD in Miss Robinson's disc drive; it's covered in your prints and those of your assistant Gloria. Mainly because it's Gloria's disc. Interestingly, Gloria's prints are all over the back seat of your car and the inside of your caravan--"

"Breaking into my caravan means anything you found is worthless."

"Motive: Miss Robinson was getting too close to your network of bully boys, she had to be stopped somehow; stealing the evidence was an essential part.

"Opportunity: I can put you in her house--"

"No you can't."

"I can put her audio collection in your car. I can--"

"No you can't!"

"Wanna bet? You're greedy and careless, Frank. You had a very rare CD in your car that you didn't buy. They are rare enough to be easily traced and the one in your car was Miss Robinson's. We know because she marked it with UV pen. Guess what happens when you shine UV light on the CD that the late and lovely Edna Savage, sadly didn't live to see burned?"

"I marked it."

"Nice slick regroup Frank, nice one. What did you write?"

"I don't need to tell you, you have to prove I didn't write it. And you can't."

"Yes, we'd need to put it up against all her other CDs wouldn't we? Which could be a problem, as you stole them."

"So you can't prove a thing. Can I go now?"

"Sure can. Detective Chief Inspector Jepson is willing and eager to read you your rights."

The stunningly beautiful blonde, leaning against the wall next to Karen, unfolded her arms and moved over to the door, smiling.

"But before you do, I'd better remind you of something that you have forgotten."

Frank stood up, edging towards the door. It was apparent that he expected to be restrained, but nobody else moved. The blonde opened the door,

"This way," she said. He slowed, possibly remembering the last time he'd challenged a girl as cool as this and spoke to Janie.

"Which is?"

"It's the first full week in May." That little snippet didn't register, so Janie enlarged upon it. "You've been playing for time, time for the Sanitation Department to empty the bins in your street. You put your bin out last night for its normal Wednesday collection this morning. So did your neighbours at 5, 21 and 23. But, due to the May Day Holiday, you're all one day early. Would you like to guess what those neighbours found in their bins when we asked them to open up for us? Evidence legitimately obtained."

"Rubbish, at a guess."

"Quite right, but that's the thing about CDs, they clean up quite well." Frank's edging progress stopped. "And guess what we found on your coffee cup?"

Frank's face said it all.

"The contents of the bin at 23 splashed when Stone opened it and disturbed something. We thought it might have splashed you too and, we were right, it did. You were anxious to visit the wash-room when you arrived, that's why we insisted you have your coffee first. Oh and one other thing, Gloria invited us into your caravan; you shouldn't have given her a key if you were planning to trade her in for a younger model."

It was obvious that Frank wasn't even thinking of the door any longer.

"Actually, two other things; we asked your wife, very nicely, if we could look in your car, for traces of Gloria, she was only too willing. It was she who found the CD, thought it was Gloria's, she's not a happy little hausfrau, panting for your return, with love in her heart. More like an amateur vet, ready to spay, with meat cleaver in hand."

Mrs. Monta took up the lead,

"So all our evidence will even stand up in court, if we bother to prosecute."

"If you're not going to prosecute why am I here?"

"We plan to do something much worse. Much worse! We'd like to tell you our plans before you go, Frank, forewarned and all that." She was indicating his seat again.

Unwillingly Frank sat down.

"We plan to inform Johnson that we will have him formally arrested next Monday and charged with running a protection racket in Crossers, with you as his first lieutenant. We intend to tell him that you have been most cooperative, once you realised we had you banged to rights. He'll have four whole days to get to you." She leaned over and dropped a bunch of keys in front of him. "Your car keys I believe, you're free to go--I'll see you next week. My guess is it will be in the Royal Hospital and that you won't be able to see me."

"You can't do that. I've told you nothing."

The body language in the room was explicit and Mrs. Monta didn't hesitate.

"Richard Keating was a friend of mine, believe me Frank, we are already trumpeting the news in glorious Technicolor, that's why we've been waiting, giving it time to spread. And we'll be adding every embellishment I can dream up, starting before you leave the building. My guess is the contract will be out by the time you get your car onto the bypass. Nobody messes with my friends."

"I'll be killed."

"I'm counting on it, you can't pretend anything but the intention was to kill Mr. Keating, we've nearly got him on that one, we're only missing a body, when he kills **you**, we'll have one, we'll have him. I can think of no better use for your worthless carcass than being the cadaver leading to a successfully prosecuted murder charge. Your car's out front, we parked it in full view of the Loop."

"Arrest me!"

Chief Inspector Jepson replied succinctly,

"I have no evidence unless Mrs. Monta provides it. If she doesn't press charges, you'll have to go free. I don't believe you'll be killed. It's Novochester, not New York."

"You have to arrest me, I'll deal, what do you want to know, I didn't kill the accountant, I didn't do anything to him, I knew nowt about the killings, that was Johnson's partner, what do you want to know?"

"Everything! Up to and including where the bodies are buried, Frank, nothing less. If I even suspect you're holding anything back, the boys will throw you straight out of the front door and lock it behind you."

"Keating's under the water tank; that waitress's under the other one. I didn't do it. I wasn't there; I knew nowt about it. Fat Sid was there, he saw it all, he's vaunting it, he told me; he was positively strutting."

Behind the union official, Stone held two fingers up, pointed to himself and departed. Nobody else in the room moved.

"It wasn't me it was Johnson. He hates me since everybody's been calling him Bullethead, that bitch!" He stabbed a finger towards Karen, leaning impassively against the side wall. She didn't even blink. "She started it, now everyone does, but he blames me for it."

"Watch the language Frank. We could always chain the pair of you to a welding station. Guess whom my money would be on?" replied Janie sweetly. Frank's clothes suddenly looked a couple of sizes too big. "Tell me about the protection racket."

"We got a cut--10% for me, 5% for the boys."

"What was 10% in a normal week?"

"£100, £150 about, usually."

"And the transhipped loads?"

"What transhipped loads?"

Janie and Shirley waved the DCI forward to arrest and caution, then all three of them started again and went through it word by word, filling in details, who did what, where and when, but especially who did what and again and again. Presently they all began, reluctantly, to accept that the union official knew nothing about transhipped loads.

When Stone returned to Headquarters, they took a break. They surrendered Frank Stooppley and much of their evidence into the care of DCI Elaine Jepson. She and a couple of burly uniforms summoned from Head Office escorted him away.

Stone was looking very solemn; he waited until the police had left with their charge before he drew his boss away from prying ears,

"We think we've found a grave," he said.

The twenty-fifth floor of the new hotel looked very strange to Karen, even for a building site. The netting all around, to keep jaywalkers from taking the quick way down, added a surreal atmosphere to an already ghostly place. Behind her, the staff hoist, from which she had just alighted, lay open. Ahead, two massive water tanks occupied almost the entire floor; between them she could just see the other temporary installations, the service hoist and the huge tool cabin, at the far end of the building. One of the water tanks was suspended on jacks, a couple of decimetres above its reinforced concrete base, whilst a figure could be seen scrabbling about deep in the gap. Karen had seen few more daunting prospects than that gap; the Tyne in flood didn't even come close, there at least you had the security of your own skill, not merely faith in someone else's workmanship. She looked pensively at the jacks; she was not alone.

"Is that safe?" Shirley asked of the contractor's foreman.

"It's designed to do it, Mrs. Monta, maintenance and all that, but better him than me."

"Come out of there--Now!"

"Coming."

"Who is it?"

Stone stepped forward,

"Thipsey, Mrs. Monta."

"Ah, yes. Leopold, he's a caver isn't he? Rescue Team."

Stone tapped his head,

"Tiles loose everywhere. He actually likes probing rock falls for trapped colleagues."

The figure made its way out of the space, inching along, the rough concrete sandwich relinquishing its filling reluctantly. Eventually, he joined the others in safety, stood up grinning and switched his caver's head light off.

"Don't go back in there until it's comprehensively chocked, that's an order."

"Okay."

The horrified foreman protested,

"That will take several days, Mrs. Monta."

"I know. Make sure it's done, nobody goes back under there until it's chocked. May I have your report please, Leopold?"

"There's a discontinuity in the concrete about a third of the way in, it's quite big, half a metre wide and a couple of metres or so long, I've chalked a rough outline."

"What do you think it is?"

"I wouldn't like to say, Mrs. Monta."

"If I told you that someone had just claimed that there is a body in that base somewhere, what would be your reaction?"

"Start digging where I've chalked out first."

"Thank you, Leopold. Report in writing first thing tomorrow please and not a word to anyone." She turned to the ashen faced foreman. "Mr. Jenkins, that water tank has to be raised and secured, at a height sufficient to allow unimpeded access to the base and if that means moving the ceiling out of the way, move it. You'll have the instructions in writing by tomorrow."

"But Mrs. Monta..."

"I want screens all around to prevent anyone seeing what's going on and all work ceases on these top floors now! The story is we suspect there could be some asbestos in that load of insulation," she pointed to a stack of boards waiting to be installed. "All work is suspended until they're checked out. That'll hold until we think of something better."

"This will mean, Police, delays, adverse publicity-'

"If Philippa is in that base, I'm sure she'll forgive us all the aggravation."

Karen had a general look around, the pipe-work and pumping arrangements were impressive; she did some rough mental calculations on the capacity of the water tanks. Little wonder they needed stout reinforced concrete bases. Presently everyone began to leave.

"Mrs. Monta," she drew her boss to one side. "I would like to go visiting, may I?"

"Take your Monta ID with you, you won't get in without it. Without mine, even I wouldn't get in."

Chapter 9

Taking Charge: May 8th-14th 2002

Karen

The patient looked up and smiled at the newcomer, it had taken her several minutes, through a sequence of checkpoints, to reach him.

"You're dead," she said. Giving him chocolates and a kiss.

He grinned back. "Officially. But actually, not quite, thanks to you the cavalry arrived like supplies to Nissan."

"Nowt to do wi' me. It was the Monta Memsahibs. Hit the panic button. Sonya, Janie and Mrs. Monta. Not me. Thank them."

"I did, they referred me to you. Thanks Karen, I owe you, big time." Embarrassed, gratified, pleased and unsure how to handle it all, Karen changed the subject,

"What happened? If it's not a rude question."

"It isn't, but I can't tell you, because I don't know. I remember going to lunch. Then, I woke up in hospital, I'm not clear when that was, but I had embroidery holding a very sore head together." He tipped his head to show the dressing. "And several bruises that I couldn't remember acquiring."

"You said something. Told Stone I was in danger. Thanks for

that. Thanks to you, we didn't lose all my notes."

He waved her thanks away, embarrassed.

"I have no recollection of it; the dogs followed the sound of my telephone."

"Janie had to keep re-dialling. The answer-phone kept kicking in,"

He nodded.

"They found me in a bag, tied and gagged and stuffed between reinforcing steel, with pumped concrete advancing my way. They grabbed me and ran. I was delirious and rambling, so the medics said, but Stone obviously listened to the ravings of a madman, thank him."

"I will. What put them onto you?"

"No idea. Stone says I was shouting 'I've found the computer,' over and over, which is stupid because nobody's lost one."

"What exactly did you say? Repeat the exact words."

"'I've found the computer,' but Stone said it sounded like 'I fountained the computer,' which is the same thing, said by an uncontrolled mouth."

"No it isn't. It's a mistake, due to delirium. Stone nearly heard right. Might have actually heard right. Then tried to make sense of the ramblings. Not his fault he got it wrong. He didn't have the key. But I have and so have you. You just don't know you have it."

He was regarding her steadily.

"How do you sign your mundane mail? Routine, production line stuff."

"Hit --" His eyes shut and his head went back. "Oh Shit!" Amnesiac no longer, apparently.

"You were saying, 'I found it in the computer.' That's what I think."

"Karen Robinson, you are good. What the bonk are you doing working as a warehouseman?"

"Right this minute, I'm not. I'm making a passable imitation of a gumshoe. So where's this computer you've found? The one with Lara's signature in F5."

"It's the office spare, the one on the trolley, in reception. The personal keys, F5 to F8 have a cover, to stop you using them by mistake and getting gobbledygook. I borrowed it, wrote my letter and the cover was off. I hit F5 on autopilot; I'm always doing it, and printed. Then, I realised what I'd done, replaced the cover and did a second copy. It was when I went to get the rubbish one back, I saw the signature, although it didn't register then. Someone must have seen me, realised I knew too much and it was only a matter of time before I twigged."

"How secure is the cover?"

"That's the point, it's screwed down; I had to screw it back down."

"You carry screwdrivers with you? Just in case?"

"There was one lying on the trolley, a complicated ratchet thing with interchangeable bits. I nicked it to return it to Maintenance before someone adopted it, what's the betting Maintenance hasn't lost one?"

"Very short odds. Have you still got it?"

"Try my jacket, in the locker."

"It's here. I'll not touch it. Leave it for Janie. Ungodly just might have used the spare bits. Left traces. That wild-eyed Mac-lover from the basement will find them."

"Jessica's lovely, but spoken for. Emily's a lucky girl, has been for yonks. She changed her name to Miller years ago."

"They're both lovely. I had sussed the relationship. Just not how committed it was. Oh No!" Karen tipped her head forwards and covered her eyes. "I don't believe it. I've known for weeks."

"Known what?"

"Who works on that computer. Processing Lara's orders. After hours."

"Well it isn't protection racket Mr. Big, he's on final warning for poor timekeeping, finishing early every night."

"Exactly. But, the office cleaner gets delayed by him. A couple of nights a week. I've seen him twice myself. Just never realised what I was seeing. He couldn't say, 'Ah, but I come back'. People would want to know why. To do what? Lara tells me that machine is never used. But, the tab key is highly polished. Normally it's the space bar and E. What's the betting they aren't? I'll check. With the cleaner, which machine. And find out which keys are polished. Fancy a wager?"

"Rearrange the following into a well-known phrase or saying, 'Off Pig!' Hi Claire, what are you doing here?"

Just as Karen had been earlier, Claire Crossers was being ushered through the door by one of Monta's security guards.

"Visiting the sick. Carrying TLC, I hope. He's in flippant mood Miss Crossers. Needs a firm hand, with lots of close contact nursing care. I'll leave you to it. Bye."

"Who's that?" an astonished Claire Crossers asked of the departing back.

"That is the reason I'm lying here and not laid out in-" The door closed behind Karen and she heard no more.

At the end of the day Karen wound her way up to Administration to collect Lara for the weekend. Paul was waiting for her.

And Claire.

"Hello Mr. Crossers. What are you doing here? You're supposed to be on holiday."

"I am and I'm going straight back, after our business is finished." He drew her through into his office. "Your application for the post of Warehouse Foreman has been accepted; you start on Monday."

"But--"

"Winston is not due to retire for a couple of months, but now that we have a suitable replacement, he has asked for leave so that he can go early to see his grandson's passing out parade in America. He will stay for up to two weeks, to mentor you, if you need him, but as from Monday you're in charge. Also, as of the meeting this afternoon, you are a member of the Board--Yes, I know you're blue collar, but Mr. Jeckobs tells me that you and he have plans to sort that problem too. Any questions?--Good. Have a nice weekend, Karen, bye."

Stunned, silent and functioning on autopilot, Karen followed her employer out of the office.

Claire was waiting outside. The beautiful teenager hugged the brand new Company Director, painfully tight, then comprehensively kissed her, all over her mouth.

"Thank you," she glanced around nervously at the now empty corridor, as she released the taller girl. "For saving you know who. When they let him out, he's going away to convalesce for a few days."

"And you're going with him."

The younger girl was ill at ease.

"He's asked me. It's just that I want more than a dirty weekend, even if it does last a fortnight."

"So does he. Why don't you ask him? Ask him straight up front."

"I couldn't."

"Just say. 'This friendship of ours. Where do you see it going? Bottom line?' Something like. If you like the answer." The tall girl shrugged, hands opened, palms up. "Take it from there. Would you settle for just the dirty weekend? If that's all that was on offer?"

The beautiful eyes, clouded with shame,

"Yes. I'd fight for more, but yes."

"I thought you might. But, I promise you; you won't have to. At the Easter dance. You know when you were dancing with him? And everyone else had vanished to irrelevance?"

The beautiful eyes widened, surprised,

"Yes."

"You were too close to notice. But, it was the same for him. You could be back inside that clinic in twenty minutes. At his bedside. Putting yourself out of all this misery and uncertainty. Putting yourself in orbit. With just one simple question."

* * *

On Monday, the time clock grudgingly acknowledged Karen's early appearance on site, to start her week, with the reminder that she would not begin earning until 07.30hrs.

"That's okay. Have your moment of triumph," she told the hated machine. "Because you are on a count down."

Most of the people around her reacted as expected to a girl talking to a machine, the two in the know grinned. Half an hour later, having sprinkled her followers through the works; Karen intercepted Winston back at the time clock.

"Congratulations."

"And you, have a lovely retirement. Would you do the admin

for me this morning? Quantum vibration is not one of my talents."

"What? I mean--talk sense girl."

"I cannot be in two places at once. Just tell them. Then go to the management meeting for me. I need to be here. I have my first tasks to do."

The rest room was full and unusually noisy. The World Cup and whether England's gifted young captain's broken foot would mend in time, on most of the lad's lips. Winston banged on the tea urn.

"Okay everyone, can I have hush? Thank you. As you know I retire soon, but I've been allowed to go early. I'll be in and out for a fortnight, then I'll have gone completely, but I'm leaving you all in safe hands. Can I present your new foreman?" He stepped to one side and indicated with his arm. "Karen Robinson." The spontaneous round of applause and genuine pleasure on several faces had Karen blushing hot. Winston nodded to her and slid out of the door.

"Thanks. Thank you that was nice. Okay, to business. Several of you have envelopes in your pockets with your name on. Take them out. Slit them open. Take the money out. Give me the empty envelopes." Several younger men twitched, but nobody moved. "It's quite safe. No one's hands will be turned to pork crackling. Mr. Stooppley will not be collecting today. He's behind bars. In a very secure dungeon. At his own request. Even though he's charged with a number of serious offences. If someone else tries to collect. I need to be ready." A thin, sad faced man called Gordon stepped forward, turned, produced an envelope and, obeying Karen's instructions, addressed the group.

"My daughter had to miss her dancing class this week for this, nearly broke my heart, time to make a stand," he turned back to his new foreman. "I'm taking a big risk Boss, trusting you, it wasn't my hand they threatened to turn to pork crackling." The empty envelope was handed over. One by one, everyone followed him. As she was handed each envelope, Karen slid a £20 note into it.

"Thank you. Thank you for that trust. Everyone please sit down, now we wait."

A moment later several men hurried into the rest room,

dressed in Crossers' coveralls and spread themselves around it, behind the door, among the warehousemen,

"They're coming." Karen nodded, turned to face the door and waited. Fat Sid entered, followed by two more overweight individuals, each with a hand secreted inside his coverall.

"Come for your protection money?" She offered the package. "Tell Stooppley it's the last you'll ever get."

"It's not Stooppley now, it's me."

"It's you what?"

"Running the protection, you pay me now." He stepped forward and grabbed the package from Karen. There was a squeal from behind him. Flint and Stone each had a minder in a double Nelson, whilst several other men with police uniforms under their coveralls, recovered baseball bats from inside clothing and set about applying handcuffs. A young sergeant stepped up to the front,

"Sidney Edward Blote, I am arresting you on suspicion of --"

Silence descended with the departure of the police.

"Right. Item one finished--Item two. The time clock. We all clocked on this morning. I intend it to be the last time. But, there will be a price to pay. Is there anyone who wants it kept? Feels strongly about it?"

Solomon, the grizzled old campaigner, daddy of the squaddies, replied,

"We've talked about this, even before you came and made it a hot topic. I'm 46, I've worked here for thirty years, my sixteen-year old daughter recently started as an office junior. I come in at half past seven and clock on, she comes in at nine o'clock and says 'Hello'. If I clock on at 07.10 I get an offensive little reminder stamped on my ticket that I don't start earning until 07.30, if she answers a telephone at ten to nine she gets thanked. If we weren't used to it, we'd consider it something to strike over."

"What's the price you mentioned?" Gordon hadn't been kidding about the protection leaving him short.

"Punctuality. I turned up here late last Tuesday. And Winston fried me. Quite rightly. What neither he nor you knew was that I wasn't late. I was early. But I wasn't here." She pointed to the floor. "Where you needed me. To pull my weight in the warehouse. Anyone keeping poor time. Arriving late, leaving early. Taking long breaks. Frequent toilet trips. Expect to be rollicked, by everybody. Keep doing it, expect to be fired. If fifteen or sixteen are doing the work of twenty. They should share the pay for twenty." There was a long silence, during which everyone glanced briefly at the two consistent offenders. "Well?" Karen too was addressing them specifically.

"I don't know why you're all looking at me."

"We're looking at you--"

Solomon interrupted her,

"Because you skive off at every opportunity. That's why. Now's your chance to prove us wrong, take it or take your cards. You should know by now that this one," he jerked his thumb in Karen's direction "Doesn't pussyfoot around, she's Winston with Stillsons. I accept the deal Big Kay, where do I sign?"

The debriefing at Monta, on her way home, had the new foreman's news filling her boss with dismay.

"That's a pig's bum, I was so sure that Bullethead would step in. Fat Sid has messed up all our plans by taking it upon himself, between us we've severed all proof to Bullethead."

"He might have been lying. Merely obeying Bullethead's orders. You need a tethered goat. One extremely angry goat offering herself. All I ask is that the protecting snipers are close by. And good."

"Whatever the truth, history suggests that Bullethead will react quickly and go off half cocked. My guess is that you will be hearing from him quite soon, as soon as the news of Fat Sid's arrest reaches him--" A mobile rang, all three girls produced one and looked at it.

"It's me." Karen flashed the screen at Shirley who nodded,

"Quite soon, like now. Tethered goat tomorrow night? We can be ready by tomorrow night." Karen nodded, answered the call and enthusiastically arranged a date with her lover for the following evening. She finished and disconnected, watching the screen carefully until it cleared, then she slid the little, leather-encased block into her bag again.

"Remind me never to trust a word you say, Karen Robinson."

"I try not to tell actual lies."

"Which is even worse. I have a friend who can grossly mislead with the absolute truth; she couldn't teach you much."

"Will I be alone? I'd feel more comfortable with Flint."

"You will appear to be alone, but we will have a small army close enough, including Flint. Had we suggested otherwise, I think he would have insisted upon it. Are you telling me you feel the same way about him?"

"Yes. Is that a problem?"

"No. I'm delighted for you both. Janie we have work to do, will you need anything Karen?"

"No--Yes. A hammer and chisel. Stone chisel. To avoid telling lies and all that."

"Okay, we'll get them to you; the hard hats and bodies are still in the third bin at the entrance."

"I'll look for them. Just in case anyone is watching."

"Okay, that's it for now ladies, tomorrow, game on."

During the following afternoon, Karen's mobile rang,

SJM
Answer?

"Hello, Mrs. Monta."

"The reception committee is in place."

"Right."

"Have you seen Stevie yet?"

"No, but she's only due back today."

"She got back this morning and reported in. It's just we haven't been able to raise her for a while, we're looking. She may have gone to see Chicago's ex. It seems that he's not happy about his divorced wife being a porn queen, but prepared to overlook the offence for money."

"Charming."

"Quite! If you see her, tell her to report in again, meanwhile take good care. We'll be watching you, if you see us, you don't know us, treat us like any other Monta people who happen to be around. It will only be from a distance until you spring the trap, be careful. Final confirmation, the first time you say 'missed', we jump in. Say it clearly."

"I will."

She disconnected and made her call,

"I thought I might find you at home. Would you mind if I'm a bit late?"

"No; of course not."

"Only I've got my hands on a new toy. Looks into concrete. I'm going to run it over Monta's new hotel site. Will you cover for me? I'll feel extra special sorry for you later."

"What are you looking into concrete for?"

"As always. For where the bodies are buried. But may be actual bodies this time. Our new accountant's disappeared. He told me he was going to the site. Last thing he did before he disappeared. I might need a strong alibi. If things go squidgy, four 'til nine. Well, before nine. I hope, okay?"

"Who knows you're roaming where you shouldn't, prying into things where people might get cross?"

"You do. A crackpot theory. Gut feeling with no evidence. The last thing I need is somebody hovering about. Asking what I'm doing."

"How are you going to prevent that, on a building site, after hours?"

"I'm going to maintain the hoists. Bag of tools. Walk around as if I owned the place. Brass neck. No problem."

"Okay, you watch your back now, make sure nobody knows. Nobody! Monta don't forgive, they terminate."

"I will."

The hammer and chisel added to the bag only served to increase its already impressive weight. Karen was glad she didn't have to carry it far.

The warehouse extension rang, the nearest warehouseman picked it up and a moment later held the receiver towards her. "Boss, for you."

"Bring a Chinese in with you."

"Okay." She knew full well that the call back had not been to order food that would have merely required 14713, but to confirm her whereabouts exactly. She hung up, thoughtful and sad.

Karen parked her car in the visitors' car park and surveyed the scene before her. Monta's new hotel was an impressive sight, the architecturally meritorious frontage drawing the eye away from the ergonomically efficient block behind it. When it was finished you would hardly notice the tower and you certainly wouldn't notice that the columns and architraves were sandstone coloured concrete, rather than the real thing.

Yes, she thought: Modern buildings are mainly factory built boxes, but there is no need for them to look like it and this one doesn't.

The storage bins were lined up neatly along the front of a site cabin, just inside the gate. She worked her way down them. Shackles and other hardware, pulley-blocks; the third one, as expected, contained hats and bodies with reflective safety stripes. She selected one with MAINTENANCE on it, put it on and adjusted a hat to fit. No-one gave her a second glance as she heaved her bag up and plodded through to the rear of the building.

The service hoist cage was a flimsy, aluminium-framed cube with mesh sides. Karen propped up her first,

Maintenance
Keep Out
Dangerous Testing
Taking Place

notice inside the hoist and retreated outside. She heaved the upper door down, being careful to keep out of the way of the lower door coming up as she did so, and sent the hoist off on its journey, then she barred the entrance gap with a substantial chain and padlock. A hooter sounded off to her right and all over the site, workers completed their current task and began heading for the exits; a couple of times the staff hoist brought squaddies down from upper floors. When she was satisfied, she erected a second, huge,

**Maintenance
Keep Out
Dangerous Testing
Taking Place**

notice in front of the chain, picked up her other notices, trekked back through and gratefully lowered her bag onto the floor of the substantial, steel, staff hoist cage.

"Maintenance!" Two approaching site workers in hard hats, carrying clipboards and plans, hailed her. "Hold the hoist please!" They strode over and joined her.

"About halfway up, we'll tell you when." One called as they neared the cage.

"Okay." Karen was impressed, she would never have known until he spoke and how the DCI had secreted all that blonde hair under her hat was a mystery. Her companions ignored her but discussed the contents of a clipboard. After half a dozen storeys Stone mentioned her name,

"Don't look," he murmured. "Don't look this way Miss Robinson, just to let you know you had the expected tail, he watched you begin work on the service hoist, then telephoned. My guess is he was reporting your arrival. Good luck." Then in a normal speaking voice. "Next floor please."

Karen obediently stopped the hoist, was thanked and murmured her own thanks in reply, with very mixed feelings. Suspicions and fears were one thing, she knew she wasn't wrong, but there could still have been an explanation, that it wasn't just betrayal. But, now she was looking it in the face and it wasn't funny and nor was it understandable. What on Earth had she done to deserve it?

Chapter 10

Payments: Tuesday May 14th 2002

Karen

Karen alighted at the twenty-fifth floor. Although half the ceiling had already been removed, the water tank had been replaced. There was no real clue that Philippa may have been found. She walked through to the rear; several people were clustered near the tool cabin.

The big man closed up to her as she laid down the heavy bag, "Can I give you a hand?"

"Thanks but it's my job. I'm just running a test. It won't take long.

And even less if the pike doesn't take the plug, she thought, but didn't say.

"Okay Karen, just shout missed as soon as you know for sure," said her Boss and she and Janie waited for Flint to join them before disappearing.

A moment later she was alone on the twenty-fifth floor. She opened the gates on the service hoist and securely chocked the cage door open. The brake mechanism was simple, reliable and easy to replace.

The staff hoist whirred faintly, Karen's heart thumped with

adrenaline, but overtly she ignored it. She finished her task and hefted her heavy bag away from the service hoist, officially, in her report, to get it out of the way, actually to give clear access to the cage and place herself nearer the tool cabin. It would be his choice, their choice, she unwillingly corrected herself. She had no qualms about loading the Russian roulette revolver for a would-be murderer; it was up to him not to pull the trigger.

Chicago's ex! Karen Robinson you have been asleep!

She stepped even closer to the safety of the tool cabin before picking up the third,

Maintenance
Keep Out
Dangerous Testing
Taking Place

notice and turning around to appraise developments. Bullethead was standing in front of the service hoist; his partner was testing the padlock on the tool cabin door, while watching her warily. Only when he was satisfied that it was securely locked did he drop a large sack down off his shoulder and stand back, concentrating solely on covering the passage to the staff hoist again. For big men, they had surrounded her very quietly.

"What's going down?"

"You are Blue Collar. You and your rebellious, busybody ways have meddled long enough, it stops tonight."

"Like Richard? I disappear? Do a Jimmy Hoffa into that supporting column?"

"Yes, I'm afraid so, my dear."

"You wouldn't."

"It's only hard the first time, Blue Collar, it's quite amazing how quickly it becomes routine."

"You can scream the place down, nobody will hear, in a few minutes, after we are finished, you will be drowning in concrete, you and your heroine, I hope the prospect pleases."

"Why did you gag Richard then? If nobody will hear me."

"He came up in a bag of tools; we couldn't have him shouting down there. Very strange, he was already dead meat and still shouting his head off. About her," he kicked the sack. "And you, my dear and your records."

"But we sorted them, as you know, now it's your turn."

"And there's another difference between you, we can do something to you that we didn't want to do to Keating. Your sound effects will add to the event."

"I'm to be raped as well."

"Oh yes, both of you," he kicked the sack again, it groaned and twitched, sluggishly rolling away from the pain, towards her. "Pleasingly ironic, don't you think, for a porn queen, who wouldn't allow rape or violence in her films, to be raped and murdered in real life?"

"You don't like being raped do you, Blue Collar, you castrate offenders, but this time, I think not?"

"Is that Stevie?"

"The Mistress Bollard. Yes."

"What have you done to her?"

"Just a headache and a few bruises as yet."

Karen didn't entirely trust that, he'd lied to her before.

Get a move on, Stevie might need treatment.

"Doesn't it worry you? The forged parts. Sending accidents waiting to happen off to innocent workers abroad."

"You have been a busy little busybody haven't you? We're providing a service; they swarm all over projects like ants. If a part fails occasionally, it just thins out the crush a bit, temporarily."

"Unlike the saving on parts, it's barely worth an entry on the balance sheet. Within days, any wastage is replaced."

Karen couldn't remember ever having seen him smile before; it was a demoniac smile, an unpleasant sight.

"Pawns. If a few consumables get killed. It's no big deal?"

"As you said, my dear, consumables. How long do you claim you've known?"

"Since the day I torched Frank's balls."

"Nice try, but utter rubbish as we both know, you would have said something. I would have known."

"We had no idea. We didn't even know we had a traitor. You

were my friend. Almost my best friend. Then, Bullethead knew about Seth. But not about Siew Mui or Lisa."

"Who?"

"Exactly. It could only have come from you. My second suspect knew only about Siew Mui. And my third, only about my friend Lisa."

"A bit thin, my dear, even by your meagre standards." The attempted put down had the opposite effect to that intended, soothing balm flowed into Karen's wounds. She replied directly to Snowy, while merely indicating Bullethead with a flick of her wrist, as if he were of no importance,

"In Bullethead's view. Seth would be the least offensive social crime. Had he known the others, he would have said. He said everything else. I didn't want to believe it. I needed time to get the proof. I got long enough. I knew whom. And, now I know why. Money, simple greed for a lost lifestyle. But not why me. Indulge me. Tell me, why me?"

"You said it yourself my dear. Control."

All the fragments jumped back into place, like a breaking window filmed in reverse. Of course, they had talked about it often, she had just left obsession out of the equation.

"It's important to show you who's the boss. You're a control freak, but today your contract has expired. Today, you will be controlled; for you that will be very hard, but it will increase my pleasure, I'm afraid. That's why Mistress Bollard is, as yet, unharmed, you important pieces need to see each other broken, had she just been a pawn, she'd have gone long since."

"Hence the rape. When you could have loving sex anytime."

"But you wouldn't do as you were told. I couldn't have that, not again."

"Again? You're talking about your wife? Mary Chicago Snowdon-Lynes?"

A hit, she could see it in his eyes; he understood she really had known who her adversary was.

"The wife who doesn't coffee with you on Thursdays."

"She will, she wouldn't be told either, but she'll learn. Of course, like you, it might be the death of her, but she'll learn. I may have underestimated you, my dear, you might have had suspicions after all."

"But it won't do her any good dead, let's get on with it." Bullethead stepped forward.

Karen's arm extension slid down her sleeve into full view.

"No! Wait Johnson, don't get too close to that wrench yet, not until we can both grab together, she's not kidding, she really does know how to use it and there's a bunny loose--how did you know about the gag?"

"You missed a trick."

The tool cabin door
swung wide open,
taking its padlock
and false hasp with it.

"She knew because I told her,"

said Richard softly, holding tightly onto the door frame for support.

A stream of Monta's boys poured past him out of the cabin; Flint moved smartly between Bullethead and Karen.

"And which computer contains Lara's signature."

Two of the boys leaped over the sack.

"She already knew who worked on it at night, after hours."

The rest grabbed the sack and hauled it away to safety.

Stone's resonant call peeled clearly down the passage. "Staff hoist secure!"

Bullethead dived into the service hoist, kicking away the safety chock.

"Don't do that," shouted Karen.

"You're dead Blue Collar, even if I do it from gaol."

Karen tried again, loudly, with panic in her voice,

"It's got no brakes."

Snowy had joined his partner.

"Sorry, my dear, I did warn you to watch your back."

This time a fearful scream.

"It's got no brakes!"

The cage's vertically closing doors slammed shut and it dropped swiftly away.

Karen spoke again, but a normal speaking voice now, resigned, almost apathetic,

"That's the hoist. With the out of spec brakes. I was just about to test it."

The cable for the hoist
speeded up to maximum,
and then kept right on,
speeding up.
The brake housing screamed,
spat parts out sideways,
and crumbled.
The cable,
now free,
plunged downwards,
out of sight,
in a shower of splintered brake housing parts.

The watching group steeled themselves, all but Karen, whilst still speaking, she moved over and unfastened the sack.

There was one solid crump, followed by several smaller tinkling ones.

DCI Elaine Jepson arrived with Stone, running.

She ran straight over to the edge of the shaft and looked down the twenty-five storeys, not even holding the rail to steady herself.

"Shit! I'll be in bother over this, Shirley."

"Why do you think I insisted that you stay with Stone?"

"To make you fireproof, Chief Inspector, even with the best-laid plans things can go wrong," explained Flint. "We needed you untainted, just in case."

Mrs. Monta joined her,

"None of us knew this was going to happen, Elaine, we didn't even know for sure what we were dealing with; you were the official backup, not a primary player. But it's a big clear up too, forgery, fraud, sundry assaults and kidnapping, three attempted murders and sadly now, I think that the only question of what we will find in the water tank base, is not what, but whom."

Stevie Bollard, bound, gagged and softly moaning, although now propped up and being released, was still out shopping. She was fully clothed, including the foundation garments of a girl who acknowledges she has a fuller figure, but wishes it were a size or two smaller. Karen released the breath she hadn't realised she'd been holding. Although not proof, it was a strong indication that Stevie's planned torture had been reserved for when it could be witnessed. It was unlikely that they would have bothered to dress her again correctly, had they got as far as stripping her earlier. The relief allowed her to add to Mrs. Monta's list,

"Not to mention those exports. Thousands of workers. All over the Third World. Trusting their lives to brakes just like those ones. Base metal safety barriers. Cinder toffee bolts. Cardboard nuts."

"Yes, the Messrs Big will not go to gaol, but neither can they do any more harm. All their minions will be picked up overnight and will go to gaol. None of us knew this was going to happen. It wasn't in anyone's brief to speculate, we knew whom, but couldn't prove it beyond reasonable doubt. Karen had to make like a tethered goat and consequently now we can prove it. None of us knew this was going to happen."

"Okay, okay, I'll take the flak."

"But from right behind me, this is private property, you have no warrant and I ordered you to stay with Stone, you played it by the book; nobody knew this was going to happen."

"The call centre has work to do, Boss."

"Yes, get them all in, Janie, around the clock, get all those dodgy parts back, all of them." She drew Karen away to one side, while Janie busied herself on her mobile

"Are you okay?"

"No. I will be. Given time." Shirley waved the big man over,

"I'd rather Flint stayed with you for a while."

"So would I." She reached out and took his hand.

"Has Snowy got any security, alarms and such?"

"He has a locked room. Deanne doesn't clean it. I've never been in. I don't think it's alarmed, but I don't know. He never set any alarms. Not that I know of."

"I'll go and check for gas leaks," whispered Stone and left.

"Take Karen home and look after her please, Flint."

"Check."

"Can we see Stevie safely into hospital first?"

"There's a paramedic team on its way up, go with them.

We'll keep the police off your back until tomorrow, write it down tonight, while it's fresh in your mind, just what you did, not why you did it, we'll answer those questions with a big and hungry eagle from the bar close by."

Back down on the ground floor, Karen walked through to the service hoist, Flint had gone to restrain her, but then thought better of it. The cage, having had to take the plunging weight of the pulley system and cross braces built into its roof, was only a few centimetres high, a smashed, squashed, basket of dirty old clothes, blood was already seeping out across the floor,

"Goodbye Snowy. Sorry. I was watching my back. I just didn't tell you how closely. Or against whom the defences were raised."

The ambulance with Stevie on board drew away, heading for Monta's clinic.

"Give me your keys, I'll drive, you're not fit yet," said Flint, then reading the resistance in her eyes. "It's okay, the boys will see to mine."

They sat quietly side by side in reception, waiting. Presently one of the senior nurses came out to see them,

"Stevie's sleeping now, we need to monitor her carefully, head trauma can have consequences. But, we are watching for those. You can see her for a second, then come back tomorrow. If there are no complications, she should be much better by then."

Having taken leave of their charge; Flint turned all his care onto his girl as they returned to Karen's car.

"Are you going to be okay, Miss? I know it's not easy to kill someone, not if you're normal that is, even someone you have reason to hate."

"Have you?"

"Falklands 'n all that."

"No, it wasn't easy. But, they were going to rape and kill Stevie. It came down to a straight choice. I prefer the outcome this way around."

"But when it came down to it, you couldn't do it; you warned them. Twice. Three times; in fact."

"It wasn't just hate."

"I know, it was an emotion that can get you killed. Pity."

"Yes. They both had the kind of pressures on them that break people. I'll need to pray for forgiveness. For loading the gun. But--if somebody's under that water tank. And I'm sure Philippa is. I won't lose any sleep. It could have been Stevie. I've idolised her for years."

"Prayer helps, not as an answer in itself, but it helps you find the answer you're searching for."

"It's the betrayal that hurts. Snowy was my friend. And you'd best hear this from me. Frequently he was my lover too."

Flint cuddled her in, leaning against the tailgate of the Astra.

"That's not exactly a surprise, Miss Robinson, after what you said to him, merely confirmation. May I help sometime?"

"Oh yes. Tonight and tomorrow I have a report to write for Mrs. Monta. Between times could you satiate me?"

"I thought Mrs. Jeevers was staying with you."

"That was last weekend. But she'll come running if I telephone. Particularly when she realises you'll be there. She'd be more than willing to make like dessert. Or a side salad. Could you help her satiate me?"

"I doubt it very much, but I'm willing and eager to try."

"My school uniform still fits me."

"Save it for when the flesh can't match the spirit Miss, about one o'clock tomorrow morning."

"One other thing, Flint. If you call me Miss once more. I'll bite you."

"Very good, Miss--Ow!"

As Flint drove them out of the car park, Karen called Lara. George answered,

"Hello George, it's Karen. Can I speak with Lara please?"

"Lara get a bag packed, you're going out to get shagged again."

Click.

Karen just waited, crackle,

"Hello, are you still there?"

"Still here darling. But pack the bag, we'll pick you up in ten minutes."

"We?"

"Me and Flint."

"Half packed already."

Karen disconnected and directed Flint to the Jeevers house.

"What's Stone up to? Checking for gas leaks."

"Snowy and Bullethead had to change their plans quickly today, they might have left the gas on." Flint's face was a blank wall; belatedly Karen's brain began functioning again.

"And while they're checking. Concrete evidence might just happen to fall into their hands. Not just word of mouth?"

"They also stole a lot of money from Crossers and Crossers' customers. Getting those parts back will be expensive; it would be nice if the villains could foot part of the bill."

"Their estate belongs to the Crown. The authorities will think so. Mrs. Monta's not going to steal-'

"Iron, steel, even aluminium alloy has nowt to do with it, we need to find all the money we can and return it to customers. It belongs to them. Red tape slows things up and gobbles cash, anyway the Treasury would just waste it."

Karen laughed, releasing herself from the tension her thoughts had built up.

"No. She won't steal it, it's just that when the finance wizards are finished their legal removal of what in justice belongs to Crossers and their customers, the estate will be considering that piracy would have been a much less painful alternative. But to do that, we have to know where to look. Stone might just stumble over that, whilst sniffing for gas."

"There's Lara. At the gate already."

"Bag and Baggage."

"Flint!"

"Said with deep friendship, just as you did last week."

"Harrumph--Hi Baggage. Jump in."

"Miss Robinson!"

"What's so funny?"

Epilogue Concluded

At work the following day, Karen gave her report its all-important final check.

'From that height a cage in free fall hits the ground at crushing speed.

Onto a solid unyielding base, the additional stresses induced by the weight of the pulley mechanism and its supports, concertina and telescope the corner struts down to just a few centimetres and any soft tissue inside the cage is reshaped to fit the available space.'

She turned back to the front page of the little booklet and scanned the conclusion,

'I recommend, in the strongest possible terms, that Mr. Johnson's covert practice of supplying below specification and forged parts to vulnerable customers, be rooted out and terminated forthwith.' Adding her signature, pedantically with the classy fountain pen, in turquoise ink.

Even in these days of razor cutting edge technology, she thought. *We can't write in black and underline in red.* She reached for a ballpoint, suppressing a smile: *Or at least, I can't, there'll be a way for sure.*[4]

She neatly double-underlined 'Conclusion' in red, checked her signature was dry, closed the notebook, snapped the elastic retainer into place, and handed the neat little folder to her boss.

"My report, Mrs. Monta."

"Thank you, Karen."

4 There is. Word can do it and InDesign does it through the Character Style route. When I first wrote Karen, I was unaware of this. I deliberately chose to leave the reference in as, **at the time**, it was true for Karen. *P.C.*

KAREN,
The Girl That Would Be A Plumber
The End

Acknowledgements

Pealle originally appeared in Karen as a supporting act, but she became so much a part of the scene and so strong a character in her own right, that I gave her her own book and removed her more personal exploits from these pages. This tightened Karen up considerably and gave Pealle a whole world to explore.

If you want to read what is no longer here, you will find it in Pealle, Sporty Sparks, by the same author.

To all those authors over the years who have given me so much pleasure a sincere and heartfelt thank you.

Arthur Ransome; Dick Francis; Robert A. Heinlein; Reginald Hill; Jane Austen; Lew Matthews; Manning O'Brine; Dornford Yeats; John Wyndham; C. S. Forester; J. K. Rowling to name but a few.

I have tried to credit you when I knowingly referred to your work. When I missed, it was innocently done, please forgive. With so many wonderful stories buried in my cortex, I must have used variations on your ideas some time.

Where I did so without credits, it was unintentional and anyway, imitation is the sincerest form of flattery, even when done by accident.

Often between writing and getting a scene to the printer, I too have seen one of my plot lines appear on the small screen.

Karen asks of her boss,

"Have you got my brain bugged?"

There are times when I think mine is.

Anyway,

Thank You! And where necessary,

Sorry,

Petra Ceason 2015.

Ownership

Original manuscript in Georgia 12 point and other fonts. This version in whatever I could get away with. In my eyes the constraints imposed by ePub make the Spanish Inquisition look like a ultra-liberal social service!

If the Ancestor had ever owned a boat, he would have called it The Double Sausage.

The publication of this First Commercial Edition funded by Double-Sausage.

Petra Ceason 2017.

If you liked this book, you may be interested in these other titles by Petra Ceason.

Delia, Chef In A Wheelchair

Due out 2017

Delia Summers is disabled, she needs special ankle supports in a built up right shoe, which she refers to as a Clump. She is a brilliant intuitive cook with an incisive brain, but she does not tolerate fools gladly.

Delia is bright, ruthlessly ambitious and in love with a married man. If that wasn't dangerous enough she's not yet sixteen and the object of desire of the wife her amour. In a short Prologue of only two sentences, we learn that someone has been murdered and the timing of the deed has devastating consequences for those putatively (un)involved.

The scene is set for love and tragedy, intrigue and murder and they are all here in generous portions, hopefully garnished with surprises, chuckles and some laughter on the way.

This is another feel good erotic story from Petra Ceason.

Rita--Who?

Due out 2017

Although Rita takes the Title Rôle, this is a Searching for Identity, Voyage of Discovery for all eight of the main characters. I have a certain amount of sympathy for some of those that end up discovering to their cost...

When Rita first appeared in a Creative Writing Homework early in 2004, our Tutor was incensed, mainly because the writing was pretty grotty, but also because,

'The Social would have something to say about an under age working girl.'

I have endeavoured to sort the grotty writing, his area of expertise, but steepled our resolve about the Social, my area of expertise.

My Acknowledgements and Thanks to an early Twentieth Century edition of Boy's Own Paper, for a vaguely remembered story idea, that I adapted to become that of Mary Richards, {and hence Mary Andrew} fighting for her life on the top of a runaway Stage Coach in America's Old West. My Apologies to Native Americans who, at that time, were portrayed as anarchic savages, and thus also in the extract. I do know that contrary to the Hollywood Studio image, you had every provocation to wage war on the invaders. Compared to many of them, you were civilised.

My thanks also to my tutor, Mr. E. E. Hughes for the imagination stimulus picture of the four men meeting, from which this crime fiction sprang. My first effort you castigated, so did my Canadian dolly, even I wasn't that keen! I like the finished erotic novel a bit better!

Petra.

Collected Short Stories And Pomes {And No It's Not A Typo}

Short stories and Geordie poems {pomes}, that started life as Creative Writing Course homeworks.

Rather than enter them for competitions, where the meaning of the winning prose is too obtuse for me to fathom, or the successful poetry has neither rhyme nor lyricism; I chose to put them in a book where folk could enjoy them for what they are.

A book of short stories usually contains between five and fifteen stories. You are reading about one with about sixty of the critters, ranging in size from precisely fifty to over five thousand words and, believe me, the harder of those two to write was the fifty!

I was kept under severe restraint whilst writing these, gagged; manacled; I'm talking SEVERE restraint here!

So Dear True Reader:-

The sex is understated, and off stage, totally unlike my usual work, but if you like Romance, Crime Fiction, the odd ghost, with just a pinch of fantasy; if you prefer your women feisty, red blooded, even, when necessary, prepared to do the asking, then this book is for you.

Enjoy,

Petra 2017.

Janie, Mechanic On A Motorbike

Janie Jones is an intelligent and resourceful school leaver who has ambitions to fly beyond an office, staff and dull.

She uses her abilities to create jobs to fit her, rather than the other way around, allowing her to broaden and enrich her life.

The triumphs and disasters; friendships; relationships; affaires; and loves of this girl-with-a-crashed-face, Janie's own description of herself, are a journey of hope and fulfilment. If you do not see an oil-painting in the mirror every morning, take heart, ninety-odd percent of us are right up there alongside. Janie makes it, and so can the rest of us. You will find encouragement here; maybe even allow yourself a small sinful smile, or three, as the dragons are slain.

Enjoy,

Petra 2017.

28/08/2017

www.ingramcontent.com/pod-product-compliance
Ingram Content Group UK Ltd.
Pitfield, Milton Keynes, MK11 3LW, UK
UKHW041432210726
13854UKWH00010B/1874